Visions and Revisions

VISIONS AND REVISIONS

*The United States
in the Global Economy*

Elliot Zupnick

Westview Press
A Member of the Perseus Books Group

Copyright © 1999 by Westview Press, A Member of the Perseus Books Group

Published in 1999 in the United States of America by Westview Press, 5500 Central Avenue, Boulder, Colorado 80301-2877, and in the United Kingdom by Westview Press, 12 Hid's Copse Road, Cumnor Hill, Oxford OX2 9JJ

Library of Congress Cataloging-in-Publication Data
Zupnick, Elliot, 1923–
   Visions and revisions : the United States in the global economy /
Elliot Zupnick.
      p.   cm.
   Includes bibliographical references and index.
   ISBN 0-8133-3552-3
   1. United States—Foreign economic relations.   2. United States—
Commerce.   3. United States—Economic conditions—1993–   I. Title.
II. Title: United States in the global economy.
HF1455.Z86   1999
337.73—dc21   98-55748
                                                                                    CIP

The paper used in this publication meets the requirements of the American National Standard for Permanence of Paper for Printed Library Materials Z39.48-1984.

10   9   8   7   6   5   4   3   2   1

To Daniel, Benjamin, and Sarah
WITH LOVE

CONTENTS

TABLES AND
ILLUSTRATIONS

ACKNOWLEDGMENTS

I owe a debt of gratitude to the many students I have both instructed and learned from over many years; to my colleagues in the Economics and Political Science Departments of Columbia University and the Graduate School of City University; to the many economists who over the years presented papers at the Columbia University's Workshop on International Economics; to the equally numerous scholars who presented papers on European and international affairs at the Columbia University's Institute on Western Europe of which I was director between 1983 and 1991; and particularly to the University Seminars at Columbia University, directed by Aaron Warner, which not only provided me with numerous opportunities to meet with and discuss my ideas with scholars from different disciplines but also extended to me financial assistance in the preparation of this manuscript for publication.

On a more personal level, I should like to extend my gratitude and appreciation to Jacob Mincer, Robert Stern, Donald Dewey, and Gerald Sirkin for many years of friendship and support as well as for reading and discussing the manuscript in whole or in part; to Aaron Warner who has shown me many kindnesses over the years; and to my nephew Eli Zupnick who graphically demonstrated the truth behind Shakespeare's adage that brevity is the soul of wit.

I owe my greatest debt of gratitude to Jane House who not only prepared the manuscript for publication but also rendered invaluable editorial assistance and, most important, support and encouragement whenever my spirit and energies flagged.

Finally, I should like to express my appreciation and gratitude to my wife, Lillian, for her editorial advice and for the myriad ways in which she helped me get through a rough patch; to my daughter, Judi, and my son, Henry, and my daughter-in-law, Judith, for their support and encouragement; and to my grandchildren, Daniel, Benjamin, and Sarah, who are a constant source of joy and wonder and to whom this book is dedicated.

Although I have received valuable advice from friends and colleagues, I am solely responsible for whatever defects remain in this book.

Elliot Zupnick

Acronyms

APEC	Asia Pacific Economic Cooperation group
CFCs	chlorofluorocarbons
EC	European Community
EU	European Union
GATS	General Agreement on Trade in Services
GATT	General Agreement on Tariffs and Trade
GSP	general system of preferences
IBRD	International Bank for Reconstruction and Development
ILO	International Labor Organization
IMF	International Monetary Fund
ITC	International Trade Commission
ITO	International Trade Organization
MFA	Multi Fibre Agreement
MFN	most-favored-nation
MITI	Ministry of International Trade and Industry
MNEs	multinational enterprises
MOFAs	majority-owned foreign affiliates
NAFTA	North American Free Trade Agreement
NICs	newly industrialized countries
OECD	Organization for Economic Cooperation and Development
OPEC	Organization of Petroleum Exporting Countries
SIMA	Special Import Measures Act
SITC	Standard International Trade Classification
TRIMS	General Agreement on Trade Related Investment Measures
TRIPS	Agreement on Trade Related Aspects of Intellectual Property Rights
UNCTAD	United Nations Commission for Trade and Development
USTR	United States Trade Representative
WTO	World Trade Organization

VISIONS AND REVISIONS

INTRODUCTION

In 1993, the U.S. Senate, after a bruising debate, narrowly ratified the North American Free Trade Agreement (NAFTA). Ostensibly addressing the specifics of this agreement, the debate was in reality most concerned with the broader question of the desirability of continuing—or extending—the globalization process. The fact that at the end of the day the agreement was ratified does not indicate, however, that this issue was laid to rest. On the contrary, the strong congressional resistance in 1997 to granting Pres. Bill Clinton fast-track authorization, which almost everybody agrees is essential if additional free trade agreements are to be negotiated, suggests that the issue is still festering. There is, moreover, every indication that this issue will play a prominent role in the 2000 presidential election. The two early frontrunners for the Democratic Party nomination, Vice Pres. Albert Gore and U.S. Rep. Richard Gephardt, have already staked out strong positions. The vice president's defense of NAFTA in his debate with third-party presidential candidate Ross Perot was a defining moment during the 1992 campaign and is likely to feature in any future campaign Gore wages. Gephardt, in contrast, has emerged as a leading opponent of extending NAFTA to include other Latin American countries.

The fact that disagreement exists over trade policy is not at all unusual. This issue, after all, has been a staple of American politics since the birth of the Republic. What is surprising, however, is that the current dispute has become so central an issue on the domestic agenda at a time when the United States is enjoying a period of apparent great prosperity. Between 1992 and 1997, 13.7 million new jobs have been created, unemployment has dropped to 4.7 percent, and the booming stock market has made the wealthy more affluent and millions of workers with pension plans more secure. Typically trade issues tend to flare up during periods of crisis and to be relegated to the back burner during periods of prosperity.

This paradox is partially resolved, however, by a realization that the prosperity of the 1990s, though real, obscures a number of deeply rooted problems in the American economy. Indeed, for many Americans, the postwar economic bloom began to fade during the 1970s. After more than twenty-five years of unparalleled growth, a number of ominous trends emerged that threatened to doom the vaunted American dream. Among the more important of these trends were a decline in the growth rates of real output and productivity, a decline in employment in the manufacturing sector, stagnant wages, and an increase in income inequality. Beginning in 1978, the earnings of those on the bottom of the income scale declined in real terms while earnings of those in the highest brackets increased. As a result, the real income of 50 percent of all income recipients in the United States was lower in 1995 than it was seventeen years earlier.

The 1980s also witnessed the emergence of large and recurrent international accounts deficits with the rest of the world. These deficits transformed the United States from the world's largest creditor country to the world's largest debtor country. The fact that a major portion of deficits was incurred with Japan and the emerging economies of East Asia—Hong Kong, Taiwan, Singapore, and South Korea—suggested a link between the deterioration of the American position in the world economy and its domestic travails. The stagnation of American wages, the decline in the number of manufacturing jobs, and the downward pressures on the earnings of the least skilled workers were widely attributed to the increase in imports of labor-intensive manufacturing goods from the low wage Asian economies and to the relocation of American industries to those areas.

The view that globalization was not in America's interest was further fueled by a growing perception that the process itself was unbalanced. The failure of American exports to keep pace with American imports, for example, was attributed to the emergence of free-riding countries that, though eager to exploit the opportunities provided by free access to American markets, maintained restrictions on imports from the United States. And though Japan was the principal target for these recriminations, other countries, particularly the emerging economies in Asia, were also faulted. To remedy the perceived asymmetries, those disaffected with the globalization process urged the United States to replace its free trade policies—which of course it never had—with fair trade policies that had as their objective the leveling of the playing field. Stripped of all its euphemisms, this proposal was little more than a call for government intervention to ensure that foreign countries reciprocate the United States for their access to American markets by absorbing an equal value of American exports. Trade managed in this manner, it was argued, would not only restore equilibrium to U.S. international accounts but also ease domestic problems caused by globalization.

These perceptions regarding the workings and the impact of globalization were clearly responsible for the opposition from organized labor and those industries that were unable to compete with foreign imports from the low-wage emerging economies. These natural opponents have been joined, however, by others who regard globalization as a threat to their particular areas of concern. Among the more important of these are the nativists, some environmentalists, and some human rights advocates. The nativists, who have long and strong roots in American history, are viscerally opposed to, and suspicious of, almost anything foreign. Thus, despite considerable evidence to the contrary, they are convinced that immigration has had an adverse effect on the American economy, that the United Nations is the enemy within our midst, that America's trading partners are untrustworthy, and that international organizations such as the General Agreement on Tariffs and Trade (GATT) and the World Trade Organization (WTO) pose a threat to American sovereignty. In recent years their most powerful mainstream voice was Pat Buchanan, who emerged during the 1992 presidential campaign as one of the shrillest opponents of globalization.

The opposition of some environmentalists and some human rights activists is based on more rational grounds. The environmentalists' concerns are threefold. First, they argue that globalization, by promoting industrialization in the emerging economies, will tend to encourage polluting activities. Second, they fear that the lax environmental standards in these countries will act as a magnet to attract industries from more advanced industrial countries that operate under more stringent standards. Finally, they are concerned that efforts by firms in the developed countries to offset this "unfair" advantage will set off a race to the bottom. Similar concerns are expressed by those human rights advocates who fear that globalization will ultimately erode labor standards and working conditions in both the developed and the emerging economies.

Although these are nontrivial concerns and demand to be considered carefully, one overarching criticism, rooted in a misunderstanding of the concept of globalization, must be emphatically rejected: that globalization and unfettered capitalism—or laissez-faire capitalism—are one and the same phenomenon and that the sins of the one can be attributed to the other.[1] Were this the case, globalization would require, among other things, a dismantling of the safety nets that were put into place to protect the poor and the underprivileged, an acceptance of the distribution of income generated by pure market forces no matter how unequal that distribution may be, complete indifference to the plight of those who are adversely affected by the globalization process, and the abolition of almost all regulatory functions of the government. In truth, globalization per se requires none of these things.

The primary thesis of this book is that globalization contributes to an increase in the wealth of nations. This, by itself, would enable those countries participating in the process to devote more resources—not fewer—to the alleviation of poverty and would, other things being equal, facilitate the reallocation of income from the wealthy to the poor if the political will to do so existed.

This is not to suggest, however, that globalization does not require a change in institutions and practices. Indeed, to compete successfully in global markets, countries would have to transform institutions and remove obstacles and regulations that repress entrepreneurship, contribute to a misallocation of resources, including scarce capital, impede the introduction of more efficient technology, impair the ability to adapt to new situations, and discourage foreign investments. It goes without saying that these imperatives are unlikely to be met where the legal system fails to provide adequate protection to property rights and respect for the sanctity of contracts; where the political system cannot or will not provide stability and security; and where the social system does not encourage transparency and displays a high degree of tolerance for corruption and nepotism.

GLOBALIZATION DEFINED

It is desirable to begin a study of globalization's impact on the U.S. economy by defining what it means and by considering individually the components that comprise it. As used in this study, *globalization* refers to the process whereby a country's economy becomes more integrated with those of the rest of the world. Changes in the degree of integration are measured by changes in the relative importance of crossborder trade in goods and services and in capital movements as well as in the country's participation in the international production system. Omitted from consideration in this study are changes related to the crossborder flow of people. This omission is due not to a failure to recognize the overwhelming importance of this phenomenon but rather to the inability to do justice to it within the framework of this study.

By every measure, the United States and almost every other country in the world experienced a burst of globalization in the post–World War II period. This process was driven largely by the interaction of policy decisions and market forces and was *enabled* by revolutionary technological developments in the transportation and communications sectors, which facilitated the movement of goods and information and drastically reduced the cost of doing so. The overwhelming influence of policy decisions upon this process is evident not only in the reduction in tariffs and the adoption of rules of good behavior, which drastically reduced the impediments to the international exchange of goods that characterized the interwar period, but also by the widespread restoration of currency convertibility, the elimination of capital controls, the easing of restrictions on the remission of earnings, and the elimination of many restrictive regulations that discriminated against foreign investors and investments. These policy decisions, undertaken both individually and collectively, contributed to an increase in the value of world trade that exceeded the increase in world output, an increase in both portfolio investments and foreign direct investments to hitherto unimaginable levels, and the growth of international production. In short, these policy decisions contributed to an expansion of the three major components that together comprise the globalization phenomenon.

THE EXPANSION OF WORLD TRADE

Between 1970 and 1996, the value of world exports increased by more than eighteenfold when measured in current dollars, from $298 billion to $5.2 trillion.[2] Since in real terms the annual rate of growth of world exports between 1960 and 1996 amounted to 6 percent while the growth of real output was somewhat less than 4 percent, the ratio of trade to output increased.

Although all countries shared in the increase in trade, they did not do so equally. Thus the industrial countries' share of total exports declined from 75 percent in 1970 to 68 percent in 1996 while the share of the developing countries increased from 25 percent to 32 percent.[3] Within the developing countries the experience of the emerging Asian economies—Hong Kong, South Korea, Singapore, and Taiwan—differed significantly from their counterparts in the Western Hemisphere—Argentina, Brazil, Chile, and Mexico. Between 1970 and 1996, the exports of these Asian economies increased from $6 billion to $378 billion while the exports of the selected Western Hemisphere countries increased from $7 billion to $182 billion. As a result of these disparate growth rates, the four Western Hemisphere countries accounted for 3 percent of total world exports in 1996 while the four "Asian Tigers"—as the emerging Asian economies have come to be called—accounted for 7 percent of total world exports. In part the difference in the export performance of these two groups of countries reflects their divergent development strategies. The Asian emerging economies adopted early on an export-oriented development strategy, whereas the Latin American countries, until only recently, placed reliance on an import-substitution strategy that consciously thwarted the globalization process.

China, a latecomer, increased its exports from $2.3 billion in 1970 to $151 billion in 1996, when it accounted for 3 percent of total world exports. As in so many other areas, the emerging economies of Africa lagged far behind: Their exports increased from $12 billion in 1970 to $103 billion in 1995, the latest year for which data are available. In that year their exports accounted for 2 percent of total world exports.[4] As for the former Soviet bloc, both choice and circumstances resulted in a high degree of isolation. In terms of globalization, this bloc fared worse than any other group.

The increase in the emerging economies' share of world exports since 1970 has played a prominent role in the globalization debate, particularly since a significant part of this increase was due to the expansion of manufactured exports. Indeed, between 1970 and 1990 the developing countries' share of total manufactured exports increased from 15 percent to 37 percent, with the share of Asian emerging economies alone accounting for 30 percent of the total.[5] Critics in Western Europe and the United States have stated that this expansion is primarily responsible for the stagnation of wages, the decline in the number of jobs in the manufacturing sectors, and the increase in the inequality of income distribution in the United States as well as for the high level of unemployment in Europe. These allegations are addressed in detail in Chapter 5.

THE EXPANSION OF
INTERNATIONAL INVESTMENTS

The increase in the crossborder movement of capital was the second major pillar of globalization. The restoration of currency convertibility, the removal of capital controls, and the relaxation of many regulations that discriminated against foreign investments resulted in a vast expansion of international capital flows. These assumed two basic forms: portfolio investments and foreign direct investments. Portfolio investments consist of the purchase of equity and debt instruments issued by governments and corporations in one country by the residents of another. Foreign direct investments involve the acquisition of businesses by residents of other countries. These acquisitions may take the form of a purchase, in whole or in part, of already existing firms or the establishment of new firms.

The Growth of Portfolio Investments

The explosive growth of portfolio investments—excluding those related to the purchase of equities—is evident from Table 1.1.

In 1970 funds raised on the international capital markets amounted to $5,753 million, all of which were the result of sales of international bonds. With the development of syndicated loans, particularly Euroloans in 1972, the value of funds raised on the international capital markets has been on an upward trajectory. With but five exceptions, the value of these funds increased every year through 1995, when it reached an astounding $832,243 million.[6] These funds were further augmented by capital movements resulting from equity and currency transactions. It is not possible with the existing data, however, to estimate the value of these flows.

This aspect of globalization has been both widely hailed and condemned. The ability to obtain capital on the international markets at relatively low rates has been a boon to many emerging economies, which previously had to rely almost exclusively on their own meager savings and the advanced countries' ever decreasing and uncertain aid programs. At the same time, as Mexico in 1994 and the emerging economies of Asia in 1997–1998 discovered, international capital moves on a two-way street. A wholesale flight of capital can quickly transform an otherwise manageable crisis into a major catastrophe.[7] The lesson to be derived from the Mexican and Asian crises, however, is not that globalization is unhealthy for the emerging economies but rather that access to the world's savings pool does not obviate the need to maintain a high degree of monetary discipline and financial regulation. Nevertheless, the problems posed by the highly volatile capital flows and the manner in which they can be curbed without impeding the flow of socially useful capital need to be addressed. Indeed, in view of the role "hot money flows"—as they have been called—have played in the 1997–1998 financial crisis, these problems have emerged as a central issue in the globalization debate.

TABLE 1.1   Funds Raised on the International Markets (breakdown by type of instrument, in millions of U.S. dollars)

	1970	1975	1980	1985	1990	1995
Euro-bonds	3528.5	8725.7	20394.2	136543.3	180133.5	371244.7
Foreign bonds	2224.2	11217.1	17924.2	31229.1	49781.6	89413.3
International bonds (total)	**5752.8**	**19942.8**	**38318.4**	**167772.4**	**229915.1**	**460658.0**
Of which:						
Straight bonds	5012.1	19189.2	29587.9	94784.1	158930.4	346662.0
Floating-rate notes	370.0	320.0	4818.1	58695.6	37072.8	78877.0
Convertibles	223.7	414.5	3912.4	7018.4	10633.6	12301.3
With equity warrants	147.0	19.1	-	4306.0	21172.3	5771.5
Zero coupons	-	-	-	1923.3	1499.0	8458.5
Syndicated Euro-loans	-	20607.2	78143.2	36135.6	122362.1	367841.2
Syndicated foreign loans	-	-	-	6938.3	2162.7	595.6
Other debt facilities	-	-	-	48920.5	6991.0	3148.3
Loans (total)	**-**	**20607.2**	**78143.2**	**91994.5**	**131515.8**	**371585.0**
Grand Total	**5752.8**	**40550.0**	**116461.6**	**259766.8**	**361430.9**	**832243.0**

Source: OECD, International Capital Markets Statistics, 1950–1995 (Paris: OECD, 1997), pp. 13–16.

Foreign Direct Investments

The increase in foreign direct investments and its consequences are arguably the most dramatic features of the globalization process. Between 1980 and 1995 the value of world stock of foreign direct investments rose from $500 billion to $2.7 trillion. These investments not only provided the host countries with additional capital; they also acted as conduits for the transmission of technology and managerial and organizational know-how. The driving force behind this expansion was 39,000 transnational corporations, 90 percent of which were domiciled in the advanced industrial countries. Between them, these transnational corporations controlled a worldwide empire consisting of 265,000 foreign-based affiliates, 27 percent of which were located in developing countries, 40 percent in developed countries, and 22 percent in central and Eastern Europe.[8]

The growing importance of transnational corporations in the global economy is suggested by Table 1.2, which shows the increase in the gross product and sales of foreign affiliates since 1982.

Particularly noteworthy are the data in the last column, which show the ratio of sales of foreign affiliates to exports of goods and services. In 1993 the value of sales of foreign affiliates exceeded world exports by 28 percent. For the world as a whole, as well as for most of its constituent groups, the sales of affiliates have become a more important mode of penetrating foreign countries' markets than the traditional arm's-length method of exporting.

THE GROWTH OF THE INTERNATIONAL PRODUCTION SYSTEM

One of the most important factors fueling this expansion in foreign direct investments was the growth of international production. This development contributed both to an increase in the number of foreign affiliates and, perhaps more important, to a change in the function of these affiliates.

Historically, foreign affiliates' major functions were to provide parent companies with raw materials for further processing or refining; to produce goods for sale in host-country markets when obstacles of various sorts—tariffs, nontrade barriers, and high transportation costs—precluded supplying these markets through exports; and to act as distributing agents for parent companies' products. For the most part, foreign affiliates were stand-alone companies. Their relationship to parent companies resembled more a collection of quasi-autonomous firms rather than components of an integrated production system.

Although foreign affiliates continue to perform these traditional functions, changes in the economic environment due to the interaction of technological developments in the transportation, communications, and information sectors, and the policy decisions that resulted in a liberalization of trade and investment, have enabled multinational enterprises to develop strategies that have revolutionized their roles in the global economy as well as the global economy itself. The implementation of these strategies, in effect, transformed foreign affiliates from stand-alone companies into components of an integrated production process that tran-

TABLE 1.2   Sales and Gross Product of Foreign Affiliates, Exports of Goods and Nonfactor Services, and GDP by Region (billions of U.S. dollars and percentages)

Region/Country	Gross Product of Foreign Affiliates		Gross Product of Foreign Affiliates as a Ratio to Home Country GDP (percent)		Sales of Foreign Affiliates			Sales of Foreign Affiliates as a Ratio to Exports of Goods and Nonfactor Services (percent)		
	1982	1990	1982	1990	1982	1990	1993	1982	1990	1993
Developed countries	410	1,102	5.2	6.7	1,770	4,272	4,525	121.2	136.3	131.5
Western Europe	180	609	5.9	8.8	785	2,360	2,564	89.3	117.6	121.7
European Union	164	572	5.7	8.7	718	2,216	2,416	87.6	118.1	122.3
Other W. Europe	15	37	9.6	10.6	68	145	148	111.7	109.9	112.7
North America	177	408	5.1	6.7	775	1,580	1,587	214.6	225.1	193.2
Others	48	86	3.5	2.5	210	332	374	95.3	78.3	72.8
Developing countries	143	274	5.7	6.6	626	1,062	1,457	113.7	111.6	133.5
Africa	23	33	6.8	8.6	99	129	143	119.5	126.4	157.7
Latin Am. and Carib.	58	97	7.5	8.9	255	377	500	226.9	236.6	293.6
Asia	61	141	4.6	5.4	265	547	802	77.9	82.4	99.1
West Asia	17	24	3.8	2.5	73	92.8	106	51.1	65.4	68.4
So., E. and SE. Asia	44	117	5.0	7.4	192	454	695	97.4	87.0	106.8
Oceania	1.2	1.7	28.6	32.2	5	7	8	346.8	303.4	230.0
Cent. and East. Europe	0.1	1.5	0.0	0.7	0.5	6	40	0.9	10.1	22.8
World	548	1,378	5.2	6.6	2,396	5,341	6,022	116.0	128.9	127.9

Source: UNCTAD, *World Investment Report 1996: Investment, Trade and International Policy Arrangements* (N.Y. and Geneva, 1996), p. 17.

scended national boundaries and ushered in, on a grand scale, the era of international production.

The new strategies embraced by multinational enterprises entailed splitting up the value chain—also known as the production process—into various activities and assigning each activity to the location where it could be performed at the lowest possible cost. The penultimate activity in the value chain consists of an in-gathering of all the intermediate products resulting from the various activities at the site chosen for the final activity, that is, the assembly of the components into finished goods. These goods are in the truest sense internationally produced. The concept of national origin, which at one time was unambiguous, is, for these goods, virtually meaningless. Indeed, in many cases the national origin of a given product is determined by some legalistic definition, which at times becomes a negotiable issue between countries.

The growth of international production has had an important impact on the determinants of the location of foreign direct investments. Whereas access to the host countries' markets and raw materials was the leading determinant in earlier times, the new strategies have elevated the importance of other factors as well. Since the minimization of the cost of production is a major objective of these new strategies, the quality of the infrastructure, the characteristics of the indigenous labor force, political stability, and prevailing wage rates play increasingly important roles in determining site location.

The internationalization of production has also had an impact on efficiency beyond that resulting from the selection of low-cost sites. The ability to slice up the value chain provides opportunities for economies of scale that otherwise would not exist. A striking but by no means unique example of this is provided by the German drug firm BASF, which concentrates its cancer and immune system research in a U.S. affiliate and disseminates the results to pharmaceutical companies located all over the world.[9]

Although a precise estimate of the number of foreign affiliates involved in international production operations is not available, an indication of their importance is suggested by the magnitude of their sales and intrafirm trade. The UN estimates that in 1993—the latest year for which data are available—worldwide sales by foreign affiliates amounted to $6 trillion. The value of these sales exceeded the value of total world exports by 28 percent.[10]

Because the very nature of international production entails a flow of intermediate products between parents and affiliates and among affiliates themselves, the growth of intrafirm trade is an even more precise indicator of globalization than total affiliate sales. Between 1984 and 1993, intrafirm exports are estimated to have increased from $816 billion to $1,587 billion. In 1993 these exports amounted to one-third of total world exports.[11]

Intrafirm trade, however, consists of all goods and services and not just intermediate goods. To obtain a finer measure of the growth of international production, a study by the Organization for Economic Cooperation and Development (OECD) attempted to estimate the proportion of manufactured imports that were intermediate inputs. This study concludes that the proportion "ranged from roughly 50 percent for Canada, Germany, the United Kingdom, and the United States, to nearly 60 percent for France and more than 70 percent for Japan." This study further notes that this trade "is growing very rapidly, maintaining its share in the expansion of trade as a whole."[12]

By separating a country's intermediate inputs into two categories—one representing inputs derived from domestic sources, the other representing inputs derived from foreign sources—the OECD developed an indicator of international linkage for each country's industries. This indicator is the ratio of foreign-derived inputs to domestic-derived inputs. Thus a ratio of one indicates that the industry derived as much of its inputs from abroad as it did from domestic sources. A ratio of greater than one indicates that a larger proportion of inputs was derived from foreign sources than from domestic sources; an indicator of less than one indicates that a smaller proportion of inputs was derived from foreign sources than from domestic sources. Estimates of this indicator for a number of prominent global industries—motor vehicles, computers, aerospace, communications equipment, and semiconductor equipment—are shown in Table 1.3. Note that the international linkage indicator for the United States in all of these industries was less than 0.5, indicating that U.S. industries placed a smaller reliance on foreign inputs than on U.S. produced inputs.[13]

As important as they are, foreign affiliates were not the only actors in the growth of international production. In addition to affiliates, multinational enterprises increasingly relied on outsourcing to unaffiliated foreign firms, on strategic alliances with foreign multinational enterprises, and on licensing and franchising. Although it is not possible with the available data to estimate the value of all of these operations, the fact that they have increased substantially in recent years is a strong indication of their growing importance. The UN, quoting a study by Hagerdoorn and Duysters, reports that "strategic alliances in high technology industries

TABLE 1.3 Ranking of Intermediate Inputs (ratio of imported to domestic sourcing[a])

Rank	Canada[b] 1986	France[b] 1985	Germany[b] 1986	Japan[b] 1985	United Kingdom[b] 1984	United States[b] 1985
1	Motor vehicles 4.8	Instruments 1.7	Computers 1.2	Aerospace 0.6	Aerospace 3.2	Other manufac.[d] 0.4
2	Computers 3.2	Nonferrous metals 1.0	Nonferrous metals 0.9	Nonferrous metals 0.4	Nonferrous metals 1.3	Computers 0.3
3	Aerospace 2.1	Chemicals 0.8	Textiles, apparel, and footwear 0.6	Computers 0.2	Chemicals 0.7	Communication and semiconductor equipment 0.3
4	Communication and semiconductor equipment 0.2	Computers 0.8	Aerospace 0.6	Petroleum refining 0.2	Computers 0.6	Motor vehicles 0.3
5	Instruments 1.4	Communication and semiconductor equipment 0.7	Petroleum refining 0.6	Food, drink and tobacco 0.1	Communication and semiconductor equipment 0.6	Instruments 0.2
6	Nonelectric machinery 1.3	Nonelectric machinery 0.5	Electrical machinery 0.4	Wood, cork and furniture 0.1	Wood, cork and furniture 0.6	Shipbuilding 0.2

continued on next page

(new materials, biotechnology and information technology) increased from an estimated 145 in 1980 to 449 in 1993."[14]

All three indicators—the expansion of trade, the increase in crossborder capital movements (in the form of portfolio investments as well as foreign direct investment), and the growth of international production—attest to the robust state of globalization in recent decades. The remainder of this study will attempt to assess, on the basis of the best available evidence, the impact of this process on the American economy and the validity of the more important arguments advanced by critics. Among other issues this study addresses the following: whether and how a liberalization of trade and investment regimes enhances economic welfare; whether the

(continued)

TABLE 1.3   Ranking of Intermediate Inputs (ratio of imported to domestic sourcing[a])

Rank	Canada[b] 1986	France[b] 1985	Germany[b] 1986	Japan[b] 1985	United Kingdom[b] 1984	United States[b] 1985
7	Other transport[c] 0.9	Petroleum refining 0.4	Chemicals 0.4	Textiles, apparel and footwear 0.1	Electrical machinery 0.5	Other transport[c] 0.2
8	Textiles, apparel and footwear 0.6	Other manufac.[d] 0.4	Instruments 0.3	Pharmaceuticals 0.1	Petroleum refining 0.5	Ferrous metals 0.2
9	Nonferrous metals 0.6	Textiles, apparel, and footwear 0.4	Nonelectric machinery 0.3	Chemicals 0.1	Motor vehicles 0.5	Motor-electric machinery 0.1
10	Electrical machinery 0.5	Ferrous metals 0.3	Motor vehicles 0.2	Instruments 0.1	Textiles, apparel, and footwear 0.5	Electrical machinery 0.1

[a] A ratio of one means that the source of this input is evenly divided between domestic and foreign suppliers; less than one means that the use of this input from domestic suppliers exceeds that of foreign suppliers; more than one means that the use of imported inputs exceeds that supplied from domestic sources.
[b] All data are expressed in current domestic currencies, except for France (constant 1980 Francs).
[c] Includes railroad equipment, motorcycles, bicycles, travel trailers and campers, and other transportation not elsewhere classified.
[d] Includes jewelry, musical instruments, toys, sporting goods, pens and pencils, and other manufacturing not elsewhere classified.

Source: Andrew W. Wyckoff, "The International Expansion of Productive Networks," *OECD Observer* 180 (Feb.–March 1993): 10.

reduction in tariffs and the removal of nontariff trade barriers were responsible for the stagnation of American wages, the increase in income inequality, the loss of good jobs in the manufacturing sector, and the burgeoning of current account deficits; whether the postwar trading system, which the United States helped to construct, contributed to the erosion of American sovereignty; whether the perception is valid that the postwar trading system enabled its trading partners to victimize the United States; whether the globalization of the capital markets has had an adverse effect on the American economy by encouraging a flight of capital and firms to low-wage countries; whether globalization poses a threat to the advanced industrial countries' more stringent environmental and labor standards; and whether the Clinton administration's emphasis on regional trade agreements represents a step toward further liberalization or a potential threat to the multilateral trading system. The concluding chapter addresses some of the current threats to a continuation of the globalization process.

Contrary to a widespread deterministic view that the globalization process is driven by technology, the underlying premise of this study is that it is policy-driven. A society that concludes that globalization is not in its interest can, through policy changes, insulate itself from whatever it fears. There is ample historical evidence to support this. As Paul Krugman has argued, the world economy prior to World War I was highly integrated. This, however, did not prevent the extraordinary fragmentation that occurred during the interwar period. The ability to stop and even reverse the globalization process makes it all the more important to understand the benefits and costs of alternative trade and investment regimes.

This study consists of three interrelated parts. Part 1 comprises Chapters 2–3, which contain a survey of the theoretical literature on the relationship between trade and economic welfare and an examination of the postwar, multilateral, rule-based, nondiscriminatory trade regime that was inaugurated in 1948 with the ratification of GATT. Part 2, comprising Chapters 4–7, is devoted to an examination of the impact of globalization on the U.S. economy. Chapter 4 is devoted to an analysis of the U.S. international accounts with special emphasis on the factors responsible for the recurrent deficits and for the transformations of the United States from the world's leading creditor to the world's leading debtor country. Chapter 5 focuses on changes in the value composition and direction of trade during the postwar period and on the impact of trade on employment, wages, and income distribution. Chapters 6 and 7 are devoted to an examination of the impact of outward and inward foreign direct investments. Part 3, comprising Chapters 8–12, is a chronicle of the deterioration of the GATT system and the attempt to reform it during the Uruguay Round. It concludes with an analysis of incipient problems confronting the global economy in the post–Uruguay Round period.

PART ONE

Free Trade:
Theory and Reality

2

THE GAINS FROM TRADE
AND THE COST OF PROTECTION

An examination of the economic performance of different countries suggests a strong positive relationship between their trade and investment regimes, growth rates, and per capita domestic product. Invariably countries that opted for liberal trade and investment regimes grew more rapidly and enjoyed higher per capita income than those that attempted to insulate their economies from foreign competition and erected obstacles to foreign direct investments.[1] This relationship is most striking when comparing the economic performance of selected Latin American countries and East Asian countries. After a brief flirtation with protectionist policies, the Asian Tigers—Hong Kong, Taiwan, Singapore, and South Korea—aggressively pursued export-oriented growth strategies. By contrast, the Latin American economies we review relied on an import-substitution strategy of development, the essence of which was to encourage domestic development by diverting demand from imports to domestic industries. The data in Table 2.1 compare how these two groups fared between 1965 and 1990.

Further support for the hypothesis that trade plays a prominent role in determining a country's economic performance is provided by students of economic growth. After identifying and isolating the factors responsible for economic growth in the United States over a long period, Moses Abramowitz, Robert Solow, and Edward Denison, among others, conclude that the increase in the quantity of labor and capital employed accounted for a relatively small proportion of the observed growth—usually no more than 20 percent—with the remainder attributable to an increase in total factor productivity resulting from improvements in the

TABLE 2.1 Growth Rates of Selected Asian and Latin American Countries, 1965–1990 (in percentages)

	Real GDP[a]		Gross Domestic Investment[a]		GDP per Capita[a]	
	1965–1980	1980–1990	1965–1980	1980–1990	1965–1980	1980–1990
Hong Kong	8.6	7.2	8.6	3.6	6.6	5.7
Korea	9.9	9.7	15.9	12.5	7.9	8.6
Singapore	10.0	6.3	13.3	3.6	8.4	4.2
Taiwan	9.3[b]	8.5	13.4[c]	4.6[d]	7.5	6.8[e]
Argentina	3.4	-0.4	4.6	-8.3	2.1	-1.7
Bolivia	4.4	-0.1	4.4	-10.7	1.9	-2.6
Brazil	9.0	2.7	11.3	0.2	6.6	0.5
Chile	1.9	3.2	0.5	4.3	0.2	1.5
Mexico	6.5	1.0	8.5	-3.4	3.4	-1.0

[a] Average annual rate of change
[b] 1971–1980
[c] Gross fixed capital formation
[d] 1980–1989
[e] 1980–1988

Source: World Bank.

quality of labor and capital as well as in the manner in which these factors of production are organized. Technological innovations, investments in human capital, economies of scale, and improvements in management and organization were the most prominent factors responsible for these developments.[2] Trade's contribution to growth results from the catalytic role it plays regarding all of these factors. The major part of this chapter is devoted to an examination of this role. Specifically, trade's impact on total factor productivity through its influence on the allocation of resources, economies of scale, industrial organization, and innovation is explored. The chapter concludes with a brief examination of the few situations where a country's economic welfare can be enhanced by adopting protectionist measures and with a still briefer discussion of the political economy of protectionism.

TRADE, ALLOCATION OF RESOURCES, AND ECONOMIC EFFICIENCY

From the earliest times, trade's biggest lure was the prospect it offered to obtain necessary or desired imports. The Old Testament informs us that Solomon, in order to obtain supplies needed to build a temple to the Lord of Israel, entered into a trade agreement with Hiram, king of Lebanon, whereby Hiram agreed to supply the Israelites with "cedars and cypresses . . . and the skilled workers necessary to hew them" in exchange for "twenty thousand measures of wheat for food . . . and twenty thousand measures of beaten oil" (1 Kings 5:10). The great Polish-born anthropologist B. K. Malinowski reported that the Trobriand Islanders incorporated the exchange of goods into their religious rituals to ensure their continued supply.[3] Marco Polo, Christopher Columbus, and even the Spanish conquistadors were seeking access to sources of supply and not markets for exports. Indeed, it was not until the time of mercantilists of the sixteenth and seventeenth centuries that the emphasis shifted from imports to exports. Writing during a period that was dominated by statebuilding and in which gold was both the symbol of and the means to power, mercantilists extolled the virtues of a trade surplus. This lesson was so deeply ingrained that it remains a potent force in the development of economic policy to this very day.

Classical economists, beginning most prominently with David Ricardo, were the first to analyze systematically the impact of trade on economic welfare.[4] In their view, trade enhanced economic welfare in two distinct ways: It enabled residents of trading countries to enjoy a wider variety of goods than otherwise would have been possible; most important, it reduced the cost of obtaining these goods. In this perspective, imports are again viewed as the welfare-enhancing component of trade. Exports, in contrast, are the payments for these imports or, in other words, their cost. The measure of a country's gains from trade is the difference between the cost of obtaining goods by producing them directly and the cost of producing the exports that are exchanged for them. Trade will enhance economic welfare when the cost of producing the desired goods directly exceeds the cost of obtaining those goods through trade. Moreover, the greater the cost difference between these two methods of obtaining the desired goods, the more welfare-enhancing trade will become.

The principle of comparative advantage, the cornerstone of classical trade theory, provides an explanation as to how trade generates gains. The principle states that when trade occurs each country tends to specialize in the production and export of those goods that it produces most efficiently and to import those goods in the production of which it is *least* proficient. Hence trade results in a reallocation of the factors of production in each country away from its most inefficient industries and toward its most efficient industries. Trade, in effect, enables a country to obtain *all* its goods—those produced domestically as well as those produced abroad—in the most efficient manner possible.[5]

Many arguments in support of protection are based on a fundamental misunderstanding of this principle. It has been argued, for example, that in an era of highly mobile capital and technology protection is necessary if developed countries' industries are to survive. In the absence of protection, we are told, the less developed countries can gain a competitive advantage across the whole spectrum of goods by combining their low-wage labor with cutting-edge technology. Not surprisingly, spokesmen for the less developed countries see a very different tableau. They point to the developed countries' superior technology and their large supply of highly skilled workers as reasons why the "trade game" is hopelessly biased against them.

Neither one of these arguments is correct. By the very nature of the case, the principle of comparative advantage precludes the possibility of any single trading partner being dominant in *all* markets. Indeed, properly construed, the principle not only highlights the goods a country will export but also the goods it will import.

The basic fallacy in the arguments that a country can become dominant in all markets is due both to a confusion between absolute and comparative advantage and to a failure to identify properly the items to be compared. It is possible for a single country to *appear* to be able to dominate most, if not all, markets. Something of this nature occurred, for example, in the period immediately following World War II, when the United States stood as a colossus over a devastated Europe and Asia. At that time many, including some highly trained economists, confused absolute and comparative advantage and concluded that because the United States was capable of producing goods A, B, C, D, . . . and N at a lower cost than any other country, it would be able to dominate all these markets to the permanent detriment of the other economies. The cost comparison that underlies this analysis is not, however, the appropriate one. What has to be compared are not the crosscountry cost differences in each industry but rather the crosscountry cost structures.

A country's *cost structure* is defined as the ratio of the cost of producing *different* goods *within* the same country. To illustrate this concept, consider a world of two countries, Alpha and Beta, whose factors of production are capable of producing two goods, wheat and cloth. In Alpha a "bundle" of factors can produce either one unit of wheat if employed in the wheat industry or two units of cloth if employed in the cloth industry. Furthermore, for purposes of illustration, assume that all the factors are fully employed in producing either wheat or cloth. Under these conditions, the production of an additional unit of wheat would require a two-unit reduction in the production of cloth. Hence, the cost of producing an additional unit of wheat is two units of cloth. This is Alpha's cost structure. Under similar assumptions, a standard bundle of factors in Beta—not necessarily the same as in Alpha's—is capable of producing one unit of wheat or three units of cloth. For reasons noted above, the cost of producing an additional unit of wheat in Beta is three units of cloth. This, then, is Beta's cost structure.

A crosscountry comparison of these two cost structures indicates that Alpha has a comparative advantage in the production of wheat and that Beta has a comparative advantage in the production of cloth. The cost of producing an additional unit of wheat in Alpha is two units of cloth, whereas in Beta it is three units of cloth. Yet the cost of producing an additional unit of cloth in Alpha is one-half a unit of wheat, whereas in Beta it is only one-third of a unit of wheat.

Were these two countries to commence trade, Alpha would specialize in the production and export of wheat and Beta would specialize in the production and export of cloth. That trade, following the course indicated by the comparative advantage principle, can enhance the economic welfare—measured in terms of the availability of goods of both economies—is easily demonstrated. Since before trade Alpha had to relinquish one unit of wheat to obtain two units of cloth, its welfare would be enhanced if, after trade, it could get from Beta more than two units of cloth for each unit of wheat. This, of course, is eminently possible. Since in the pretrade period Beta had to give up three units of cloth to get a unit of wheat, it would be more than willing to offer Alpha, say, two and a half units of cloth for a unit of wheat. In short, the *difference* in the cost structures of the two countries creates a window of opportunity. By engaging in trade at any rate of exchange between one unit of wheat for two units of cloth and one unit of wheat for three units of cloth, the economic welfare of both countries would be enhanced.

This is an important conclusion. Trade is not a zero-sum game. The gains that each country derives from trade are not at the expense of the other but rather are the fruit of the increase in efficiency that results when each country specializes in the production and export of those goods that it is capable of producing most proficiently.

DETERMINANTS OF COMPARATIVE ADVANTAGE

Although the principle of comparative advantage is the bedrock of international trade theory, it cannot by itself provide insights into a specific country's trade pattern. To understand why a country has a competitive edge in some markets and not in others, it is necessary to know the determinants of comparative advantage. This knowledge is important, however, not only for the insights it provides regarding actual trade patterns—why Germany exports this and the United States exports that—but also (and from the perspective of this study even more important) because it sheds additional light on the relationship between trade and growth.

The three major determinants of comparative advantage are crosscountry differences in technology, factor endowments, and economies of scale. For analytical purposes the influence of each of these determinants is treated separately, yet in reality they interact with each other so that a country's competitive edge in any particular good is frequently a product not of one but of several determinants. Of the three determinants, the influence of technology is the most obvious and requires the least explication. Countries whose firms develop or exploit the most advanced technologies gain a competitive edge over those that do not. Ralph Waldo Emerson's dictum regarding the advantage of building a better mousetrap—particularly if this advantage is combined with a lower price—still holds. Technological developments explain in large part Britain's dominance in manufacturing during the early part of the nineteenth century, Germany's successful challenge to that dominance during the latter part of that century, and why the advanced industrial countries today *are* advanced. As we will illustrate below, the desire to acquire the latest technology is a major factor influencing the decision by some developing countries to adopt more liberal trade and investment policies.

The Role of Factor Endowments

The role of factor endowments in the determination of comparative advantage has received much attention during the past fifty years. Much of this attention was motivated by the Hecksher-Ohlin hypothesis, which posited that a country with an abundant supply of a particular factor of production will tend to enjoy a comparative advantage with respect to those goods in the production of which this factor is intensive.[6] To illustrate this point, assume two countries, the United States and China, two factors of production, labor and capital, and two commodities, designated as X and Y. For the purpose of isolating the impact of factor endowments on the determination of comparative advantage, it is assumed that the technology is identical in both countries and hence does not affect the outcome. Good X is assumed to be capital-intensive relative to good Y, in that when the two goods are produced using the most efficient method, more capital per unit of labor is required to produce a unit of X than is required to produce a unit of Y. If it is now assumed that the United States has an abundant supply of capital relative to labor and that China has an abundant supply of labor relative to capital, the Hecksher-Ohlin hypothesis predicts that the United States would have a comparative advantage in the production of good X—the capital-intensive good—and China would have a comparative advantage in the production of good Y, the labor-intensive good. When trade with China and the United States begins, the United States would export capital-intensive goods and China would export labor-intensive goods.

In fact, American-Chinese trade at present is not unlike the pattern predicted by the Hecksher-Ohlin hypothesis. It must be emphasized, however, that this does not condemn China to a permanent role as a global hewer of wood and drawer of water. A country's factor endowments are neither natural nor static. At any given point in time they reflect its past history and development. The present endowment of the United States, for example, is largely the result of huge investments in both physical and human capital. It is not at all surprising that the comparative U.S. advantage is in the capital-, skill-, and knowledge-intensive areas. By contrast China, until recently one of the poorest countries in the world, has a scarcity of both physical and human capital. What it does have in abundance is a large, unskilled labor force. China's current comparative advantage in the production of unskilled labor–intensive goods is a manifestation of this.

This, however, is not a chronic condition. Japan's transformation from an exporter of unskilled labor-intensive goods during the prewar period to a preeminent exporter of knowledge and skill-intensive goods is a testimony not only to the ability of a country to reinvent itself but also to the rapidity with which this can be done. Israel provides still another example of this. Within a period of a short lifetime this country, largely because of the massive inflow of highly educated and skilled immigrants, transformed itself from a rather primitive agricultural exporter to an important producer and exporter of skill- and knowledge-intensive goods. Further examples of economies in transition are provided by the Asian Tigers.

It should be noted that factor endowments influence the pattern of trade and are in turn influenced by it. This suggests another channel through which trade may influence a country's economic growth. For example, because the United States has an abundant supply of skilled labor and a scarcity of unskilled labor, it would tend to export skilled labor–intensive goods and to import unskilled labor–intensive goods. Hence, trade would result in an increase in the demand for skilled labor and a decline in the demand for unskilled labor, thereby increasing the gap between the earnings of skilled and unskilled workers. In creating additional incentives to acquire skills, trade would thus tend to increase the American endowment of the factor—human capital—that many economists consider to be the most important contributor to a country's economic growth.[7]

This does not imply, however, that trade will make rich countries like the United States richer and poor countries like China poorer. It is true that for China the initial impact of trade would be to increase the demand for and the remuneration of unskilled labor. By itself this would suggest a decline in the inducement to acquire skills, inasmuch as the rate of return on human capital as measured by the difference between skilled and unskilled wages will have narrowed. This tendency is offset, however, by two forces pushing in the opposite direction. First, by increasing China's real income, trade would enable that country to devote more resources to skill acquisition than would otherwise be the case. Second, by making China less competitive in the production of unskilled labor–intensive goods, the increase in wages would provide an incentive to develop comparative advantage in other sectors. This process has, in fact, already occurred in those economies—Hong Kong, South Korea, and Singapore, to name but a few—that have made the transition from exporters of unskilled labor–intensive goods to exporters of relatively highly skilled labor–intensive goods as a result of an increase in the wages of unskilled labor.[8]

The Role of Economies of Scale

Economies of scale complete the triad of the determinants of comparative advantage. Amazingly, this determinant was not considered important until fairly recently.[9] What pushed it into the spotlight was the realization that a very large part of international trade—that between the advanced industrial countries—could not be explained either by differences in technology or in factor endowments. This trade—as even a cursory examination of the import and export matrices of any advanced industrial country would reveal—consists for the most part of an exchange of similar albeit not identical goods. The importance of intraindustry trade to the United States is suggested by Table 5.6 in Chapter 5, which shows the imports and exports of selected items in 1996.

Economies of scale occur when an expansion of a firm's output is associated with a reduction in its unit cost of production. These economies may be due to a number of factors, the most prominent of which are the firm's ability to spread fixed costs over a larger number of units and the ability to exploit the opportunity to restructure its organizations and to adopt more efficient methods of production that were not previously available to it at lower levels of output. For whatever reason they occur, economies of scale enable firms to attain a competitive edge vis-à-vis their smaller rivals. And like superior technology or differences in factor endowments, these economies can be adduced to explain why firms in certain countries enjoy a comparative advantage vis-à-vis their competitors in global markets.

Critics of free trade argue that a comparative advantage that reflects economies of scale is somehow less compelling than one that reflects superior technology or differences in factor endowments. Since serendipity frequently plays a role in determining which firms get to enjoy economies of scale, critics argue that a strong case can be made for government intervention in the form of subsidies to domestic firms or tariffs on imports to level the playing field. It is difficult, however, to accept this argument. The competitive edge that firms enjoy as a result of economies of scale is not derived at the expense of rivals. The possibility that this advantage might have been enjoyed by other firms if circumstances were different—if these other firms had begun operations earlier, if their management, sales forces, advertising campaigns, brand names, and service departments were better than they were—does not make the existing economies of scale enjoyed by the first comers any less real than if the advantage were derived from superior technology. Moreover, the loss that would result if subsidies or tariffs eliminated the economies of scale—as they would if they resulted in a reduction in the output of the advantaged firms—is as real as that which would result from banning the use of a superior technology.

Economies of scale are, of course, closely associated with specialization. They emerge because of decisions made by firms to concentrate efforts in selected niches of industries. This tendency, however, not only generates economies of scale over a broad spectrum of goods but also lays the groundwork for the vast network of intraindustry trade. The exploitation of economies of scale thus increases economic welfare in two distinct ways: It results in lower costs of production, and it increases the variety of goods available to consumers and producers. Moreover, by increasing the degree of specialization, it could, as Adam Smith suggested more than two hundred years ago, contribute to growth by stimulating innovations and inventions.

Economies of scale find their most fertile soil in oligopolistic industries that are characterized by a relatively small number of firms. Typically, the small number of firms in oligopolistic industries reflects high barriers to entry, resulting from either large capital requirements or large development costs. The large production runs necessary to amortize these costs and to keep prices at a reasonable level suffice to ensure that the number of firms in the industry will remain small. Among the oligopolistic industries that play a major role in the global economy are automobiles, pharmaceuticals, computers, computer software, aerospace, and transportation equipment.

The existence of economies of scale increases total factor productivity by reducing the unit costs of production. By enabling firms to expand their output beyond that dictated by domestic demand alone, international trade contributes to a country's growth rate.

THE DYNAMIC IMPACT

Thus far, gains from trade resulting from a more effective allocation of resources and economies of scale have been highlighted. Although these gains are not insubstantial, they might be overshadowed by others that are frequently ignored or minimized because they are basically nonmeasurable. In a study initially published in 1942 entitled *Capitalism, Socialism, and Democracy*, the great economist Joseph Schumpeter attributed the growth of economic welfare during the past two centuries to a process he called "creative destruction." In his view, the driving force of a dynamic economy is

> competition from the new commodity, the new technology, the new source of supply, the new source of organization. . . . Competition which commands a decisive cost or quality advantage and which strikes not at the margins of the profits and the outputs of existing firms but at their foundations and their very rise. This kind of competition . . . is the powerful lever that in the long run expands outputs and brings down prices.[10]

This process is even more potent when played out on a global scale. The reorganization and restructuring of the American automobile industry to improve efficiency, the widespread adoption of the agile production system that originated in Japan, the innovations and investments in the American textile industry that kept it competitive despite the challenge posed by the emerging economies, the improvement in American competitiveness that has resulted in its being ranked the highest in the world in a recent study,[11] all reflect, in whole or in part, the American response to the intense global competition it encountered in the post-1970 period. In an important study of the factors responsible for national differences in manufacturing productivity, Martin Baily and Hans Gerbach concluded that although capital and scale played a role "innovations such as designs for manufacturing and workplace organization turned out to be more important."[12] They found that a firm's ability to adapt to revolutionary developments, moreover, was clearly related to the degree of its exposure to global competition.

> In particular it is noted that industries in a given country compete against companies with the best manufacturing processes wherever these leading companies are located, so that they themselves become best practice producers. Vigorous global competition against the best practice producers not only spurs allocation efficiencies, it also fuels structural changes in industries and encourages the adoption of more efficient product and process designs.[13]

This process of revolutionary rationalization has resulted in, among other things, the downsizing of American corporations, which in turn has been singled out as one of the most egregious aspects of globalization. This criticism, however, is misplaced. It is at best a criticism not of globalization but rather of market capitalism. And though it is true that liberal-

izing trade has both extended the sphere in which competitive forces operate and intensified the degree of market discipline, it has not altered
either the structure or the logic of the system. Moreover, if it is a fact that
economies that place reliance on market forces outperform those that rely
on central control—and the history of the past seventy-five years would
seem to leave little doubt about this—the extension of the market through
the process of globalization should be welcomed rather than condemned.
The American corporate downsizing that has been the cause of much
angst in recent years should be regarded not as a symptom of corporate
greed but rather of the waste and inefficiency that have infected the
American economy and constrained its growth. The implicit argument
that existing jobs should be preserved at all costs is no different in principle from the argument frequently voiced in Eastern and Central Europe
that the reforms introduced after the collapse of communism should be
reversed because the elimination of subsidies to and the protection of
hopelessly inefficient industries have produced widespread economic
distress and unemployment. It is amazing the way in which many
Americans, untrained in economics, see the fallacy of this argument while
not realizing that it is equally applicable to the denunciation of corporate
downsizing. A recent editorial in *The New York Times*, which in a series of
articles both publicized and implicitly deplored American downsizing, is
a case in point. Referring to a belated effort by the Bulgarian and
Rumanian economies to adopt reforms, the editor noted:

> Earlier this month, the Rumanian government shut seventeen money-losing
> state factories, relics of the communist era. The closure is the latest sign that
> Rumania is braving worker protests to stitch through harsh but necessary
> free market reforms. . . . The pain of subsidy cuts and closure of inefficient
> state industries will try [Rumania's] commitment . . . to reforms. . . . The
> temptation to flinch will be great but [it] should not forget the misery
> brought by the reluctance to shed old habits.[14]

On a smaller scale, is not the American corporate downsizing analogous?

This, however, is not to suggest an unconcern for or an insensitivity to
the plight of those who are adversely affected by the globalization
process. A market-based economy has proved to be a powerful engine of
growth. At the same time, however, it has not brought about an equitable
distribution of the fruits of growth. One can applaud the production performance of the market-based economy while deploring the existence of
extreme poverty amid unimaginable plenty. Regarding the devastated
economies of Eastern and Central Europe, it has been widely recognized

that the success of reform will depend upon international assistance in the form of aid and foreign investments. Yet the same need for assistance exists for those adversely affected by the globalization process within the affluent societies. The notion that a closer integration of the U.S. economy with that of the rest of the world requires the dismantling of the safety net or that the globalization process relieves society from any responsibility to assist those adversely affected by it has no basis in fact. Indeed, since globalization will tend to enhance a country's economic welfare, just the reverse may be true. The increase in real income resulting from the liberalization of trade should make it economically easier to aid those adversely affected by the globalization process. But acceding to those who demand an end to integration through the imposition of trade and investment barriers on the grounds that liberalization has had some adverse effect is a recipe for failure and will inevitably inflict more harm on those groups that these policies are ostensibly designed to assist.

The most important component of any program designed to help those adversely affected by the closer integration of the U.S. economy with that of the rest of the world is the pursuit of policies that promote job creation and education. In at least one respect the United States in recent years has fared very well indeed. Between 1992 and 1997 13.7 million new jobs were created, and available data suggest that after relatively brief layoff periods the vast majority of workers who were downsized found jobs as good or almost as good as those they lost.

To resist industrial rationalization, whether in central and Eastern Europe or in the United States and France, on the grounds that it results in unemployment and dislocation is in principle no different from resisting technological progress. In the short run, the perception of the Luddites of the early Industrial Revolution who threw their sabots into the machine was correct: The old machines resulted in a loss of jobs and worker displacement. With the hindsight of history, however, it is clear that the adoption of their programs would have been disastrous. Nor, in the light of twentieth-century economic history, can there be any doubt that any short-term gains, resulting from an attempt to insulate economies from competitive pressures exerted by foreign firms, would be quickly offset by long-term losses.

THE USE OF TARIFFS FOR PURPOSES OTHER THAN PROTECTION

Although tariffs and other trade barriers are most frequently used to protect industries that are unable to compete in the marketplace, they are sometimes deployed to raise revenues, to achieve noneconomic objectives, to augment the economic welfare of the country by exploiting its market power, and to provide temporary protection to infant industries with the implicit understanding that they will be removed when the infants mature. In this section, the case for using tariffs for these purposes is briefly examined.

Before the introduction of the income tax, tariffs were a major source of revenue for the U.S. federal government. At the present time, however, the revenues derived from tariffs in the United States and in most advanced industrial countries are insignificant. For some less developed countries, however, tariffs remain an important source of revenue, and the potential loss of these revenues is a factor contributing to the reluctance of these countries to reduce or remove existing tariffs.

Tariffs are frequently deployed to attain social objectives. They have been used to, among other things, offset market distortions resulting from monopolistic practices or rigid wages that impair the market's allocation mechanism; to alter the composition of a country's imports in order to conserve foreign exchange for more essential purposes; to expand the domestic production of goods that are deemed essential for national security; to redistribute income; and to protect the health and welfare of the public. Despite the fact that tariffs can achieve these and similar objectives, they are for the most part second-best solutions. The primary reason is that they are insufficiently focused and hence tend to generate undesirable side effects that could be avoided by using more focused measures.

Tariffs always impact two sectors of the economy: the supply sector and the demand sector. By increasing the domestic price of a good, the tariff induces both an increase in domestic production and a decline in the quantity demanded. If the objective was to reduce the quantity of the good demanded, then the increase in domestic output is an undesirable side effect. But if the objective is to increase domestic output—because this is deemed desirable on national security grounds—the induced decline in demand is an undesired side effect. These side effects can be avoided by adopting measures that have more focused impacts than tariffs. A consumption or use tax, for example, is a more efficient way to induce a decline in demand; a production subsidy is a more efficient way to stimulate domestic output.[15]

It will be noted in Chapter 3 that even though GATT did not ban the use of tariffs to achieve social objectives it did encourage countries to opt, where possible, for measures that have the least impact on trade. Since tariffs are almost always second-best alternatives, this approach is beneficial to the trading community as a whole as well as the specific country.

THE OPTIMAL TARIFF

International trade that reflects the principle of comparative advantage will lead to an enhancement of world economic welfare. The actual distribution of the gains from trade between participating parties will depend, however, on the terms of trade or the ratio of export prices to import prices. The higher this ratio, the more favorable a country's terms of trade. Normally terms of trade are determined by impersonal market forces. However, if a country has market power in the sense that it can influence the prices of the goods it imports or those it exports, it can change the terms of trade in its favor. During the 1970s, for example, the Organization of Petroleum Exporting Countries (OPEC), in a display of its market power, ratcheted up the price of petroleum by restricting its supply, thereby improving the terms of trade of its members. Similarly, a country with market power can improve its terms of trade by levying tariffs on goods it imports, thereby inducing a decline in the demand for and the world price of these goods. If the objective in levying the tariff is to maximize the country's economic welfare, tariffs will be raised to the optimal level, defined as that level at which the country's *gains* from trade—not to be confused with the terms of trade—are at a maximum. Since *gains* from trade are determined by both the terms and the volume of trade, a rise in tariffs from a suboptimal to the optimal level will increase a country's economic welfare as the gains resulting from the improvement in the terms of trade will more than offset the losses resulting from the induced decline in the volume of trade. Any rise in tariffs above the optimal level, however, will result in a net decline in a country's economic welfare as the losses due to the reduction in volume will more than offset the gains resulting from the improvement in the terms.

Although the optimal tariff argument is theoretically sound, it is doubtful that it has any practical significance. First, unlike the gains that accrue to a country when it moves from a state of autarchy to trade, the gains that accrue to it by deploying optimal tariffs are at the expense of its trading partners. If these partners follow suit and seek to improve their economic welfare by exploiting their market power, trade could be transformed from a benign and welfare-enhancing activity to a highly belligerent one. Second, the information required to calculate optimal tariffs is rarely available. Since the optimal tariff for most goods is zero, it is almost certain that a country is more likely to improve its welfare by adopting an across-the-board zero-tariff policy than by trying to estimate the value of specific optimal tariffs. Finally, even if nonzero optimal tariffs can be calculated, their deployment will almost certainly favor the larger, affluent countries at the expense of the smaller, more vulnerable ones and hence will tend to increase the already large disparities between the incomes of the wealthy countries and those of the poor.

STRATEGIC TRADE POLICY

Strategic trade policy is akin to the optimal tariff policy in that both are designed to improve a country's gains from trade at the expense of its trading partners. Whereas the optimum tariff policy attempts to do this by improving a country's terms of trade, the strategic trade policy is designed to help a domestic firm—the national champion—wrest monopoly profits from its foreign competitor through the use of subsidies.[16] This strategy assumes the existence of an industry consisting of, say, two firms, one domestic and the other foreign. Because of large development and startup costs, each firm requires a large production run to enable it to exploit economies of scale. It is assumed further that the market for the product is limited so that were both firms to operate at an optimal level neither would be profitable. At the same time, were the industry to be monopolized, the remaining firm would be able to earn substantial monopoly profits. Under these circumstances, proponents of strategic trade policy assert that a government can influence the outcome by granting subsidies to its national champion. These subsidies would enable the firm to continue to operate even at a loss. In time, the foreign firm, incurring losses, would quit the industry and the hitherto subsidized firm would be in a position to earn monopoly profits. Since these rents are expected to exceed the subsidies granted to the firm, strategic trade policy would enhance the economic welfare of the country.[17]

The problems attending the use of this policy are too obvious to require extensive analysis. First, the notion that the other government would not retaliate in kind and hence derail the strategy at its very inception is far-fetched. Second, the information that is required for this strategy to succeed is almost never available. Third, the potential gains resulting from the use of this strategy are overall too small to be worth the trouble. These drawbacks are so severe that even Paul Krugman, who contributed importantly to the theory underpinning strategic trade policy, does not believe there is a place for it in any government's policy toolbox.[18]

THE INFANT INDUSTRY ARGUMENT FOR TARIFFS

Tariffs to protect and nurture infant industries until they reach maturity and are capable of standing on their own feet have been advocated for more than two centuries. This argument has particular appeal in emerging economies, where it is felt that without this protection they would be permanently excluded from industries in which the only source of their competitive disadvantage is that they are latecomers. A classic statement of this argument was advanced by Alexander Hamilton in his essay "On Manufactures," written shortly after the U.S. War of Independence.

To justify protection, however, even on a temporary basis, some conditions must be satisfied. It is not sufficient simply to demonstrate that the industry to be protected is a qualified infant in the sense that it has a good chance to become an effective competitor if it can overcome the hurdles of being a late bloomer. In addition, it must be shown that the industry cannot be nurtured to maturity *without* public assistance. This means demonstrating that for one reason or another placing reliance exclusively on the private sector to grow the industry to the required size is likely to prove futile. One reason generally given for not being able to rely on the private sector is that there are imperfections in the capital market that preclude the possibility of raising the requisite capital, particularly if the interim during which operations are not likely to be profitable is long. This situation, however, does not justify granting protection for reasons already noted. Capital imperfections constitute a form of market distortion. The use of tariffs to correct this distortion is a second-best alternative. It would be more efficient to address the distortion directly or, if necessary, to offer the industry a temporary production subsidy.

A second argument advanced for an infant industry tariff has greater merit: Although the prospective returns of the industry seeking protection are sufficiently large to justify borrowing, some of these returns cannot be appropriated by private investors. This would be the case, for example, if a portion of the returns consisted of an improvement of labor or management skills or an acquisition of knowledge regarding production techniques and organization, which, once acquired, become public goods. These "neighborhood effects" benefit the society at large and, of course, are extremely valuable. Public assistance in the form of tariffs or (perhaps better still) subsidies is, in this situation, clearly justifiable on welfare grounds.

A word of caution, however, is in order. The bill of particulars that must be met to justify tariffs on infant-industry grounds is stringent. Very few industries that have been granted such protection over the years have in fact lived up to expectations. Much more often than not infant-industry arguments have been used as a tactic to obtain a tariff that has no other function but to protect an inefficient industry permanently from foreign competition.

THE POLITICAL ECONOMY OF PROTECTION

Trade's bounties are manifold. As a result of trade, nations enjoy a higher real gross domestic product than would otherwise have been possible. This is due in part to the direct increase in efficiency resulting from the re-allocation of resources from less efficient to more efficient industries. It is also due to the opportunities trade provides to exploit economies of scale, to learn and benefit from the experience of other nations, to respond to the imperatives to invest, innovate, restructure, and adjust, in short, to do all that is necessary to keep the economy dynamic and avoid the onset of senescence. It is indeed difficult even to imagine an economy remaining dynamic while shut off from its neighbors. That being the case, how does one explain why protectionism—despite all the advantages that international trade confers—remains very much alive, not only in the emerging economies but also in the most advanced industrial economies as well? The simple answer is that although trade improves the economic welfare of the world as a whole it does create losers as well as winners. The old adage that a rising tide raises all ships is only partially true; it raises only those ships that survive it, not those that are sunk by it. Trade can and does inflict pain; inefficient domestic firms and workers with little skills are at risk from labor-intensive imports from the low wage emerging economies. The fact that the gainers gain more than the losers lose is little consolation to those faced with the loss of businesses and jobs.

In democratic societies where the fate of proposed legislation depends very much on the strength of those lobbying for it and against it, the odds favor those who would benefit from protection rather than those who are harmed by it. The reason for this is that losses tend to be highly concentrated, whereas the much larger gains are widely dispersed. Thus even if in the aggregate gains are vastly greater than losses, no individual stands to gain very much, whereas the losses to individuals can be very high.[19] The levying of a tariff on apparel to protect domestic U.S. industries from the competition of foreign imports, for example, may cost each American a few dollars a year more because of the higher prices they would have to pay for apparel. Yet the failure to impose a tariff could cause the disemployment of thousands of workers and the closing of hundreds of mills. The concentration of the losses results in a very high cost to the industry affected, and the threat of competition provides them with strong incentives to mobilize their forces and to fight against the removal of a tariff or for the imposition of one.

Where democratically elected legislatures are responsible for trade policies, as in the United States, the pressure for protectionism is considerably increased. Indeed, it is in the trade domain that the adage that all politics is local is most relevant. A member of Congress whose constituents' jobs are threatened by imports is likely to press for the imposition of tariffs even if aware that protectionism will have an adverse effect on the nation's economic well-being. Moreover, since the imperatives driving some members of Congress today to press for protection are likely to apply to other members at some point in the future, back-scratching allies are rarely in short supply. Indeed, the wonder is not that protectionist pressures persist despite the potential gains from trade but rather that so much progress has been made in recent years toward reducing trade barriers. Much of the credit for this, at least in the United States, is due to Congress's ceding some of its constitutional responsibilities for trade matters to the executive branch. More interested in promoting broad foreign goals than in protecting local industries, the administration is better positioned to deny protection than the less-insulated Congress. An additional counterweight to the demand for protection is the growing importance of foreign markets to many of the large and influential corporations. Fearing retaliation abroad, these corporations have in recent years lobbied intensively against the erection of new trade barriers and for the removal of old ones.[20]

An example will indicate just how important this development has been in the formation of U.S. trade policies. In 1992, a small ceramic processing company located in Milford, Massachusetts, applied to the department of commerce for trade protection on national security grounds. Its petition argued that it was one of the few remaining firms producing ceramic parts, essential for computers and advanced weapons systems, and that it was endangered by intense competition from a Japanese firm, Kyocera Inc., which dominated the market. Leading the opposition to this petition were "many giants of American industry . . . including the American Semiconductor Industry Association, IBM and the Aerospace Industries Associations," all of whom had strong ties with Japan and feared they would become targets for retaliation. Describing the process, Joseph Massey, a former assistant trade representative, commented,

"Foreigners don't vote, so they seek allies . . . lobbyists get a polite reception but if AT&T or Motorola comes they get listened to."[21] It need hardly be added that faced with this opposition the petition from a small Milford, Massachusetts, company was rejected.

It should be noted that the cost of lobbying for and against protection is very high. Professor Anne Krueger and others have suggested that since the consumers ultimately have to pick up the bill for lobbying as well, it is legitimate to include these costs in any estimate of the costs of protection to the American economy.

Protectionist measures do, of course, save jobs—but only at a very high cost. Gary Hufbauer and Kim Elliot estimated that in the early 1990s, 191,000 jobs were "saved" in twenty-one highly protected industries that employed 1.8 million workers.[22] The average tariff for the products of these industries amounted to 34.5 percent. The cost to the consumers in the form of higher prices due to these tariffs amounted to an astonishing $170,000 per job. In the luggage industry, the cost to the consumer for each job saved amounted to $934,000. In the ceramic tile industry the cost per job saved was $400,000; in the apparel industry it amounted to $170,000. The *President's Economic Report 1995* estimated that the cost of import barriers to American consumers amounted to an astonishing $70 billion per year.[23]

Conclusions

The conclusions that emerge from this chapter can be summarized succinctly. Trade benefits society by increasing the availability of goods, by enabling it to use its resources more effectively, by exposing it to competitive pressures that contribute to its dynamism, and by enabling it to keep in touch with the latest developments in technology and organization. The arguments that protectionist measures are necessary to achieve social objectives are faulty. More effective measures than tariffs are available for this purpose. This is particularly true with regard to the use of tariffs to save jobs. The cost for each job saved in this way can scarcely be justified on rational grounds.

3

GENERAL AGREEMENT ON
TARIFFS AND TRADE

High on the agenda of the Bretton Woods conference, which was convened in 1944 to develop an institutional structure for the postwar international economy, were proposals for the International Monetary Fund
(IMF), the International Bank for Reconstruction and Development
(IBRD) now known as the World Bank, and the International Trade
Organization (ITO). Each of these institutions was designed to redress
problems that together contributed to the collapse of the international
economic system during the interwar period. It quickly became apparent,
however, that a fundamental difference between the American and
British delegations regarding the functions of the proposed ITO could not
be reconciled, and it was agreed to table discussions on trade matters.

The problems to be addressed in this area were severe. The passage of the
Smoot-Hawley Tariff Act in 1930—against the opposition of the entire membership of the American Economic Association—raised American tariffs to
historically high levels and predictably triggered a reaction from American
trading partners. Within a period of two years, twenty-five countries imposed their own retaliatory tariffs. This destructive round of beggar-thy-
neighbor policies contributed to a precipitous decline in world trade between 1929 and 1934. During the same period, the U.S. real gross domestic
product declined by 23 percent, real exports by 39 percent, and real imports
by 31 percent. In addition, the collapse of the gold standard system, the
adoption of disinflationary policies, and the severe shortage of international
liquidity undermined the multilateral trading system that characterized the
pre–World War I period. This system was soon replaced by a byzantine network of bilateral agreements and quantitative restrictions.

Realizing the folly of continuing the destructive trade war, U.S. Secretary of State Cordell Hull urged Congress in 1934 to enact the Reciprocal Trade Agreement Act. This act authorized the president to negotiate with other countries for tariff reductions of up to 50 percent on a reciprocal basis. It also provided that any tariff concessions granted to one country would automatically apply to countries with which the United States had a most-favored-nation (MFN) treaty. An escape clause, which authorized countries to withdraw concessions in the event that they led to a "damaging" increase in imports, was an integral part of each reciprocal trade agreement and ensured that industries would not be severely damaged by an increase in imports resulting from the tariff reductions. Between 1935 and the outbreak of the war, the United States negotiated tariff reduction treaties with thirty-two countries. Together with a degree of economic recovery, these reductions contributed to an expansion of trade, including a 44 percent increase in real American exports between 1934 and 1939.

The task of repairing the international trading system, interrupted by the outbreak of the war, was not resumed until 1946, when, in response to a United Nations resolution, preparatory meetings were held to draw up a charter for the ITO. While the ITO charter was being drafted, the General Agreement on Tariffs and Trade was negotiated at a meeting held in Geneva in 1947. The original intention was to incorporate this agreement into the ITO. However, when it became apparent that the proposed ITO was not acceptable to the U.S. Congress, the Truman administration withdrew it and salvaged GATT by successfully arguing it was negotiated under authority granted in 1945 by the extension of the Reciprocal Trade Act and hence did not require Senate consent. Thus, in this roundabout manner, an agreement that was signed into law by the United States on October 30, 1947, and by twenty-two other countries was magically transformed into a quasi-international organization.[1] This quasi-international organization guided the postwar trading system until 1994, when it was replaced by the WTO. During this period it convened eight rounds of tariff negotiation sessions that resulted in a reduction in the average tariff rates from 40 percent to 5 percent.

GATT's Guiding Principles

GATT was informed by a strong awareness that trade could not reassume its pre–World War I role as an engine of growth unless the more egregious practices that were adopted during the interwar period were curbed. The more important of these practices, as already noted, were high tariffs designed to protect inefficient domestic industries and to export unemployment; the resort to discriminatory and frequently exploitative bilateral trading arrangements, which in some cases deteriorated to the level of primitive barter; and the widespread use of quotas and other quantitative restrictions to limit imports.

The determination to redress these problems is reflected in the basic principles that underlie the GATT system. These principles entailed commitments to reduce trade barriers and to ensure that the system operated in a nondiscriminatory manner and that its rules and regulations were transparent. The reduction of trade barriers was to be achieved through multilateral negotiations at periodic tariff reduction rounds and the binding of these tariffs so that they could not be raised again.[2] Nondiscrimination was ensured by extending unconditional most-favored-nation status to all participating partners so that any tariff concession granted to one partner would automatically apply to all and by adhering to the principle of national treatment. This principle committed each participating partner to treat imports, once admitted into the country, "no less favorably" than domestically produced goods, insofar as regulation, taxation, advertising, and distribution were concerned. Adherence to this principle would thus prohibit, among other things, the levying of nonborder taxes exclusively on imported goods or the application of regulations restricting the proportion of imported inputs permitted in the production of domestic goods.[3]

Finally, the transparency objective was to be achieved by the absolute prohibition of quotas and other quantitative restrictions and by keeping traders fully informed regarding the regulations and customs procedures to which they would be subject. The importance of transparency is difficult to exaggerate, as illustrated in another context by the remarks of the (human) world chess champion, Gary Kasparov, who, when asked to comment on the chaotic situation in the Kremlin following Pres. Boris Yeltsin's reelection to the presidency in 1996, remarked, "I play a game where there are rules. . . . I see the movements of every piece on the board but this is something different. If there are rules to this game, they are rules made and understood by one man only."[4] This is precisely what the transparency principle was meant to avoid.

THE EXCEPTIONS TO GATT'S PRINCIPLES

Inevitably there were exceptions to the principles underlying the GATT charter, the most important reason being a recognition by the architects of the GATT system that there is an incipient conflict between the obligations a country assumes upon becoming a member of a rule-based trading system dedicated to the dismantling of trade barriers and its ability to maintain sovereign rights to determine domestic policy. Many of the exceptions spelled out in the GATT charter were designed in part to ensure participants that although the fundamental objective of GATT was to encourage the expansion of trade the intention was *not* to achieve this objective at the expense of sovereign rights. Thus Articles 20 and 21 of the GATT charter explicitly endorse each country's right to adopt whatever domestic policy measures it requires for national security reasons, for the protection of the life and health of humans, animals, and plants, for the protection of intellectual property rights and national treasures, for the conservation of resources, for the prevention of the importation of goods made with prison or enforced labor, and for the enforcement of its antitrust and customs regulations. The only constraint placed on the participating parties was that measures to implement these policies would *not* be applied "in a manner which would constitute a means of arbitrary or unjustifiable discrimination between countries" and that they not be "disguised restrictions on trade."[5]

In addition to these exceptions, which were motivated by concerns for maintaining sovereign rights, the GATT charter authorized three exceptions to the nondiscriminatory principle. The first was an authorization to establish customs unions and free trade areas, despite the fact that the elimination of tariffs on intra-area trade while maintaining them on goods derived from countries outside the area was prima facie discriminatory.[6] The charter does specify, however, that to qualify as a free trade area or a customs union the participants must agree to remove tariffs on *all* intra-area trade within a reasonable period of time and that the external tariffs be no higher than they were before. The requirement that tariffs be eliminated across the board was designed to avoid the use of a customs union or free trade area to disguise covert discrimination.[7]

The second exception to the nondiscriminatory principle was initiated in 1971, when in response to pressures exerted by the developing countries GATT granted a ten-year waiver authorizing developed countries to apply lower tariffs on imports derived from them. This waiver did not *mandate* a general system of preferences (GSP) but rather, in the words of one legal authority, "established the GSP framework[, leaving] a great deal of individual discretion . . . to each of the sovereign industrial nations implementing it."[8] At the expiration of the waiver period, a "decision" by the contracting parties in the form of a declaration entitled

"More Favorable Treatment, Reciprocity, and Fuller Participation of Developing Countries"—popularly known as the Enabling Act—in effect made the GSP a permanent feature of GATT.[9]

A third exception, spelled out in GATT Article 12, authorizes the use of discriminatory restrictions on imports to alleviate balance of payments problems. This provision was originally motivated by the existence of a severe dollar shortage during the early postwar period and was designed to enable countries to restrict imports from the United States for which scarce dollars had to be paid while maintaining them from nondollar sources. This exception, however, provided many developing countries with an opportunity to discriminate long after the rationale for it disappeared.

GATT's Escape Hatch

Despite these exceptions, nondiscrimination, transparency, and the removal of trade barriers formed the cornerstones of the postwar international trading system. To become operational, however, the system required both an escape hatch and a dispute settlement mechanism. The escape hatch was politically necessary to provide countries with a "legal" way to temporarily suspend some of their obligations when, as a result of unforeseen circumstances, adherence would result in serious injury to import-competing industries; and to permit them to defend themselves against what many regarded as unfair trading practices, particularly those involving dumping and the use of export subsidies to gain a competitive edge. A dispute settlement mechanism was indispensable given that conformance with GATT's rules and regulations was the responsibility of the participating parties and that differences in the interpretation of these rules and regulations could lead to disputes that had to be peaceably resolved.

The Safeguard, or Escape, Clause

The GATT charter authorizes participating parties to initiate actions to suspend their obligations under three circumstances. The first, spelled out in the safeguard clause (commonly known as the escape clause), was designed to protect domestic industries when, as a result of tariff concessions, they suffered *serious* injury resulting from an unexpected surge of imports (Article 19). The escape clause is almost identical to that first introduced into the Reciprocal Trade Agreement that the United States negotiated with Mexico in 1945. The rationale for this clause, which authorizes a country to "suspend the obligation in whole or in part or to withdraw or modify the concessions" granted, is to provide import-substitute industries the time necessary to adjust to an *unexpected* large increase in imports resulting from the negotiated reduction in tariffs. By stipulating that the suspension or withdrawal should be for only as long "as necessary to prevent or remedy such injury," the charter emphasizes its temporary nature. Moreover, by requiring that countries offer compensation for any withdrawal or modification of concessions—either by offering other concessions of equal value or by allowing its trading partners to withdraw a previously granted concession—the framers of the charter attached a cost in the hope it would discourage use of the escape clause.[10]

Despite these efforts to limit the authority of GATT signatories to withdraw or modify concessions, ambiguity in the escape clause's language, particularly regarding the term *serious injury*, has been criticized on the grounds that it gives countries too much latitude. A leading authority on international trade law, professor John Jackson, notes that "almost any import barrier can find legal cover in the language of Article XIX when responding to the prerequisite of an escape clause situation."[11] This absence of precision has been a major cause of many disputes between the participating parties from GATT's inception to the present day.

In defense of the framers of the GATT charter, however, it should be noted that they were between a rock and a hard place. There is no question that "the effectiveness of GATT crucially depends on its ability to control the use of contingent protection by its members," yet framers had to avoid not only the use of loose controls, which would allow "each country to define for itself the conditions under which it could use contingent protection," but also tight controls, which would have induced governments to "seek to solve their problems" when confronted with the demands from injured import-substitute industries by placing reliance on GATT-prohibited actions.[12]

Antidumping and Antisubsidy Clauses

The GATT's antidumping and antisubsidy clauses make up the second and third components of the escape hatch.[13] Unlike the safeguard clause, which authorized a country to withdraw or modify concessions—not because its trading partners were guilty of unfair practices but rather because of miscalculating the impact of the concessions it offered on imports—the antidumping and antisubsidy clauses were designed to be weapons participants could use to defend themselves against practices by their trading partners that they regarded as unfair. These clauses authorize countries to levy special taxes on imports—designated as antidumping duties and countervailing duties—when those imports are priced below their "normal value." The general idea is to permit the injured countries to level the playing field by depriving exporters of any unfair advantage resulting from dumping or the granting of subsidies.

Before examining GATT's provisions in detail, it should be noted that despite the almost universal condemnation of dumping and subsidies it is not clear that either practice in fact harms importing countries. Indeed, many economists view them as more beneficial than harmful. By making goods available to the consumers of the importing countries at reduced prices, subsidies and dumping increase consumer welfare. And though it is true that domestic producers can be harmed by lower prices, the losses pale to insignificance when compared with the gains accruing to consumers. The ready acquiescence to the producers' demands for the right to retaliate reflects the dominance of producers over consumers in determining trade policy.

There are, however, two situations where dumping and/or subsidies could have invidious effects. The first is when dumping becomes a component of a predatory strategy aimed at the monopolization of a market by driving out competition in order to raise prices. Retaliatory action is justified under these circumstances, as is conceded by all.[14] One would be mistaken, however, to assume a priori that every case of discriminatory pricing—that is, charging a higher price in the domestic market than in the foreign market—is evidence of predation. Indeed, it can be demonstrated that setting different prices in the two markets is a rational response to differences in demand conditions.[15]

The second situation justifying retaliatory action is when a country puts into place general subsidies that by design or otherwise offset a tariff concession offered to trading partners. By reducing the *domestic* price of goods, the subsidy in effect reduces the value of its concessions and "impairs and nullifies" the benefit that the trading partners anticipated receiving when they offered concessions in return.

Inasmuch as the United States has made antidumping duties and countervailing duties the instruments of choice in restricting imports, it is of some importance to examine carefully the apposite GATT provisions. GATT does not proscribe the practice of selling goods in a foreign market at less than normal value. It does target the sale of goods at below-normal values if this "causes or threatens to cause *material* injury to an established industry . . . or materially retards the establishment of a domestic industry." It defines the phrase *less than a normal value* as including a price "less than the comparable price" for the product when sold in the exporting country or, if the product is not sold in the exporting country, at a price less than either the "highest comparable price for the like product for exports to any third country . . . or the cost of production of the product in the country of origin plus a reasonable addition for selling costs and profits."[16]

Only after it is demonstrated that dumping has occurred *and* that it has resulted in or threatens material injury to a domestic industry will the GATT rules permit the imposition of an antidumping duty (even on a product with a bound tariff).[17] In principle, this duty should not exceed the dumping margin, that is, the difference between the normal price—however that is derived—and the actual export price. It should, moreover, be phased out when dumping ceases.

The situation with regard to subsidies and the appropriate response to them is even more complex than that of dumping. Most economists agree that subsidies have an adverse effect on the welfare of the subsidizing country and a favorable one on that of the rest of the world. Stripping the analysis to its essentials, a country that subsidizes its exports is presenting a gift to the importers of their goods. This has led some economists to argue that it would be foolish for importing countries to levy a countervailing duty to offset subsidies. In general, however, this argument has fallen on deaf ears. Over the years, the granting of subsidies has been regarded as a hostile act and an unfair trading practice, and the demand for some kind of antisubsidy policy was too intense for framers of the GATT charter to ignore.

Any antisubsidy policy would inevitably have to deal with two problems: The first concerns the nature of retaliatory actions against subsidies that cause material injury to some of the importing countries' industries. The second addresses the more basic question of delineating between subsidies that are permissible—and hence not subject to retaliatory action—and those that are not permissible and therefore subject to such action. The first problem was easily resolved: Countervailing duties could be levied if a subsidy that is characterized as nonpermissible inflicts material damage on the importing countries' industries. The second problem, however, has proved to be more intractable.

Broadly speaking, subsidies fall into two categories: export subsidies and general subsidies. Since export subsidies are specifically designed to improve the competitive position of exporters, a case of sorts can be made for the imposition of retaliatory tariffs to offset this advantage if the domestic industries in the importing countries can demonstrate that subsidies have caused them to suffer material injury. In contrast, general subsidies are usually motivated by the desire to achieve domestic objectives. The primary motive for agricultural subsidies, for example, is to improve the economic welfare of farmers. The fact that these subsidies have important, albeit possibly unintentional, impacts on trade cannot be denied. There is no question, for example, that the European Community's (EC) agricultural subsidies were responsible for its transformation from a major agricultural importing unit to a major agricultural exporting unit. Were GATT to prohibit the granting of subsidies of this nature, or authorize the imposition of retaliatory tariffs to counter them, it would in effect be violating one of its basic principles: not to restrict participating countries' ability to formulate domestic policies. As we shall see, it was not until the Uruguay Round that this question received the attention it deserves.

The initial GATT charter's treatment of subsidies was sparse. Its most notable components were: an authorization to levy countervailing duties against subsidized exports when they caused material injury to domestic industries; and a prohibition against granting new subsidies to goods on which tariffs were bound. The second provision reflected a recognition of the fact that subsidies could inhibit imports by reducing the prices of domestically produced goods and that they were in effect a substitute for tariffs.

Over the years, GATT's policy regarding subsidies was broadened. In 1955 a distinction was introduced between export subsidies and general subsidies.[18] The GATT charter was amended to proscribe export subsidies on nonprimary goods when they resulted in export prices that were lower than those charged in the domestic market.[19] And though export subsidies on primary goods were not restricted, GATT urged all participating parties to refrain from taking action that would result in their obtaining a "more than equitable share of world export trade in that product"[20] without, however, defining what an *equitable share* was.

In 1979, during the Tokyo Round of tariff reductions, a comprehensive subsidy code was drawn up. This code consisted of two parts. The first addressed various issues regarding countervailing duties and the procedures to be employed in levying them, as well as an attempt to define the concept of material injury. The second part addressed conditions under which subsidies could and could not be employed. Basically, it restated the previous agreement's position regarding the use of export subsidies on primary products and placed an absolute prohibition on the granting of export subsidies to nonprimary goods. In addition, Article 2 of the new code addressed, for the first time, the impact of general subsidies on international trade. Article 2 stated that although there is no intention to regulate general subsidies that were put into place to achieve nontrade objectives, when these subsidies do in fact have trade impacts participating parties should attempt to avoid them. Although it would be difficult to describe Article 2 as a major breakthrough, the reason for its indecisiveness is abundantly clear. The participating parties were again torn between a desire to rein in the use of general subsidies and a reluctance to relinquish any control over domestic policies to an international organization. It was not until the Uruguay Round that this question was addressed in a more definitive manner.[21]

GATT's Dispute Settlement Mechanism

Given the ambiguity in many aspects of the GATT code, an efficient dispute settlement mechanism would seem to be an urgent necessity. Yet the mechanism that was eventually put in place suffered serious flaws. Articles 22 and 23 of the GATT charter outline the dispute settlement mechanism. Article 22 encourages members to consult with each other on GATT–related measures before they are put into effect. This provision is designed to encourage participating parties to express views—and reservations—regarding measures under consideration in foreign countries in the hope such consultations will avoid potential disputes. Article 23 deals with the actual dispute settlement mechanism.

To set the mechanism into motion, a GATT signatory must claim that actions taken by another participating party resulted in a "nullification and impairment" of its benefits. Although the GATT charter did not spell out the actions that lead to such a charge, GATT panel decisions identified three situations that would constitute a prima facie case for nullification or impairment: breach of an obligation; use of domestic subsidies to inhibit imports; and use of quantitative restrictions.[22]

Upon receiving a complaint, GATT was authorized to investigate the facts in the case and issue a ruling. Initially, disputes were heard by all the GATT participants during semiannual plenary sessions. This proved too cumbersome, however, and in due course a working party was established to hear all disputes. In 1955 the procedure was again changed, and each case was heard by a panel of experts established specifically for it. In any event, the group hearing the dispute was required to submit a recommendation to the contracting parties for final approval. To become operative, the recommendations had to be unanimously approved. This proved to be the Achilles' heel of the dispute settlement mechanism in that both parties to the dispute were, in effect, granted veto power. As will be noted below, the ineffectual dispute settlement mechanism provided the rationale for many extra-GATT initiatives by the United States and other countries and the motivation for establishing a stronger WTO in 1994.

THE SPECIAL STATUS OF AGRICULTURE AND THE TEXTILES AND APPAREL TRADE

An account of the GATT system would be incomplete without considering the special status of trade in agriculture, textiles, and apparel. As originally conceived, GATT rules and discipline were to extend to the full range of tradable goods; international tradable services were not considered sufficiently important at the time and hence were exempt from that discipline. In fact, however, two goods sectors, agriculture and textiles and apparel, remained immune to GATT discipline. In the case of agriculture, GATT authorized the United States to apply quotas to restrict imports of agricultural goods when domestic production restrictions designed to raise prices were in effect. Subsequently, the United States applied for and received a waiver to impose quotas on agricultural imports even when these goods were not subject to production limitations. This opened the floodgates. Other participating parties, particularly in Europe, decided, not unreasonably, that what is good for the goose is good for the gander, and agricultural import quotas sprouted as rapidly as alfalfa. The violations of the GATT rules in this sector were so rampant that many commentators erroneously concluded that agriculture was specifically exempted from GATT discipline.

With regard to trade in textiles and apparel, GATT-prohibited arrangements were so widespread that GATT undertook the task of systematizing them and made efforts to integrate them into the system. The first step down this road was taken in 1955, when Japan acceded to U.S. demands to "voluntarily" restrict its exports of textiles and apparel to the U.S. market. Other advanced countries, equally concerned about their markets being inundated with inexpensive textiles and apparel exports from Japan, sought similar restrictions. In 1961, the various voluntary export restrictions that the advanced industrial countries negotiated first with Japan and later with other less developed countries were consolidated into an arrangement that included sixteen importing and exporting countries and covered sixty categories of goods. Over time, this arrangement developed into the Multi-Fiber Agreement. By 1991, when the last Multi-Fiber Agreement expired, this arrangement covered thousands of categories of goods. Its participants included all the major import and export countries, and it became an integral part of the GATT framework. The decision not to renew the Multi-Fiber Agreement was a prelude to eliminating it during the Uruguay Round. But until negotiations were completed, the old agreement was extended indefinitely.[23]

Multilateral negotiations between exporting countries and importing countries determined the overall quota for every category of goods covered by the Multi-Fiber Agreement. Individual quotas were then determined through bilateral negotiations between individual countries. These arrangements restricted the exports of virtually every developing country, raised the prices consumers had to pay for textiles and apparel, and were extremely discriminatory. In short, they violated the most basic principles underlying GATT.

GATT: Taking Stock

GATT as a quasi-institution ceased to exist in 1994. Its functions were assumed by the newly created World Trade Organization, and its charter, in amended form, reemerged as GATT II. In view of the fact that the original GATT's life span coincided with the beginning, the flowering, and—at least in the views of some observers—the withering of the globalization process, it is not inappropriate to take stock of its role and its accomplishments.

In February 1997 columnist Thomas L. Friedman of *The New York Times* reported the following story about the Zapatista guerrillas in Mexico:

> Last year the Zapatistas held a conference in the jungles of Southern Mexico entitled "The Intercontinental Forum in Favor of Humanity and Against Neo-Liberalism." The closing session . . . ended with the Zapatistas doing a kind of drum roll and announcing the most evil, dangerous institution in the world today. To a standing ovation, the Zapatistas declared the biggest enemy of mankind to be the WTO—the World Trade Organization in Geneva which promotes global free trade.

Since WTO had inherited GATT's mantle and had done little to distinguish itself from its predecessor at the time the Zapatista conference was held, it would not be unfair or inappropriate to substitute GATT for WTO as the biggest enemy of mankind.

It would be difficult on the basis of the evidence to support the Zapatistas' choice for biggest enemy of mankind. Although GATT has been both highly lauded and passionately maligned, it has deserved neither. This minimalist quasi-institution was not responsible for the dismantling of tariff barriers—for which it was either given credit or assigned blame—or guilty of encroaching on the sovereignty of countries great and small, as American and Mexican critics have alleged. Indeed, its role in world affairs resembles more that of a referee than an active player. GATT's basic functions were modest and mundane, consisting primarily of codifying the multilateral rules of commerce unanimously agreed to by contracting parties; arranging for the convening of periodic multilateral negotiating rounds, during which contracting parties exchanged trade concessions; establishing panels to adjudicate disputes regarding the legality of actions undertaken by participating parties; and publishing periodic reports on the state of world trade.

One of the outstanding characteristics of GATT when contrasted with the Bretton Woods institutions—the IMF and the IBRD—was the almost complete absence of independent authority. As an institution, GATT was not authorized to play a leadership role in the development of the global economy, and it did not assume one. Globalization was not a managed process. It developed from the spontaneous actions and reactions of numerous agents—private and official—pursuing private and national interests, as the case may be.

Contrary to widespread belief, GATT's charter, which guided but did not determine the development of the postwar trading system, was neither a free trade tract nor a game plan for laissez-faire capitalism. The fact that this charter was, at least in part, informed by a liberal philosophy is of course undeniable. Its major objective after all was to create an environment favorable to the expansion of trade. At the same time, however, the charter strongly reflected the mercantilistic bias that an expansion of exports was desirable and that the accompanying expansion of imports was at best a necessary evil. This bias is reflected in the emphasis on reciprocity during the tariff negotiating sessions; in the nullification and impairment provision that authorized a country to withdraw previously extended concessions if the benefits it expected to obtain in return were impaired or nullified by the actions of its trading partners; and in the license granted to a country to take retaliatory action against a trading partner whose offense consisted of nothing more than attempting to sell goods at discounted prices. This mercantilistic bias is no accident. In an economic world in which free trade is scarcely an ideal that any country aspires to, the promise of an increase in exports was the carrot that was necessary to get countries to agree to lower trade barriers. Indeed, in the course of events, when it became apparent that adherence to the rules of the game did not ensure balanced trade, the system began to implode. And though a number of systemic defects, including a defective dispute settlement mechanism and an inadequate administrative staff, have been singled out as being responsible for these developments, in reality primary responsibility rests with those participating members who, for one reason or another, had become dissatisfied with the system they created and decided to take matters into their own hands. In the final analysis, GATT's major role was that of guardian of the multilateral arena. What happened inside and outside this arena was determined not by GATT but rather by the participating parties. If the Zapatistas, in condemning GATT, were reacting to injuries sustained as a result of Mexico opening its market to foreign goods and investments or its failure to protect those harmed by these actions, they hung the wrong villain. These actions are the responsibility of the Mexican government and not that of GATT, which has no control over Mexico's trade policy or its welfare safety net.

PART TWO

The Impact of Globalization on the U.S. Economy

4

U.S. International Accounts, 1970–1996

American perceptions regarding the world economy and the U.S. role in it were radically transformed during the 1970s and 1980s. The United States entered the postwar period in a triumphalist mood. It alone among the major belligerents emerged from the war with its economy not only intact but stronger than it had been during the prewar period. Early fears that the end of the war would again envelope the country in a crippling depression were quickly dispelled. Moreover and contrary to widespread expectations, the United States not only did not retreat into isolationism, as it had done so often in the past, but assumed a leadership role in reconstructing the shattered economies of former allies and enemies and in fashioning the international economic institutions it believed were essential to prosperity for itself and the rest of the world.

These institutions—IMF, IBRD, and the proposed ITO (which in somewhat attenuated form materialized as GATT)—were the infrastructure for a liberal trade and investment regime. As already noted, GATT's fundamental objective was to establish a multilateral trading system committed to reducing trade barriers and based upon the principles of nondiscrimination, national treatment, and transparency. The major objective of IMF was to discourage countries from resorting to currency revaluations to gain a competitive edge over trading partners and to provide liquidity to countries experiencing temporary balance of payments problems in order to obviate the necessity to restrict imports. IBRD was designed to provide less developed countries with seed capital to promote growth.[1]

These institutions performed better than expected during the quarter-century following the end of the war. After an initial period of reconstruction partially financed by the United States in the guise of the Marshall Plan, the United States and the rest of the world enjoyed a period of growth and prosperity unparalleled in modern history. During this period there was a general consensus that the postwar international economic system served well American interests and the interests of its trading partners.

By the 1980s, however, this consensus had shattered. The earlier view that globalization contributed importantly to American prosperity was seriously challenged and replaced by a growing perception that it was at least partially responsible for some of the more intractable problems facing the United States. In this revisionist account, the emergence of large and persistent U.S. balance of payments deficits assumed iconic proportions. For many Americans the deficits were not only symbolic of the declining importance of the United States in the world economy—what professor Jagdish Bhagwati called the diminished giant syndrome—they were also held responsible for a number of adverse domestic developments, including the loss of jobs in the manufacturing sector, wage stagnation, and an increase in income inequality. This perception contributed to an increase in the demand for protection, which was further exacerbated by the conviction that a beleaguered United States had fallen victim to the machinations of trading partners who, though delighted to exploit the opportunities that access to the affluent American markets provided, were reluctant to reciprocate by opening up their markets to American exports.

In view of the role these balance of payments deficits have played in recent years in shaping perceptions about the U.S. position in the world economy and U.S. international economic policy, it is essential to explore the factors responsible for them, their impact on the U.S. economy, and the policies necessary to restore balance to the international accounts. This chapter and Chapter 5 are concerned, in part, with these questions.

U.S. INTERNATIONAL ACCOUNTS

Table 4.1 shows the evolution of the U.S. international accounts between 1975 and 1996. These accounts are a record of all crossborder transactions involving monetary payments between residents of the United States and non–U.S. residents.[2] Transactions that result in monetary payments from foreign residents to American residents are designated as credits, whereas those that result in monetary payment from American residents to foreign residents are recorded as debits. The transactions are shown in two separate but interrelated subaccounts: current account and capital account.

TABLE 4.1 U.S. International Transactions, 1970–1996 (billions of U.S. dollars: credits (+), debits (-))

| | Current Accounts | | | | | | | | Capital Accounts | | | | | | | Stat. Discr. |
| | Goods | | | Services | Investment Income | | Uni-lateral Trans-fers, Net | Bal-ance on Curr. Acc't | U.S. Assets Abroad, Net | | | | Foreign Assets in the U.S., Net | | | Total: Sum of Items w/Sign Reversed |
	Exports	Imports	Net Goods	Net Services	Receipts on U.S. Assets Abroad	Pay-ments on Foreign Assets in U.S.			Total U.S. Assets Abroad	U.S. Official Reserve Assets	Other U.S. Gov't Assets	U.S. Private Assets	Total	Foreign Official Assets	Other Foreign Assets	
1970	42.5	-39.9	2.6	-0.7	11.7	-5.5	-6.2	2.3	-9.3	2.5	-1.6	-10.2	6.4	6.9	-0.6	-0.2
1975	107.1	-98.2	8.9	3.5	25.4	-12.6	-7.1	18.1	-39.7	-0.9	-3.5	-35.4	17.2	7.0	10.1	4.4
1980	224.3	-249.7	-25.5	6.1	72.6	-42.5	-8.3	2.3	-87.0	-8.2	-5.2	-73.7	62.6	15.5	47.1	20.9
1985	215.9	-338.1	-122.2	0.3	93.7	-73.1	-22.7	-124.0	-39.9	-3.9	-2.8	-33.2	146.4	-1.1	147.5	17.5
1987	250.2	-409.8	-159.6	6.2	100.5	-91.3	-23.9	-168.1	-72.6	9.1	1.0	-82.8	248.4	45.4	203.0	-7.7
1990	389.3	-498.3	-109.0	27.8	163.3	-139.4	-34.6	-91.9	-74.0	-2.2	2.3	-74.2	141.0	33.9	107.1	24.9
1995	575.9	-749.4	-173.6	71.5	196.9	-190.1	-34.0	-129.1	-307.2	-9.7	-0.5	-297.0	451.2	110.7	340.5	-14.9
1996	612.1	-803.2	-191.2	80.1	206.4	-203.6	-40.0	-148.2	-352.4	6.7	-0.7	-358.4	547.6	122.4	425.2	-46.9

Source: U.S. Department of Commerce, Survey of Current Business (July 1997): 64–65.

The current account shows the crossborder payments resulting from the import and export of goods and services; from incomes earned and transmitted by Americans on their foreign-based assets and by foreigners on their U.S.-based assets; and from unilateral transfers that include official foreign aid to foreign countries and private remissions. The capital account is a record of those transactions that reflect investment activities. These transactions result in changes in the value of American-held assets abroad and in the value of foreign-held assets in the United States.[3]

An examination of Table 4.1 illuminates the nature of the underlying changes in the economic relationship between the United States and the rest of the world. The two most important developments, which also had the greatest impact on the American psyche, were the emergence of large and persistent current account deficits in the post-1982 period and the transformation of the United States from the world's leading creditor country to the world's leading debtor country. Between 1982 and 1996, the United States incurred a cumulative deficit on current account equal to $1.4 trillion. During the same period, the United States became a debtor nation as the value of foreign investments in the United States exceeded the value of U.S. investments abroad. These developments were not unrelated: The financing of the large and persistent current account deficits was the major factor responsible for the increase in U.S. indebtedness to the rest of the world.

THE REACTION TO U.S.
CURRENT ACCOUNT DEFICITS

Understandably, a sea change like this would evoke a lot of hand-wringing. The professional Cassandras spoke openly of an imminent slide of the U.S. economy to a third world ranking. An announcement by two Boston-based economists regarding the deindustrialization of America was accepted as a fait accompli, and the Democratic Party's 1984 nominee for president, Walter Mondale, openly declared that, if elected, his goal would be to restore America's rightful position as a producer of computer chips and not potato chips.[4] Scholars tooled up their computers to begin learned treatises that would appear a few years later lamenting or celebrating—depending upon the political complexion of the authors—the rise and fall of the American century and economy.[5]

Motivating this anguish and oratory was the realization that behind the deterioration of current accounts were the disparate growth rates of imports and exports. Between 1982 and 1987 the value of imports grew by 66 percent, whereas the value of exports increased by only 18 percent. To those opposed to the globalization process, these disparate growth rates were a smoking gun. They regarded the stagnation of U.S. exports as evidence that foreigners, particularly Japanese, were denying U.S. firms access to their markets. The rapid expansion of imports, in contrast, was seen as reflecting the openness of American markets that permitted—if not encouraged—the flood of manufactured goods from low-wage developing countries. The $44 billion increase in imports from Asia's newly industrialized countries (NICs) between 1982 and 1987, which accounted for 29 percent of the total increase in imports during this period, was offered as support for this hypothesis. In the view of these critics, the restoration of balance to the current accounts required a leveling of the playing field. Specifically, the United States had to replace its free trade policy—which of course it never had—with a fair trade policy.[6]

Under this policy U.S. markets would be open only as much as those of U.S. trading partners. The concept of reciprocity was thus given new meaning. In GATT, and earlier in the U.S. prewar reciprocal trade agreements, *reciprocity* referred to an exchange of concessions of roughly equal trade values. Under this definition, the United States would agree to reduce tariffs on, say, Japanese computers if Japan agreed to reduce its tariffs on U.S. aircraft. The hope—and perhaps expectation—was that as a result of these tariff reductions the value of U.S. aircraft exports would increase by roughly the same amount as the value of its computer imports. The new concept of reciprocity, however, amounted virtually to a replacement of the open trading system by a managed trading system. Thus, if Japan wished to maintain its 20 percent share in the U.S. markets for widgets, for example, it would have to accept an arrangement for the United States to have a share of the Japanese gadget market with an equivalent impact on the value of American exports.

As we illustrate below, policies reflecting these views were put into place during the 1980s. Yet deficits on current accounts persisted. The root cause of these deficits was neither the lack of access to foreign markets nor the expansion of manufactured imports from low-wage developing countries; rather they were due largely to the adoption of macroeconomic policies that induced Americans to live beyond their means.

SAVINGS, INVESTMENTS, AND CURRENT ACCOUNT DEFICITS

A nation incurs a current account deficit when national expenditures on consumption and investment goods exceed national income (or the net value of goods and services produced). Not unlike a family, a nation can spend more than it earns (produces) only by borrowing the difference. In the case of a family, the source of the loan may be the savings of another family belonging to the same nation. In the case of a nation, however, the source of the loan must be the savings of another country. The current account deficit is the form that the loan assumes. In fact, it is a precise measure of the amount of excess expenditures (or so it would be in the absence of statistical discrepancies).

A slight reformulation of this proposition illuminates the proximate cause for current account deficits: National savings are equal to the difference between national income and national expenditures on consumption goods. Thus, savings set an upper limit to the amount that a nation can spend on investment goods without resorting to borrowing. If expenditures on investment goods were to exceed this limit, the excess would have to be obtained by borrowing from abroad. Regarded in this way, a current account deficit is exactly equal to the difference between expenditures on investment goods and national savings.

Table 4.2 shows U.S. savings, investments, and current account balances (net foreign investments) in selected years between 1975 and 1996. To illustrate the relationship between these three variables, consider the data for 1985. In that year, the sum of gross domestic private investments and gross government investments amounted to $865 billion. These expenditures exceeded gross domestic savings by $119.4 billion. The recorded current account deficit in that year amounted to $116.9 billion. The difference between the current account deficit and the excess of investments over savings—$2.5 billion—is equal to the statistical discrepancy.

The recurring deficits on the current account are a reflection of the low personal savings rate in the United States and the macroeconomic policies in effect during the 1980s, which resulted in huge federal government deficits that had to be financed from the already small savings pool. The existence of a chronic savings shortage in the United States is suggested by the data in Table 4.3. This by itself, however, does not explain why the current account deficit ballooned during the 1980s. For an explanation of this phenomenon it is necessary to review briefly the macroeconomic policies pursued in that period. To curb the inflationary pressures that had been building up in the U.S. economy as a result of the precipitous oil price hikes of the 1970s and an accommodating monetary policy, the Federal Reserve Board adopted a tight monetary policy during the early 1980s. At the same time, however, the Reagan administration introduced its experiment in supply-side economics, a central feature being a reduc-

TABLE 4.2 Gross Saving and Investment, 1970–1996 (billions of U.S. dollars)

| | Gross Saving | | | | | | | Gross Investment | | | | | Addenda | |
| | Gross Saving Total | Gross Private Saving | | | Gross Government Saving | | | Total Gross Investment | Gross Private Domestic Investment | Gross Gov't Investment | Net Foreign Investment | Statistical Discr. | Gross Saving as Percent of GNP | Personal Saving as Percent of Disposable Personal Income |
		Tot. Gross Private Saving	Personal Saving	Business Saving	Total Gov't Saving	Federal Gov't	State and Local Gov't							
1970	197.3	163.8	62.0	101.8	32.6	2.2	30.4	199.1	150.2	44.0	4.9	1.9	18.9	8.5
1975	297.3	301.2	107.8	193.5	-3.9	-49.9	46.0	309.5	225.4	62.7	21.4	12.1	18.1	9.3
1980	547.2	489.2	169.1	320.1	56.8	-26.8	83.6	574.8	465.9	96.4	12.5	27.6	19.4	8.5
1985	745.6	730.5	216.4	514.1	15.2	-116.9	132.0	748.0	715.1	149.9	-116.9	2.4	17.7	7.2
1987	779.6	726.0	179.9	546.1	53.6	-77.2	130.8	764.2	747.2	173.5	-156.4	-15.4	16.6	5.3
1990	903.1	860.3	221.3	639.0	42.7	-94.0	136.7	920.5	799.7	199.4	-78.6	17.4	15.7	5.3
1995	1,165.5	1,093.1	254.6	838.5	72.4	-103.6	176.0	1,137.2	1,038.2	213.4	-114.4	-28.2	16.0	4.8
1996	1,267.8	1,125.5	239.6	885.9	142.3	-39.2	181.5	1,207.9	1,116.5	224.3	-132.9	-59.9	16.6	4.3

Source: U.S. Department of Commerce, Survey of Current Business, various issues.

TABLE 4.3 Ratio of Gross Fixed Capital Formation to GDP and Ratio of Savings to Disposable Personal Income in Selected Developed Countries, 1980–1995

	United States	France	Germany	Italy	Netherlands	United Kingdom	Japan	Canada
Ratio of gross fixed capital formation to GDP (current prices):								
1980	19.6	23.0	22.6	24.3	21.6	17.9	31.6	23.3
1990	16.2	21.4	20.9	20.3	20.9	19.5	31.7	21.1
1992	15.0	20.1	23.1	19.2	20.0	15.7	30.4	18.7
1993	15.4	18.5	21.8	16.9	19.3	15.0	29.5	18.1
1994	16.2	18.0	22.0	16.6	19.3	14.9	28.7	18.6
1995	16.7	18.0	21.7	17.0	19.7	14.9	28.4	17.6
Ratio of savings to disposable personal income:								
1980	8.2	17.6	14.2	21.6	11.0	13.4	17.9	13.3
1990	5.0	12.5	14.7	18.2	15.6	8.1	12.1	9.5
1992	5.9	13.6	13.9	17.7	13.0	12.2	13.1	10.2
1993	4.5	14.1	12.9	15.8	12.0	11.4	13.4	9.4
1994	3.8	13.6	12.2	14.8	11.3	9.6	12.8	7.8
1995	4.5	14.3	12.3	13.1	(NA)	10.1	13.4	7.3

Source: U.S. Department of Commerce, Statistical Abstract of the United States, 1998.

tion in tax rates, which would then stimulate economic activity to such an extent that the induced increase in tax revenues would more than offset the decline in tax revenues resulting from the original cuts. When this expectation was not realized, the budgetary deficits increased (Table 4.2). Since these deficits had to be financed out of the savings pool, the savings available to finance investments were reduced still further. Were it not for the ability of the United States to borrow from abroad, domestic investments could not have exceeded the low level of savings that remained available to finance them. Far from indicating foreign intrigue or an unlevel playing field, current account deficits provided the United States with the means to sustain a relatively high level of investment despite its low savings rate and large budget deficits. Indeed, between 1982 and 1996 10 percent of total U.S. investments were financed by current account deficits.

It should be noted that the macroeconomic policies of the 1980s contributed in yet another way to the perception that globalization no longer promoted U.S. interests. The combination of a tight monetary policy and an expansionary fiscal policy drove up U.S. interest rates, which in turn caused an appreciation of the dollar as foreign investors increased their holdings of U.S. securities. The overvalued dollar induced a switch in expenditures both at home and abroad away from U.S. goods to more competitively priced foreign goods. It was this overvaluation, rather than the combination of open U.S. markets and closed foreign markets, that was responsible for the increase in the trade and current account deficits that characterized the early 1980s.

THE BURDEN OF A
CURRENT ACCOUNT DEFICIT

The conclusion reached above—that the current account deficits contributed to the well-being of the United States by enabling it to sustain a higher level of investment than would otherwise have been possible—is not to suggest, however, that these deficits are not also a source of concern or that a sanguine attitude can be taken toward them. Indeed, for most countries, large and recurrent deficits constitute a threat of immense importance. The need to rein in deficits that have grown unduly large has been one of the more important destabilizing factors during the postwar period. For these countries, the level of their international reserves and/or their ability to borrow funds from the IMF, other monetary authorities, and private investors set an upper limit to the level of tolerable current account deficits. When this level is surpassed, however, corrective actions, accompanied by painful side effects, must be undertaken. The 1994 Mexican financial crisis and the 1997–1998 Asian crisis provide dramatic but not unique illustrations of this.

In 1990 Mexico incurred a current account deficit equal to $7.4 billion, which was more than offset by an $8.4 billion net capital inflow. Encouraged by the apparent attractiveness of Mexico to foreign investors, Mexico's government and monetary authorities initiated expansionary policies that resulted in an increase in the current account deficit in 1992 to $24 billion. Refusing to recognize an incipient problem, and encouraged by a $27 billion net capital inflow, the Mexican government continued on its expansionary course, driving up the current account deficit to $30 billion in 1984, thereby increasing Mexico's foreign debt and reducing the level of its international reserves.[7]

At this point investor confidence was undermined and a massive flight of capital, including Mexican-owned capital, ensued; in 1995 net capital *outflows* amounted to $11 billion. This left the Mexican government with no alternative but to introduce drastic austerity measures, to sharply devalue the peso, and to reduce the level of government expenditures. To prevent an even greater crisis, the IMF extended loans to the Mexican government, and the United States developed an emergency plan that would ultimately lead to an additional $50 billion line of credit. For the most part, this rescue operation succeeded. The Mexican economy recovered quickly, and the emergency loans extended by the United States were repaid before their due dates. With international confidence restored, foreign investments resumed, and the growth process was revived. In 1996, Mexico's current account deficit amounted to $2 billion, and net capital inflows amounted to $4.8 billion.

The collapse of the Asian economies during 1997–1998 was even more dramatic. For somewhat more than two decades these economies grew at an unprecedented rate. This growth was fueled largely by an increase in the employment of labor and capital.[8] The large reserve of labor in the rural areas ensured a steady supply of workers to the expanding industries. To sustain the high growth rates, however, these economies placed increased reliance on foreign capital. Indeed, the resulting current account deficits were largely financed by short-term borrowing from foreign banks and by drawing down the level of international reserves. By the middle of 1997, short-term debts exceeded international reserves by more than threefold in South Korea and by slightly less than twofold in Indonesia and Thailand.[9]

The mounting current account deficits and the increase in the ratios of short-term loans to international reserves set off alarms in mid-1997. Foreign banks, fearing defaults, refused to renew loans when they fell due. Other investors, both foreign and domestic, liquidated investments and moved receipts to safer havens abroad. Speculators, suspecting that the exchange rates (which were fixed in terms of the dollar) could not be sustained much longer, sold the beleaguered countries' currencies. The outflow of funds resulting from these developments led to drastic devaluations; to take but one example, Thailand's baht lost 80 percent of its value in less than two weeks. These devaluations wiped out large proportions of the country's wealth, forced numerous banks and industries into bankruptcy, and left those whose debts were denominated in foreign currency in a hopeless situation. Moreover, as a condition for obtaining much needed hard currency from the IMF, these countries had to agree to adopt reforms and introduce austerity measures, which, though contributing to long-run solutions, exacerbated short-run problems.[10]

THE SPECIAL POSITION
OF THE UNITED STATES

The United States has thus far been able to avoid the pain associated with large current account deficits. This is due to the fact that its current account deficits, though large in absolute terms, are relatively small compared to its gross domestic product as well as to the role of the dollar as an international reserve and transactions currency. Countries hold international reserves as a contingency to finance occasional deficits on their international accounts and to help ward off speculative attacks on their currencies. Traditionally, reserves were held in the form of gold. By the end of the nineteenth century, however, some countries began to hold a portion of their reserves in the form of currencies. The prewar sterling bloc, for example, consisted of countries with strong ties to Britain, which held reserves in pound sterling. Likewise, French colonies formed a franc bloc. During the postwar period, however, the dollar emerged as the international currency of choice. And though the relative importance of the dollar as a reserve currency has declined somewhat over the years, it still accounts for approximately one-half of the world's currency reserves.

Several factors can be adduced to explain the dollar's dominance as a reserve currency. The shortage of gold, which became particularly acute when the rapid expansion of trade during the postwar period created the need for additional reserves, is surely one of them.[11] Others include the strength of the dollar as the currency of the most economically powerful country in the world; the highly developed capital markets in the United States, which provide countries the opportunity to hold reserves in interest-bearing form and ensure a high degree of liquidity; and the fact that the dollar was widely used during the postwar period as an international transaction currency. It is interesting to note that more than 50 percent of total world trade—including all trade in petroleum—is denominated in dollars.

As long as other countries are willing to hold and to add dollars to reserve accounts, there is little pressure on the United States to adopt the painful remedies necessary to restore balance to its international account. There is, however, no assurance that this situation will continue indefinitely in the face of recurring current account deficits and mounting foreign debt. Countries and individuals are prepared to hold their reserves in currency form only as long as they are convinced that the currency will retain its value. Persistent deficits could conceivably trigger a flight from the dollar, with disastrous effects not only on the U.S. economy but on the international financial system as well. It must be emphasized, however, that the probability of this occurring in the foreseeable future is not very high. With the future stability of the European Union's (EU) single currency, the Euro, still to be determined, the dollar's position as the international currency of choice appears to be robust.

THE BURDEN OF FOREIGN DEBT

There is, however, an additional reason why a reduction in the current account deficits would be desirable. These deficits have contributed to a buildup in foreign-held debt, which requires payments for interest. Unlike the servicing of domestically held debt, which entails but a transfer of funds from one group of Americans, the taxpayers, to another group, the bondholders, the servicing of foreign debt imposes a *real* cost on the country. This cost is measured by the value of goods and services that have to be sold abroad to service the debt, which means they are not available for domestic consumption or investment. In 1996 the cost of servicing U.S. debt held abroad amounted to $71.3 billion. It is interesting to note that this sum is equal to 48 percent of the current account deficit during that year.

This is not to infer, however, as some observers have in fact done, that the United States is already suffering a debt crisis comparable to that of the heavily indebted countries during the 1980s. The burden of the foreign debt to the United States is vastly different from that of those countries. The proportion of a country's export receipts required to service its foreign debt is widely regarded as a good measure of the burden of this debt. In 1984, for example, near the height of the debt crisis, Argentina devoted 25 percent of total export receipts to servicing debt. During that year, 38 percent of Bolivia's export receipts, 30 percent of Uruguay's export receipts, 32 percent of Algeria's export receipts, and 40 percent of Morocco's export receipts were required to service those countries' debts. By contrast, in 1996 the cost of servicing the U.S. debt was equal to 7 percent of the value of its exports. It should be obvious that the size of the foreign-held debt would have to increase many times before a crisis developed like those that enveloped many Latin American countries during the 1980s. This, however, is small comfort to those who question the morality of a system that permits the United States, the most affluent country in the world, to absorb a portion of the world's savings while other, more needy countries have to go without.

Since current account deficits are the mirror image of the excess of national expenditures over national income or output, they can be eliminated only by bringing income and expenditures into balance. Hence the policies advocated by the protectionists—increasing tariffs, imposing quotas, adopting numerical targets for exports—will have no effect on the deficits unless they also have incidental side effects that reduce the gap between domestic expenditures and domestic output. Although these side effects might exist, a more direct approach would be both more effective and less painful. The two main ingredients of this approach are a reduction of the government deficits—a process that is already under way—and an increase in private savings.

BILATERAL CURRENT ACCOUNT BALANCES

Although trade policies are unlikely to have a significant impact on a country's overall current account, they can affect *bilateral* current account balances. Table 4.4 shows U.S. current account balances vis-à-vis specific trading partners in 1996.

Unlike the overall balance on current account, which is determined by the disparity between domestic expenditures and domestic income, the bilateral balance between, say, Japan and the United States is determined by, among other things, relative growth rates in the two economies, cyclical developments, relative prices, exchange rates, and the degree of openness of the two economies. Since imports are sensitive to changes in

TABLE 4.4 U.S. Bilateral Current Account Balances, 1996 (billions of U.S. dollars)

Selected Country	Current Account Balances
Western Europe	-18.7
Canada	-10.7
Western Hemisphere and Latin America	-13.0
Japan	-45.9
Emerging economies of Asia and Africa	-76.3
All countries	-148.2

Source: U.S. Department of Commerce, Survey of Current Business (July 1997): 93 ff.

income, a higher growth rate in the United States than in Japan, for example, would tend to induce a larger increase in U.S. imports from Japan than of U.S. exports to Japan. Likewise, nonsynchronous business cycles in the two countries could lead to a disparate growth of imports and exports. A boom in the United States in conjunction with a recession in Japan—as happened in 1998—will eventually be reflected in an increase in the U.S. bilateral current account deficit with Japan as imports into the United States increase more rapidly than exports. Changes in relative prices and in exchange rates involving not only the United States and Japan but third-party countries as well will also impact the bilateral current account.

An awareness of the various factors that influence bilateral account balances brings back into focus the question of Japan's and, currently, China's and the other Asian economies' role in the U.S. current account. In 1996 Asia, including Japan and China, accounted for 80 percent of the total U.S. current account deficit. This can be explained in part by the recession in Japan and the prosperity in the United States. Relative prices, in contrast, are clearly responsible for a significant part of the deficit with China. At the same time, however, the degree of openness of these countries to imports is also a factor in the equation.

Although much of the Japanese-bashing in recent years, which attributes the overall U.S. current account deficit to invisible barriers that keep U.S. exports out of the Japanese market, is off the mark, it is true that if Japan's markets were more accessible the U.S. deficits with that country would have been lower and U.S. economic welfare would have increased.

There are two reasons for this. First, a more open market would have provided the United States with an opportunity to direct some of its resources away from the less efficient industries producing for the domestic market to the more efficient export industries, thereby increasing their productivity. This, of course, is but a restatement of the classical argument that trade contributes to economic efficiency. Second, if the Japanese market was more open, the increased demand for U.S. export goods might have contributed to an improvement in U.S. terms of trade by increasing the prices of American exports. Thus, although the large and persistent overall U.S. deficits cannot be attributed to difficulties in penetrating the Japanese market, success in getting that country to remove its nontariff trade barriers is likely to benefit both the United States and Japan. It should be noted, however, that the essence of this argument is that any expansion of trade is beneficial. The fact that it might also lead to a reduction in a country's bilateral current account balance is, at best, of secondary importance. Indeed, since opening markets will have a beneficial effect on U.S. real income, it could even lead to a larger overall current account deficit while reducing the bilateral deficits with specific countries.

U.S. CAPITAL ACCOUNTS

In 1987 the United States was transformed from a creditor to a debtor nation. By 1996 the United States was the world's leading debtor, with a net international investment position equal to minus $870 billion.[12] This development, of course, was not unrelated to the outcome on current accounts. Indeed, the cumulative deficit during this period of $1 trillion was a major contributing factor to the deterioration in the U.S. investment position.

The evolution of the U.S. international investment position between 1982 and 1996 is shown in Table 4.5. Between these two years, the U.S. net international position, measured in current prices, deteriorated by $1.3 trillion as a result of a $3.9 trillion increase in foreign assets in the United States and a smaller $2.6 trillion increase in U.S. assets abroad. An examination of the composition of foreign assets in the United States indicates, among other things, the importance of foreign investments in the financing of the large U.S. budgetary deficits during this period. Between 1982 and 1996 foreign holdings of U.S. debt increased from $158 billion to $1.1 trillion. In 1996, foreign investors held approximately one-third of the total U.S. Treasury outstanding debt. Were it not for the ability to sell U.S. securities abroad, the financing of the large budgetary deficits would almost certainly have driven up U.S. interest rates and would have con-

TABLE 4.5   International Investment Position of the United States, 1982–1996
             (billions of U.S. dollars, at current cost)

	1982	1990	1996
U.S. assets abroad	1,119	2,066	3,721
Foreign assets in U.S.	740	2,317	4,591
Net U.S. international investment position	+379	-251	-870
U.S. government assets abroad	218	257	244
U.S. private assets abroad	901	1,809	3,477
Direct investment	387	620	971
Portfolio investment	74	229	1,273
Claims on foreigners	440	961	1,233
Foreign official assets in U.S.	189	375	805
U.S. government securities	132	295	610
Foreign private assets in U.S.	551	1,942	3,786
Direct investment	177	467	729
Portfolio investment	118	629	1,965
Claims on Americans	255	844	1,091
Addendum: Foreign holdings of U.S. securities			
Official	133	295	610
Private	26	162	739[a]
Total	159	457	1,349

[a] including $209 billion in U.S. currency

Source: Russel B. Scholl, "The International Investment Position of the United States in 1995," *Survey of Current Business* (July 1996): 44, and "International Investment Position of the United States in 1996," *Survey of Current Business* (July 1997): 33.

strained U.S. investments. In contrast, had foreign investors been absent, the value of the U.S. dollar would have depreciated, thereby inducing an increase in U.S. exports and a reduction in U.S. imports.

One interesting feature of the foreign holdings of U.S. assets is worthy of note. In 1996 foreign holdings of U.S. currency amounted to $209.6 billion, an amount equal to 53 percent of the total U.S. currency in circulation. The

U.S. dollar is apparently an important reserve currency, not only for foreign governments and central banks but for foreign individuals as well.

The purchase by foreigners of privately issued stocks and bonds also played a major role in the increase in foreign-owned U.S. assets. Between 1982 and 1996 these holdings increased by $1.1 trillion. About two-thirds of this increase—amounting to $780 billion—occurred between 1990 and 1996 and undoubtedly played a major role in the spectacular U.S. stock market rally during this period.

Compared to the expansion of foreign holdings of U.S. securities, the increase in the foreign direct investments in the United States was relatively modest and amounted to $552 billion. This expansion, however, significantly reduced the gap between U.S. foreign direct investments abroad and foreign direct investments in the United States. In 1982 the value of U.S. foreign direct investments abroad was more than double that of foreign direct investments in the United States. By 1996, the value of U.S. foreign direct investments abroad exceeded the value of foreign direct investments in the United States by only 33 percent.

Of the $2.6 trillion increase in the value of U.S. assets abroad between 1982 and 1996, $584 billion were accounted for by an increase in U.S. foreign direct investments and $1.2 billion in U.S. holdings of foreign stocks and bonds. The remainder, which accounted for 30 percent of the total increase, resulted from a $794 billion increase in U.S. claims against foreigners reported by both banks and nonbank institutions. A large proportion of these claims represent short-term loans to foreigners.

This completes the overview of U.S. international accounts in recent years. Chapter 5 explores more closely the impact of U.S. trade on the U.S. economy, whereas Chapters 6 and 7 examine in greater detail the impacts of foreign direct investments.

5

U.S. TRADE

Trade, together with the widespread perception of a flight of U.S. industry to low wage emerging economies, are, for many Americans, the most visible and divisive aspects of globalization. This chapter addresses the impact of the expansion of trade during the postwar period on the U.S. economy, including the changing trade patterns and the relationship between trade, wages, and employment, whereas Chapter 6 explores the impact of U.S. foreign direct investments abroad.

To proponents of globalization the expansion of trade during the postwar period, driven by the removal of protective barriers, by rapid world economic growth, and by technological developments, was a major contributing factor to the prosperity, dynamism, and efficiency of the U.S. economy. To its detractors, however, the increased integration of the U.S. economy with that of the rest of the world is regarded as being at least partially responsible for the loss of relatively high paying manufacturing jobs and for exacting downward pressures on wage levels. The extent to which U.S. opinion is divided on this issue is reflected in the closeness of the 1993 congressional vote on the bills to establish the North American Free Trade Agreement and to ratify the Uruguay Round agreement, which were widely regarded as votes on the desirability of continuing the globalization process.

Together with almost every other country, the United States experienced record-breaking growth in trade in the postwar period. Because the growth rates of exports and imports exceeded the growth rate of output, the ratio of exports to gross domestic product increased from 4.9 percent in 1965 to 11.1 percent in 1996, and the ratio of imports to gross domestic product increased from 4.3 percent to 12.5 percent. Although high by historic standards, the degree of integration of the U.S. economy with the

TABLE 5.1   Trade as a Percentage of Gross Domestic Product in Selected Countries,
1996

	Exports	*Imports*
Canada	29	29
France	24	22
Germany	23	23
Italy	24	20
Japan	9	9
Netherlands	54	48
United States	11	13
United Kingdom	29	29

Source: International Monetary Fund, *International Financial Statistics* (derived).

rest of the world as measured by these trade ratios is still considerably less than that of other advanced industrial countries (see Table 5.1).

Trade, moreover, is but one of the channels for the crosscountry sale of goods and services. Another, which has become even more important than arm's-length trade in recent years, is the sale of goods and services by foreign affiliates of transnational corporations. In 1995, for example, sales by foreign-based affiliates of U.S. corporations amounted to $1.6 trillion. When the value of these sales is added to U.S. exports, the ratio of total sales by U.S. corporations to foreigners is significantly increased.

THE GEOGRAPHIC
DISTRIBUTION OF U.S. TRADE

The expansion of U.S. merchandise trade was associated with significant changes in the geographic distribution of both its exports and its imports (see Tables 5.2 and 5.3). To fully grasp the significance of these changes, particularly with regard to U.S. exports, it is necessary to view the data from several, sometimes overlapping perspectives. When this is done, two changes in particular stand out. The first is a pronounced shift of the center of gravity away from Western Europe and toward Asia and the Pacific Rim; the second is the increase in the relative importance of developing economies as markets for U.S. goods.

Between 1975 and 1996 the share of U.S. merchandise exports to Western Europe declined from 28 percent to 22 percent. During the same period the share to Asian countries increased from 28 percent to 35 per-

TABLE 5.2   U.S. Exports by Geographic Regions, 1975–1996
(billions of U.S. dollars and percentages)

	1975		1980		1996	
	$	% of Total	$	% of Total	$	% of Total
Total	107	100	224	100	612	100
Western Europe	30	28	68	30	137	22
Eastern Europe	3	3	4	2	7	1
Canada	23	21	42	19	135	22
W. Hemisphere & Latin America	17	16	38	17	109	18
Japan	10	9	21	9	66	11
Oceania	3	3	7	3	16	3
Other Asia	20	19	44	20	146	24
Addendum:						
Mexico	5	5	15	7	57	9

Source: U.S. Department of Commerce, *Survey of Current Business*, various issues.

cent. This increase was driven both by the extraordinarily high growth rates that these countries enjoyed during the past two decades and the unilateral reduction in trade barriers by some of them.

The increase in the relative importance of the emerging economies in the Western Hemisphere and in Asia as markets for U.S. goods is almost as dramatic. These countries' share of U.S. exports rose from 35 percent in 1975 to 42 percent in 1996; the share of the emerging Asian economies rose from 19 percent to 24 percent; and the share of those in the Western Hemisphere increased from 16 percent to 18 percent.

Turning to the geographic distribution of U.S. imports, two changes are noteworthy. The first is the increased dependence of the United States on North American countries as a source of supply; between 1975 and 1996, the combined share of U.S. imports supplied by Canada and Mexico increased from 25 percent to 29 percent. The second significant development was the growing importance of emerging economies as a source of supply, which paralleled their growing importance as a market for U.S. exports. Largely as a result of the expansion of those countries' labor intensive manufactured exports, their share of U.S. imports increased from 41 percent in 1975 to 45 percent in 1996.

TABLE 5.3   U.S. Imports by Geographic Regions, 1975–1996[a]
(billions of U.S. dollars and percentages)

	1975		1980		1996	
	$	% of Total	$	% of Total	$	% of Total
Total	98	100	250	100	803	100
Western Europe	21	21	47	18	162	20
Eastern Europe	1	1	1	—	7	1
Canada	22	22	43	17	158	20
W. Hemis. and Latin America	16	16	37	15	128	16
Japan	11	11	31	12	115	14
Oceania	2	2	6	2	8	1
Other Asia	25	25	83	33	232	29
Addendum:						
OPEC	19	19	55	22	44	5
Mexico	3	3	13	5	74	9

[a] adjusted to balance of payments basis

Source: U.S. Department of Commerce, *Survey of Current Business*, various issues.

The increased importance of North American countries and emerging economies as markets for U.S. exports and as suppliers of U.S. imports is also evident from an examination of Table 5.4, which shows the ten largest purchasers of U.S. exports and the ten largest suppliers of U.S. imports in 1996. Four the largest purchasers of U.S. exports and five of the largest suppliers of U.S. imports are emerging economies. In 1996, the combined value of U.S. exports to Mexico, South Korea, Taiwan, and Singapore amounted to $118 billion, 19 percent of the total. The combined value of imports from these countries and China amounted to $198 billion, 25 percent of the total.

THE COMPOSITION OF U.S. TRADE

Turning to the composition of U.S. trade, the two most dramatic changes that occurred between 1970 and 1996 were the declining importance of agriculture in the structure of U.S. exports and the rise and fall of petroleum as a factor in U.S. imports (see Table 5.5). The decline in the relative

TABLE 5.4 Leading Markets for U.S. Exports and Leading Suppliers of U.S. Imports, 1996 (billions of U.S. dollars; percentage of total)

Leading Markets for U.S. Exports			Leading Suppliers of U.S. Imports		
Market Country	$	% of Total	Supplier Country	$	% of Total
Canada	134	22	Canada	156	19
Japan	67	11	Japan	115	14
Mexico	57	9	Mexico	74	9
United Kingdom	31	5	China	51	6
South Korea	26	4	Germany	39	5
Germany	23	4	Taiwan	30	4
Taiwan	18	3	United Kingdom	29	4
Netherlands	17	3	South Korea	23	3
Singapore	17	3	Singapore	20	3
France	14	2	France	19	2

Source: U.S. Department of Commerce, Statistical Abstract of the United States, 1997.

importance of agriculture reflected two developments: the green revolution, which by increasing the productivity of agriculture in many countries made those countries less dependent on agricultural imports; and the highly protectionist agricultural policies adopted by the European Community (now the European Union), which transformed itself within a relatively short period of time from a net importer of agricultural goods to a net exporter. The impact of these developments on U.S. exports is all too apparent; between 1970 and 1996 the agricultural share of U.S. exports declined from 17 percent to 10 percent.

The rise and fall of the importance of petroleum in the U.S. import matrix was the second dramatic change in the composition of U.S. trade. The petroleum drama began in 1973, when a hitherto little-known group, OPEC, established a cartel to restrict the production of petroleum in order to raise its price. The cartel's early success resulted in both an increase in the value of petroleum imports into the oil dependent countries, including the United States, and an intensification of conservation efforts designed to reduce demand for energy. In the course of time, these efforts, combined with the inevitable internal disputes regarding the distribution of the production quotas between the cartel's participating countries, led to a collapse of petroleum prices.

TABLE 5.5 U.S. International Trade in Goods by Principal End-Use Category, 1970–1996 (billions of U.S. dollars)

| | | Exports | | | | | | Imports | | | | | |
| | | | Nonagricultural Products | | | | | | | Nonpetroleum Products | | | |
	Total Exports	Agri. Products	Total	Indus. Supp. and Mat.	Cap. Goods. Except Automot.	Automotive	Other	Total Imports	Petro- leum and Other Prods	Total Nonpet. Products	Indus. Supp. and Mat.	Cap. Goods Except Automot.	Automot.	Other
1970	42.5	7.4	35.1	12.3	14.7	3.9	4.3	39.9	2.9	36.9	12.4	4.0	5.5	15.0
1975	107.1	22.2	84.8	26.8	36.6	10.6	10.8	98.2	27.0	71.2	24.0	10.2	11.7	25.3
1980	224.3	42.0	182.2	65.1	76.3	17.4	23.4	249.8	79.5	170.2	53.0	31.6	28.3	57.4
1985	215.9	29.6	186.3	54.8	79.3	24.9	27.2	338.1	51.4	286.7	62.6	61.3	64.9	97.9
1990	389.3	40.2	349.1	96.9	152.5	36.5	63.2	498.3	62.3	436.1	82.9	116.1	88.5	148.6
1995	575.9	57.2	518.6	135.5	233.8	61.8	87.6	749.4	56.2	693.3	128.8	221.4	123.8	219.2
1996	612.1	61.5	550.6	137.9	253.1	65.0	94.5	803.2	72.7	730.5	136.8	229.0	128.9	235.8

Source: Council of Economic Advisors, President's Economic Report, 1998, p. 400.

These developments are mirrored in the changes in the relative importance of petroleum in the U.S. import structure. Thus, in 1970, before OPEC's attempt to cartelize the industry, petroleum imports accounted for 7 percent of total U.S. imports. By 1980 these imports accounted for an incredible 32 percent of the total. From this high peak the importance of petroleum in the U.S. import matrix declined. In 1996, it accounted for 9 percent of total U.S. imports, approximately equal to its share during the precartel period.

The decline in the relative importance of agriculture in U.S. exports and in petroleum in U.S. imports contributed to a higher concentration of both U.S. exports and imports in the manufacturing sectors. Between 1970 and 1996 the ratio of manufactured exports—excluding industrial supplies and materials—to total exports rose from 54 percent to 67 percent, and the share of manufactured imports to total imports rose from 61 percent to 74 percent.

The Importance of Intraindustry Trade

Accompanying this increase was the growing importance of intraindustry trade. As noted in Chapter 2, this trade consisted of the (almost) simultaneous import and export of similar albeit not identical goods. In 1996 intraindustry trade within the four-digit Standard International Trade Classification (SITC), which consists of highly disaggregated product groups, accounted for more than 50 percent of total U.S. trade. Table 5.6 gives important examples of this phenomenon. This development, however, should not come as a surprise in view of the fact that a large part of this trade is carried on with advanced industrial countries, whose factor endowments and technologies are broadly similar to those of the United States. This trade consisted of, among other things, the exchange of advanced technology products. In 1994 trade in these products accounted for $121 billion of U.S. exports and $98 billion of U.S. imports, respectively 24 percent and 15 percent of the totals (see Table 5.7).

Differences in factor endowments and technologies do, however, continue to play an important role in U.S. trade, particularly that with emerging economies. In the not-too-distant past, trade between developed and less-developed countries consisted almost exclusively of the exchange of developed countries' manufactured exports for the less-developed countries' raw materials. With the industrialization of emerging economies during the past two decades—particularly in Asia—the nature of this trade has been transformed. In some ways this trade has become more

TABLE 5.6 Intra-Industry Trade, 1996 (billions of U.S. dollars)

	U.S. Exports	U.S. Imports
ADP equipment, office machines	40	66
Chemical, medical	7	7
Chemical, organic	15	15
Electrical machinery	57	75
Gen. indus. machinery	26	25
Metal working machinery	5	7
Paper and paperboard	10	12
Power generating machinery	22	22
Rubber tires and tubes	2	3
Scientific instruments	20	12
Specialized indus. machinery	26	18
Telecommunications equipment	20	34
Vehicles, parts	25	21

Source: U.S. Bureau of Census, *U.S. Merchandise Trade*, Series FT 900.

like that between advanced industrialized countries, in that it consists primarily in the exchange of manufactures. Unlike trade between advanced industrialized countries, however—which is driven primarily by economies of scale rather than by differences in technology and factor endowments—this trade consists largely of the exchange of labor-intensive, light manufactures from the emerging economies for the high-skill, capital-intensive goods from advanced industrial countries. In 1994 60 percent of U.S. imports from the emerging economies, amounting to $125 billion, consisted of labor intensive manufactured goods.

Trade in Intermediate Goods

There is, however, another important difference between this trade and trade between advanced industrial countries: A significant portion of U.S. trade with emerging economies consists of intermediate goods. The growth of trade in intermediate goods is due largely to the development by transnational corporations of global production strategies, which were made feasible by the reduction in trade barriers and the technological breakthroughs in the communications and transportation sectors. More than ever before, it is now possible for transnational corporations to slice

TABLE 5.7 U.S. Trade in Advanced Technology Products, 1990–1994 (billions of U.S. dollars)

Product Category	Exports					General Imports				
	1990	1991	1992	1993	1994	1990	1991	1992	1993	1994
Total	93.4	100.0	105.1	108.4	120.8	59.3	63.1	71.8	81.2	98.4
Advanced materials	6.4	6.2	0.6	0.7	0.9	1.0	1.1	0.4	0.5	0.6
Aerospace	37.0	41.9	42.5	37.4	35.0	10.7	12.1	12.8	11.6	11.4
Biotechnology	0.6	0.7	0.7	0.8	1.0	(Z)*	(Z)	(Z)	0.1	0.1
Electronics	7.5	8.9	16.5	19.6	25.8	11.0	12.4	15.4	19.4	25.9
Flexible manufacturing	3.1	3.3	3.4	4.0	5.2	1.7	1.8	1.7	2.2	2.9
Information & communications	31.4	30.7	32.5	36.7	42.9	30.2	29.2	33.9	40.1	49.9
Life science	4.9	5.5	5.8	6.1	6.8	3.4	4.3	4.8	4.7	4.8
Nuclear technology	1.3	1.3	1.5	1.4	1.6	(Z)	(Z)	(Z)	(Z)	(Z)
Opto-electronics	0.5	0.6	0.6	0.7	0.9	1.1	2.0	2.6	2.5	2.5
Weapons	0.7	0.9	0.8	0.7	0.7	0.1	0.2	(Z)	0.2	0.1

* Z = less than $50 million

Source: U.S. Department of Commerce, Statistical Abstract of the United States, 1997, table 1339.

up the production process in ways that enable them to improve their competitive positions. One of the elements in these strategies, which can become very complex, is to assign every value-added activity to a locale where it can be undertaken most effectively and ultimately to integrate the resulting intermediate components into finished goods for distribution to global and regional markets.

This globalization of the production process has had a revolutionary impact on what was at one time called the takeoff stage of development in emerging economies. This stage was typically characterized by the establishment of stand-alone industries making products that were highly intensive in unskilled labor and that required very little capital, physical or human. The textile and apparel industries are textbook examples of industries that played pivotal roles during the early stages of development in many emerging economies, including Japan. Although these industries continue to play that role, the options currently available are much broader. Increasingly, transnational corporations involved in the production of technologically advanced products have placed reliance on emerging economies for value-added activities that are labor-intensive. The computer industry is a case in point. A recent study noted that

> a growing portion of computer parts and peripherals are imported from foreign-owned firms. . . . Asian origin parts and peripherals represented more than 80 percent [of these imports] in 1994. In fact, most computers assembled and sold in the United States contain disk drives from Singapore, monitors from South Korea, and mother boards from Taiwan. The composition of these computers reflects the continuing globalization of the computer manufacturing industry.[1]

Intrafirm imports and exports provide some indication of the importance of trade in intermediate products. Intrafirm trade consists of trade between parent companies and their foreign affiliates as well as trade among the affiliates themselves. In 1995 intrafirm exports from U.S.-based parents to their foreign affiliates amounted to $145 billion and accounted for 25 percent of total U.S. exports. Intrafirm imports from affiliates to their American parents amounted to $124 billion, 16 percent of total U.S. imports.[2] And though it is true that a part of this trade consisted of shipments of finished goods, a significant portion—including trade in semiconductors, electronic products, and the like, which make up most of the exports between emerging economies and the United States—is accounted for by the transshipment of intermediate goods between the parent companies and their foreign subsidiaries.

Intrafirm trade is, however, but one of the modalities used by transnational corporations to exploit the opportunities offered by the globalization of the production process. Although it is not possible to evaluate its precise importance, the practice of outsourcing has become a prominent feature of the globalization process.

THE IMPACT OF GLOBALIZATION ON SPECIFIC MANUFACTURING INDUSTRIES

Although the expansion of trade and the internationalization of the production process have resulted in a greater integration of the U.S. economy with the world economy, the impact of these developments on specific industries has not been uniform. An attempt to measure this impact on U.S. manufacturing sectors was recently undertaken by José Campa and Linda Goldberg.[3]

Campa and Goldberg rely on four measures to evaluate the external orientation of all twenty SITC two-digit manufacturing industries. These measures are the industry's export share, import share, imported input share, and an overall measure of net external orientation. An industry's export share is the ratio of the value of its exports to total shipments or sales; its import share is the ratio of the value of imports to the value of total domestic consumption of that industry's products; the imported input share is the ratio of the value of imported inputs to the value of output produced by that industry; and an overall measure of "net external orientation," which is defined as "the difference between an industry's export share and its imported input share in production."[4] Three of these measures for 1975, 1985, and 1995 are shown in Table 5.8; Table 5.9 shows the change in the net external orientation of U.S. manufacturing industries between 1975 and 1995.

An examination of Table 5.8 reveals that all measures indicate a greater integration of the U.S. manufacturing sector with that of the rest of the world. For the manufacturing sector as a whole, the export share increased from 8.4 percent in 1975 to 13.4 percent in 1995. The import share increased from 6.3 to 16.3 percent, and the imported input share increased from 4.1 to 8.2 percent. In 1995 the export shares of ten of the twenty two-digit industries exceeded 10 percent, as contrasted with 1975, when only five industries' export shares exceeded 10 percent. The most highly integrated industries, by this measure, were industrial machines and equipment, the electronic and other electric equipment industries, the instruments and related industries, the transportation equipment in-

TABLE 5.8 Export Share, Import Share, and Imported Input Share of U.S. Manufacturing Industries in Selected Years

Industry/Products	1975			1985			1995		
	Export Share	Import Share	Imported Input Share	Export Share	Import Share	Imported Input Share	Export Share	Import Share	Imported Input Share
Food and kindred products	3.3	3.7	2.8	3.6	4.3	3.6	5.9	4.2	4.2
Tobacco products	6.9	0.6	1.4	8.1	0.5	1.6	14.9	0.6	2.1
Textile mill products	5.1	4.3	3.0	3.6	7.7	5.4	7.6	9.1	7.3
Apparel and other textiles	2.0	8.5	1.3	1.8	22.4	2.3	7.4	31.4	3.2
Lumber and wood products	7.2	6.9	2.2	5.3	10.5	3.5	7.6	10.3	4.3
Furniture and fixtures	1.3	3.0	3.6	1.6	9.2	5.3	5.5	14.1	5.7
Paper and allied products	5.9	5.9	4.2	4.3	7.1	5.1	9.0	10.0	6.3
Printing and publishing	1.6	1.0	2.7	1.2	1.2	3.0	2.4	1.6	3.5
Chemicals and allied prods.	10.1	3.6	3.0	11.7	6.5	4.5	15.8	11.0	6.3
Petroleum and coal products	1.7	9.7	6.8	3.1	9.5	6.8	3.9	5.7	5.3
Rubber and misc. products	4.8	4.9	2.7	3.9	6.3	3.9	9.2	12.8	5.3
Leather and leather products	3.9	17.7	5.6	6.1	49.6	15.7	14.4	59.5	20.5
Stone, clay and glass prods.	3.4	3.4	2.1	3.4	7.6	3.6	5.6	9.5	4.7
Primary metal products	5.1	9.8	5.0	3.7	16.6	9.2	11.2	17.4	10.6
Fabricated metal products	6.3	3.0	4.7	4.7	5.5	7.8	7.9	8.5	8.7
Industrial mach. and equip.	23.3	6.3	4.1	20.1	13.9	7.2	25.8	27.8	11.0
Electron. and other elec. eq.	11.1	8.5	4.5	10.1	17.0	6.7	24.2	32.5	11.6
Transportation equipment	15.8	10.4	6.4	13.0	18.4	10.7	17.8	24.3	15.7
Instrmnts. and related prods.	16.8	7.4	3.8	15.5	13.7	5.4	21.3	20.1	6.3
Other manufacturing	9.9	13.4	4.6	8.1	35.0	8.5	13.5	41.1	9.9
Total manufacturing	8.4	6.3	4.1	7.9	11.0	6.2	13.4	16.3	8.2
Industry rank correlations w/1975 values	−	−	−	0.901	0.850	0.934	0.765	0.614	0.812

Source: José Campa and Linda S. Goldberg, "The Evolving External Orientation of Manufacturing: A Profile of Four Countries," *Federal Reserve Bank of New York: Economic Policy Review* 3:2 (July 1997): 57, table 1.

dustry, the chemical and allied product industries, and tobacco products. The least-integrated industries as measured by export shares were printing and publishing, rubber and miscellaneous products, stone, clay, and glass products, paper and allied products, and food and kindred products.

In 1995 the import shares of fourteen of the twenty two-digit industries exceeded 10 percent, as contrasted with only 3 percent in 1975. Industries with import shares exceeding 20 percent in 1995 included apparel and other textiles, leather and leather products, industrial machinery and

TABLE 5.9 U.S. Net External Orientation Over Time

Export Share Exceeds Imported Share by:	1975 Number of Industries	1975 Share of Manufacturing Shipments	1985 Number of Industries	1985 Share of Manufacturing Shipments	1995 Number of Industries	1995 Share of Manufacturing Shipments
More than 10 percent	2	11.3	2	11.8	4	23.9
5 to 10 percent	5	27.9	2	9.4	1	10.2
0 to 5 percent	9	48.5	4	37.2	10	49.2
0 to -5 percent	3	5.6	10	36.3	4	16.3
-5 to -10 percent	1	6.8	2	5.2	1	0.3
More than -10 percent	0	0.0	0	0.0	0	0.0

Source: José Campa and Linda S. Goldberg, "The Evolving External Orientation of Manufacturing: A Profile of Four Countries," *Federal Reserve Bank of New York: Economic Policy Review* 3:2 (July 1997): 58, table 2.

equipment, electronic and other electric equipment, transportation equipment, instruments and related products, and other manufacturing.

Regarding imported inputs, the shares of five industries exceeded 10 percent in 1995. This is in marked contrast to 1975, when the highest imported input share was 6.8 percent in the petroleum- and coal-producing industry. The industries with the largest imported input shares in 1995 were leather and leather product industries, the transportation equipment industry, the electronic and other electric equipment industries, the industrial machine industries, and primary metal products.

An examination of Table 5.9 reveals a significant shift in the net external orientation of the United States between 1975 and 1985 and again between 1985 and 1995. Between 1975 and 1985 the number of industries in which export shares exceeded imported input shares declined from sixteen to eight. As will be noted below, the appreciation of the dollar during the early part of the 1980s, which increased the foreign price of U.S. exports and reduced the dollar price of U.S. imports, was mainly responsible for this outcome. With the subsequent depreciation of the dollar, a reverse shift occurred. By 1995, the export shares of fifteen of the twenty industries exceeded their imported input shares.

THE TRADE DEFICIT

The size, persistence, and geographic distribution of U.S. merchandise trade deficits have generated the most controversy of any aspect of globalization. These deficits have not only been used as an indicator of the negative impact that trade has had on U.S. wages and employment; they have also come to symbolize the perceived inherent asymmetries in the trading system. Despite the fact that the United States was—and is—a military and an economic superpower, many Americans have cast their country in the role of hapless victim. In their perception, the deficits on trade accounts reflected nothing more than the refusal of foreigners to provide U.S. firms access to their markets while exploiting the opportunities provided them by the relatively open U.S. market. The true picture, however, is somewhat more complex.

An examination of Table 5.10 reveals that between 1965 and 1970 the United States earned a surplus on merchandise accounts in every year. By contrast, between 1971 and the present the United States incurred a deficit on merchandise accounts in all but two years, 1973 and 1975. These deficits, moreover, which started modestly enough, began to balloon in 1977, when the deficit increased from $9.5 billion in the previous year to

TABLE 5.10 U.S. Merchandise Accounts, 1965–1996[a]
(billions of U.S. dollars)

	Exports	*Imports*	*Balance*
1965	26.5	21.5	5.0
1966	29.3	25.5	3.8
1967	30.7	26.9	3.8
1968	33.6	33.0	0.6
1969	36.4	35.8	0.6
1970	42.5	39.9	2.6
1971	43.3	45.6	-2.3
1972	49.4	55.8	-6.4
1973	71.4	70.5	0.9
1974	98.3	103.8	-5.5
1975	107.1	98.2	8.9
1976	114.7	124.2	-9.5
1977	120.8	151.9	-31.1
1978	142.1	176.0	-33.9
1979	184.4	212.0	-27.6
1980	224.3	249.8	-25.5
1981	237.0	265.1	-28.1
1982	211.2	247.6	-36.4
1983	201.8	268.9	-67.1
1984	219.9	332.4	-112.5
1985	215.9	338.1	-122.2
1986	223.3	368.4	-145.1
1987	250.2	409.8	-159.6
1988	320.2	447.2	-127.0
1989	362.1	477.4	-115.3
1990	389.3	498.3	-109.0
1991	416.9	491.0	-74.1
1992	440.4	536.5	-96.1
1993	456.8	589.4	-132.6
1994	502.4	668.6	-166.2
1995	575.9	749.4	-173.5
1996	612.1	803.2	-191.1

[a] Adjusted to balance of payments basis.

Source: U.S. Department of Commerce, *Survey of Current Business*, various issues.

$31 billion. From that year on, the deficit increased by fits and starts until 1987, when it reached $159 billion, an amount equal to 3.4 percent of the U.S. gross domestic product. From that peak, the deficit declined to $74 billion in 1991, then increased again to $191 billion in 1996, an amount equal to 2.5 percent of gross domestic product.

The U.S. balance on merchandise accounts for the years 1980, 1987, and 1996 reveals much about the pattern of U.S. trade over the past decade and a half. In 1980, the deficit was in large part a consequence of a steep price increase of oil engineered by the OPEC cartel in 1973 and 1974. By 1987, however, OPEC was no longer a significant factor; internal disputes, which impaired the cartel's ability to regulate production and hence prices, as well as conservation efforts by the importing countries contributed to the decline in petroleum prices and hence in the value of U.S. petroleum imports.

As we discuss in Chapter 4, the roots of U.S. trade deficits during the post-1980 period are to be found in the early part of the decade, when the Federal Reserve Board embarked on a deflationary policy that by raising interest rates led to an appreciation of the dollar vis-à-vis the currencies of most U.S. trading partners. The impact of the dollar's appreciation on the U.S. competitive position in global markets is all too apparent from an examination of Figure 5.1. This chart shows clearly the relationship between the appreciation of the dollar and the unit labor costs in U.S. manufacturing relative to those of other advanced industrial countries. When measured in national currencies, U.S. labor costs declined slightly between 1980 and 1988 relative to those of U.S. trading partners. Because of the appreciation of the dollar, however, unit labor costs measured in terms of dollars increased during this period by approximately 40 percent relative to those of the other advanced industrial countries.

Table 5.11 shows the impact of the dollar's appreciation on the U.S. competitive position in somewhat greater detail. When measured in national currencies, hourly compensation costs in the United States rose at an annual rate of 5.7 percent between 1980 and 1985, a rate *lower* than that of all the countries listed (except for Japan and former West Germany). When measured in dollars, however, the hourly compensation costs in the United States rose by *more* than any other country listed. Indeed, by this measure the hourly compensation costs of Mexico, France, Germany, Italy, Spain, Sweden, and the United Kingdom all declined.

This decline in the U.S. competitive position had predictable results: U.S. exports languished while U.S. imports soared. Between 1980 and 1987, the value of U.S. imports increased by 64 percent, from $250 billion

FIGURE 5.1 Unit Labor Costs in U.S. Manufacturing Relative to Those of the Other G-7 Countries, 1979–1993.

Index: 1979 = 100

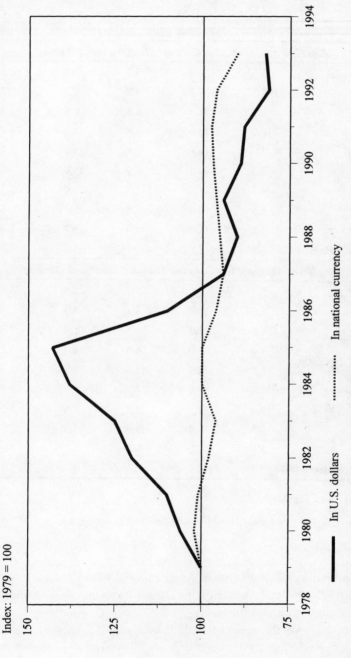

Note: Curves represent U.S. indexes relative to trade-weighted indexes for the six other G-7 countries.

Source: U.S. Department of Labor, *Monthly Labor Review* (Oct. 1994).

TABLE 5.11 Annual Percent Changes in Hourly Compensation Costs in Selected
Countries, 1975–1994, When Measured in U.S. Dollars and When
Measured in National Currency

	1975–1994	1975–1980	1980–1985	1985–1990	1990–1994
When Hourly Compensation Costs Are Measured in U.S. Dollars					
United States	5.3	9.2	5.7	2.8	3.5
Canada	5.2	7.8	4.8	7.7	-0.2
Mexico	3.1	8.5	-6.4	0.6	12.3
Japan	10.9	13.0	2.8	15.1	13.7
France	7.2	14.6	-3.4	15.2	2.8
Germany[a]	8.0	14.2	-4.9	18.0	5.6
Italy	6.8	11.8	-1.3	18.4	-2.3
Spain	8.3	18.4	-4.6	19.4	0.3
Sweden	5.2	11.7	-5.0	16.7	-2.6
United Kingdom	7.6	17.5	-3.7	15.2	1.7
When Hourly Compensation Costs Are Measured in National Currency					
United States	5.3	9.2	5.7	2.8	3.5
Canada	6.9	10.8	8.1	4.3	3.8
Mexico	38.5	23.2	51.6	62.4	17.6
Japan	4.9	7.0	4.0	4.2	4.2
France	8.7	14.3	12.3	4.2	3.3
Germany[a]	5.6	7.5	4.7	4.7	5.7
Italy	12.0	18.0	15.9	7.9	5.2
Spain	13.2	23.8	13.4	7.9	7.3
Sweden	8.7	12.2	9.5	8.3	4.0
United Kingdom	9.7	16.4	8.3	8.1	5.7

[a] Former West Germany

Source: U.S. Dept. of Labor, *Monthly Labor Review* (Oct. 1995): 8.

to $410 billion, while the value of American exports increased by 12 percent, from $224 billion to $250 billion. The trade deficits, in turn, increased from $25 billion to $160 billion.

Table 5.12 shows the geographic distribution of U.S. merchandise trade deficits for selected years between 1970 and 1996. The important role that Japan and the emerging economies of Asia have played regarding these

TABLE 5.12   U.S. Merchandise Trade Balance with Selected Countries,
             1970–1996 (billions of U.S. dollars)

	Total	Canada	Western Europe	Japan	China	Asian NIC[a]
1970	2	-1	3	-1	NA	NA
1975	9	1	9	-1	NA	NA
1980	-26	-1	21	-10	NA	NA
1985	-122	-16	-23	-46	0	-21
1990	-109	-10	2	-42	-10	-19
1996	-190	-24	-25	-49	-39	-7

[a] Hong Kong, Singapore, Taiwan, and South Korea.

deficits over the past decade is apparent. In 1996 these countries accounted for 50 percent of the total. It should be noted, however, that between 1985 and 1995 Japan's share in the U.S. merchandise trade deficit
declined from 38 percent to 26 percent while the share of the emerging
economies of Asia, including China, increased from 12 percent to 24 percent. The change in China's role in the U.S. deficit was the most dramatic.
In 1996, the U.S. trade deficit with China amounted to 20 percent of the
total deficit.

The fact that one-half of the total U.S. merchandise deficit was incurred
with Japan and the emerging economies of Asia contributed importantly
to the perception that the United States was not playing on a level field.
Underscoring that view is the fact that all these countries aggressively pursued export-oriented growth policies and, with the exception of Hong
Kong, have to some degree protected domestic markets. Although this
may be the case, the remedies suggested to restore balance to the U.S. trade
accounts, that is, the adoption of protectionist policies, were ill-advised.

As we note in Chapter 4, the U.S. deficits are due not to the restraints
employed by foreign countries to inhibit imports but rather to the imbal-
ance between U.S. savings and investment. The trade deficits are the
means by which U.S. borrowings from abroad (to finance the excess investments over savings) are actually transferred. Were Japan and the
Asian Tigers to take steps to reduce trade barriers—both hidden and
overt—their share of the deficits would surely fall, but the overall U.S.
deficit would not be affected unless the difference between its domestic
investments and domestic savings was also reduced.

Motivated by a desire to reduce costs of production as well as the fear
of U.S. retaliation, many Japanese firms have moved production facilities

to lower wage Asian economies as well as to the United States. Although this has had some constraining impact on the Japanese trade surplus, it has also contributed to the growth of other Asian countries' surpluses with the United States.[5]

U.S. TRADE IN SERVICES

In recent years, the deficits incurred by the United States on merchandise accounts were partially offset by surpluses on service accounts. Between 1975 and 1996, U.S. exports of services increased from $18 billion to $224 billion while imports increased from $16 billion to $143 billion. The resulting $81 billion surplus in 1996 was equal to 42 percent of that year's merchandise deficit.

Table 5.13 shows the growth and composition of U.S. service trade between 1975 and 1996. Although the category of travel, passenger fares, and other transportation accounts for the largest proportion of trading services, the relative importance of this category has declined during the past few decades. Between 1975 and 1996, its share of U.S. service exports declined from 61 percent to 53 percent while its share of U.S. service imports fell from 87 percent to 65 percent. The share of royalties and license fees in U.S. service exports also declined from 22 percent in 1975 to 13 percent in 1996, but its share of U.S. imports increased to 5 percent during the same period. The largest gains in shares were made by trade in other private services, a category that includes, inter alia, education, financial, insurance, telecommunications, business, professional, and technical services. This category's share of U.S. service exports increased from 17 percent of the total in 1975 to 33 percent in 1996 while its share in U.S. service imports increased from 11 percent to 30 percent during the same period. Net exports in this category amounted to $31 billion, accounting for 38 percent of the total surplus in the service sector.

Despite the expansion of U.S. exports of other private services, this sector has become a source of contention between the United States and some of its trading partners. The reason is that many of the services that fall into this category require hands-on contact between the providers of those services and their clients. In these circumstances, a prerequisite for effective access to foreign markets is that providers be allowed to establish a physical presence in markets they wish to penetrate and that, once admitted, they be granted national treatment, that is, they not be made subject to rules and regulations less favorable than those applied to nationals. Since many countries impose discriminatory restrictions on for-

TABLE 5.13 U.S. Trade in Private Services, 1975–1996 (billions of U.S. dollars)

	Total			Travel, Transportation, and Passenger Fares			Royalties and License Fees			Other Private Service[a]		
	Export	Import	Balance	Export	Import	Balance	Export	Import	Balance	Export	Import	Balance
1975	18	16	2	11	14	-3	4	—	4	3	2	1
1980	39	33	6	26	26	—	7	1	6	6	3	3
1985	63	58	5	37	46	-9	7	1	6	20	10	10
1990	137	101	36	81	72	9	17	3	14	39	24	15
1995	204	134	70	110	88	22	28	6	21	67	39	28
1996	224	143	81	118	93	25	30	7	23	74	43	31

[a] This category includes education, financial services, insurance, telecommunications, business, and professional and technical services.

Source: U.S. Department of Commerce, Survey of Current Business, various issues.

eign service vendors, access to these markets is impaired. As a result, the value of the sale of services by U.S.-owned affiliates in host countries was, unlike the situation regarding goods, less than the value of arm's-length exports. In 1994, the last year for which data are available, U.S. affiliates' sales of services to unaffiliated foreigners amounted to $133 billion, compared to $210 billion for exports.[6]

The determination of the United States to open these markets to its service sectors was a strong motivating factor in calling for the Uruguay Round negotiations. And though some progress has been made in the course of these negotiations to alleviate the problem of access, it has not been resolved. As noted below, this remains a high priority in the U.S. trade agenda.

TRADE AND THE LEVEL OF EMPLOYMENT

Under the best circumstances, the large and persistent deficits on trade accounts would have raised hackles; the robust mercantilistic philosophy, which regards exports as virtuous and imports as, at best, a necessary evil, would have assured that. In the event, however, the increased integration of the United States into the world economy was perceived to be directly responsible for a number of adverse domestic developments, which included, among other things, a decline in the economy's growth rate, a reduction in the number of jobs in the manufacturing sector, and stagnation of wages accompanied by an increase in income inequality to a degree not witnessed since the 1940s. This perception fueled increasingly strident demands for a retreat from the liberal trade policies that informed the U.S. international economic agenda since the end of the war and their replacement by new policies designed to level the playing field. To help assess both the validity of this perception and the need to revise the U.S. international economic agenda, the remainder of this chapter is devoted to an examination of the impact of trade on the level and sectoral distribution of employment, on earnings, and on the distribution of income.

A letter to the editor in *The New York Times* by a resident of East Twickenham, England, articulated a widely held fear that globalization represents a threat to the economic security of workers and farmers. The letter notes that "workers and farmers all over the world are responding to globalization by calling for protection of jobs and communities. South Korean workers have been in the streets. In Mexico thousands marched in support of the Zapatista rebels who want their livelihoods protected. In

India half a million people protested against the General Agreements on Tariffs and Trade." Only in the United States, the correspondent writes with obvious frustration, "inertia seems to reign in the face of growing job insecurity." "Perhaps," he continues, "it is time Americans joined workers in other parts of the world to defend their jobs and communities against the adverse effects of globalization."[7]

Although the correspondent from East Twickenham is correct in claiming that the perception that globalization poses a threat to jobs is widespread, he fails to state that the vast majority of economists—in the United States and elsewhere—do not share this perception. The reason for this is that there is almost universal agreement among economists that the level of employment is determined primarily by a country's macroeconomic policies and the efficiency of its labor market and not by its trade policies. Assuming that macroeconomic policies are compatible with the attainment and maintenance of full employment—appropriately defined—the existence of unemployment is symptomatic of an inefficient labor market.

Efficient labor markets have two principal characteristics. First, firms will hire workers as long as the anticipated increase in revenues associated with the sale of output is equal to or exceeds the costs of hiring. Second, any excess supply of or demand for labor will be eliminated within a relatively short period of time by requisite changes in wages and in other costs of hiring. Thus, an excess demand for labor will induce an increase in wages, whereas an excess supply of labor—unemployment— will induce a decline. The existence of persistent unemployment is the result of a downward wage rigidity and is the telltale sign that the market is inefficient.[8] The most common reasons for downward rigidity are government regulations, including but not restricted to minimum-wage legislation and the manner in which social service benefits are financed; centralized bargaining, which results in a failure to accommodate regional differences in the supply of and demand for labor; and union and other institutional regulations and policies.

Although not a determinant of the level of employment, changes in trade patterns do, of course, impact the sectoral demand for labor. The increase in apparel good imports from low-wage developing countries in recent years has been associated with a decline in the domestic apparel producers' demand for labor. Whether or not this leads to unemployment, however, depends on the efficiency of the labor market. If the market is efficient, the cost of hire will tend to decline to a new equilibrium level, and disemployed workers will be absorbed elsewhere, albeit not necessarily with the same wage package they previously enjoyed. From the workers' point of view, the economic impact of the increase in imports is best measured by the difference between their former wage package and their new wage package. Yet if the labor market is inefficient and the disemployed are either prevented from accepting wage packages below specified levels or are unwilling to accept them because of the availability of more attractive alternative income programs—unemployment insurance, welfare programs, and the like—unemployment will result.

As a matter of historical record, the U.S. labor market has proved to be extraordinarily efficient in recent years. Despite the increase in manufactured imports from emerging economies and persistent trade deficits, the U.S. economy generated 32 million new jobs between 1980 and 1997, and the level of unemployment was driven down to less than 5 percent. It should be noted, however, that during this period U.S. real wages were virtually stagnant, and the wages of unskilled and less-educated workers declined, whereas the wages of more-skilled and better educated workers increased. This resulted in increased income inequality. Whether and to what extent these developments can be attributed to the increase in imports from the developing economies is examined below.

The contrast between the American experience and that of key Western European countries during this period is striking. Buffeted by the same forces operating on the U.S. economy, Western European countries were afflicted by high unemployment rates and the inability to generate new jobs. At the same time, however, these countries succeeded in preventing an increase in income inequality. Thus, it is plausible in these circumstances to conclude that the downward rigidity in the costs of hire in Western Europe's labor market was a major factor responsible for the different outcomes. This rigidity was the result of more stringent government regulations, more powerful unions, and more comprehensive safety nets than existed in the United States. In effect, Western European policies provided a high degree of protection to those who had jobs, but this came at a very high cost to those who did not.

Trade and the Manufacturing Sector

In the campaign leading up to the 1996 presidential election, Patrick Buchanan, who was seeking the Republican Party nomination, and Ross Perot, who was pursuing a third-party candidacy, zeroed in on the loss of jobs in the manufacturing sector as the factor mainly responsible for the malaise of the middle classes. This loss of jobs was attributed both to the increase in U.S. imports from developing economies and the flight of U.S. industries to low-wage emerging economies. In the absence of these jobs, they argued, it would be difficult if not impossible for the middle class to maintain its social status and its economic position in the U.S. economy. This in turn could have a profound impact on the political, social, and civil institutions upon which the country was founded and previously prospered.

This apocalyptic vision was not new to the American scene. In the 1980s, for example, citing the difficulties U.S. manufacturers were experiencing in exporting goods, Barry Bluestone and Bennet Harrison raised the specter of the deindustrialization of the U.S. economy. When the value of the dollar fell during the mid-1980s from the heights it reached earlier in the decade and exports again became profitable, the deindustrialization specter receded from sight. In light of this experience, it would be prudent not to accept at face value claims from the likes of Buchanan and Perot but rather to examine the evidence to determine just how much of a threat the increase in imports from the emerging economies poses to the U.S. economic system.

Although the change in trade patterns contributed to the relative decline in the manufacturing sector in recent years, more powerful and more deeply seated factors were clearly at work. As Table 5.14 illustrates, this sector's importance in the U.S. economy was in decline throughout the entire post–World War II period. The reduction in the percentage of manufacturing employees to the total work force, from 33 percent in 1950 to 15 percent in 1997, reflected not trade developments but rather the well-known tendency for consumers to allocate a larger proportion of their expenditures to services as their incomes rise as well as to the greater increase in productivity in the manufacturing sector relative to the service sector, which enabled an increase in manufacturing output with fewer workers. It is of some interest to note, moreover, that even before the increase of manufactured imports from the developing economies the decline in manufacturing employment was heavily concentrated in the least skill-intensive industries. When measured in labor efficiency units—that is, the number of workers adjusted for changes in productivity—employment in the low-tech manufacturing industries declined from 12.5 percent of total manufacturing employment in 1940 to 4.8 percent in 1990.[9]

Some insight into the impact of imports on the U.S. manufacturing sector is provided by a study by Robert Bednarzik of the U.S. Department of Labor.[10] Defining import-sensitive industries as those in which 30 percent or more of the supply brought to the domestic market is composed of im-

TABLE 5.14   Industrial Distribution of Employment in the United States
(millions and percentages)

	Total Employment	Manufacturing Employment	Manufacturing as % of Total	Services Employment	Services as % of Total
1950	45.2	15.2	34	29.7	66
1960	54.2	16.8	31	33.7	63
1970	70.9	19.4	27	47.3	66
1973	76.8	20.1	26	51.9	67
1980	90.4	20.3	22	64.7	72
1985	97.4	19.4	20	72.5	74
1990	109.4	19.1	17	84.5	77
1995	117.2	18.5	16	92.9	79
1997	122.3	18.5	15	97.5	79

Source: U.S. Department of Labor, *Monthly Labor Review*, various issues.

ports, Bednarzik identified forty-eight four-digit SIC industries as being import-sensitive between 1982 and 1987 (see Table 5.15). These industries, which employed approximately 2 million workers in 1987, belong mainly to three manufacturing groups: leather, apparel, and miscellaneous manufacturing. Between 1982 and 1987, when employment in the manufacturing sector as a whole increased by 243,000 jobs, the import-sensitive industries, as defined, lost 281,000 jobs.[11]

Based on the not unreasonable assumption that the level of earnings can be used as a proxy for skills, the fact that the average hourly earnings in the import-sensitive industries were below those of the manufacturing sector as a whole is significant. In 1987, whereas the average hourly earnings for production workers in the manufacturing sector amounted to $9.30, hourly earnings for production workers in the import-sensitive industries were $8.06. In the apparel, leather, and toy industries, where many import-vulnerable workers were employed, average hourly earnings ranged from $5 to $6.30.[12] This would suggest that unskilled workers were among the most vulnerable to imports. Further support for this conclusion is provided by Bednarzik's findings that a high proportion of the employment in the apparel and leather industries consisted of blacks, Hispanics, part-time workers, and younger workers between the ages of sixteen and twenty-four.[13] And although the evidence strongly suggests that some manufacturing workers were disemployed as a result of the imports from developing economies,[14] the

TABLE 5.15 Distribution of Four-Digit SIC Manufacturing Industries, by Average
Import Penetrations Rates, 1982–1987

Penetration Rate[a]	Number of Industries	Frequency	Cumulative Frequency
All four-digit SICs	377	100.0	—
Under 1 percent	30	8.0	8.0
1 to under 2 percent	35	9.2	17.2
2 to under 5 percent	60	16.0	33.2
5 to under 10 percent	88	23.3	56.5
10 to under 20 percent	81	21.5	78.0
20 to under 30 percent	35	9.3	87.3
30 to under 50 percent	34	9.0	96.3
50 percent or more	14	3.7	100.0

[a] Import penetration is a ratio of import value to new supply (imports plus domestic product shipments).

Note: Sums of individual items do not necessarily add to totals, due to rounding.

Source: Robert Bednarzik, "An Analysis of U.S. Industries Sensitive to Foreign Trade, 1982–87," *Monthly Labor Review* (Feb. 1993): 17.

widely held view that trade squeezed out highly paid workers from the manufacturing sector into low-priced, "hamburger-flipping" jobs is somewhat exaggerated. For the most part, the disemployed workers were the unskilled, young, and lesser educated, whose wages in the manufacturing sector did not differ significantly from wages in their new, service-sector jobs.

This is consistent with a finding by other investigators that workers laid off from industries experiencing increased import penetration tend to receive higher wages in their new jobs compared to others who lose their jobs for reasons other than import pressures. The explanation for this is not that import displacement *causes* higher earnings but rather that "workers in industries in which import penetration is growing have low absolute levels of earnings. Pay for workers losing low wage jobs is less likely to fall and is perhaps more likely to increase."[15]

THE IMPACT OF TRADE ON WAGES
AND ON INCOME INEQUALITY

As we already note, efficient U.S. labor markets virtually ensured that a decline in demand for U.S. labor resulting from an increase in imports would be manifested not in a decline in employment but rather in a decline in wages (a proxy for the cost of labor). A recognition of this has led some economists, and many more noneconomists, to argue that trade was responsible both for the stagnation of U.S. wages during this period as well as for the very pronounced increase in income inequality. How valid is this claim? Before examining this question, it is necessary to review the nature of the problem.

Between 1960 and 1973, real compensation per hour for the American worker increased by 38 percent, an average annual rate of 2.7 percent. By contrast, between 1973 and 1996, U.S. wages were virtually stagnant; the increase in real compensation per hour amounted to but 8 percent during the entire period, or 0.34 per annum. At the same time, there was a significant increase in the inequality of income distribution. This combination of income inequality and (almost) stagnant wages resulted in a hollowing out of the income distribution. By the end of the 1980s, a larger percentage of workers was "at the top and at the bottom of the distribution, and a smaller percentage [was] in the middle."[16]

The major burden of the decline in the growth rate of income and the increase in income inequality was borne by younger workers whose formal educations did not extend beyond high school. These workers suffered a decline not only in relative incomes but in absolute incomes as well. In 1987, their earnings were less than they were in 1979. One manifestation of this is the decline in the proportion of workers between the ages of twenty-five to thirty-four who earned $20,000 or more per annum, from 57 percent in 1979 to 46 percent in 1987.[17]

Increases in both the educational premium and the experience premium were the principal factors responsible for the growth of income inequality during the 1980s. Thus, in 1979 college graduates between the ages of twenty-five and thirty-four earned 13 percent more than high school graduates in the same age cohort. By 1987, however, the real median income of high school graduates declined by 12 percent, whereas those of college graduates increased by 8 percent, resulting in a rise in the educational premium from 13 percent to 33 percent.[18] The increase in the experience premium—measured by age—during this period, though substantial, was somewhat less dramatic. Between 1979 and 1987, the gap between the median earnings of high school graduates aged forty-four to fifty-four, and those between the ages of twenty-five and thirty-four, rose by 10 percentage points. And though the real income of both age cohorts declined during this period, that of the younger group declined by more.[19]

This, however, is precisely the group that previously found middle-class jobs in the now declining manufacturing sector. It required but a short step for some observers to conclude that the travails experienced by this group were due in large part to trade deficits in general and to the increase in manufactured imports from emerging economies in particular.

Mainstream economic theory lends some support to this view. According to the factor endowment hypothesis, the opening of trade between two countries will result in each specializing in the production and export of those goods that are intensive in its abundant factor. Thus, if the United States has an abundant endowment of human capital and China has an abundant supply of unskilled labor, the opening of trade between these two countries would lead to an increase in the production of human capital–intensive goods in the United States and an increase in the production of unskilled labor–intensive goods in China. At the same time, the United States would reduce its production of unskilled labor–intensive goods and China would reduce its production of human capital–intensive goods. Hence, the price of human capital—skilled labor—would rise in the United States and fall in China, whereas the price of unskilled labor would fall in the United States and rise in China. In short, as a result of trade, the price of each country's abundant factor—human capital in the United States and unskilled labor in China—would rise above their pretrade levels, whereas the price of their scarce factors—unskilled labor in the United States and skilled labor in China—would fall.

A Nobel Prize–winning economist, professor Paul Samuelson, carried this analysis several steps further.[20] First, he showed that under extreme assumptions—including, among others, that the technology of both countries is identical, that full employment prevails at all times for all factors of production, that goods are produced in both countries efficiently, and that all transactions and transportation costs are equal to zero—the price of the factors in the two countries would converge. He then went on to demonstrate—this time with fellow economist Wolfgang Stolper—that a rise (or fall) in the relative price of the traded good would lead to a rise (or fall) of the price of the factor that is intensive in that good.[21] Thus, if trade with China leads to a relative decline in the price of unskilled labor–intensive goods in the United States, the real wage of unskilled labor in the United States would fall. Thus, both the factor-price equalization hypothesis and the Samuelson-Stolper hypothesis would seem to implicate the trade deficits and the increase in labor-intensive imports from emerging economies in the stagnation of U.S. wages, in the decline in the

number of jobs in the manufacturing sector, and in the increase in the inequality of income distribution.

The fact that one can use the factor-price equalization hypothesis to
"tell a story" about income distribution that is not incompatible with actual developments during the 1980s, is, however, no proof that it is a correct interpretation of events. An alternative hypothesis, advanced by professor Jacob Mincer and others, is that nonneutral, or biased changes in
technology that favored the better-educated, skilled workers at the expense of less-educated, unskilled workers were responsible for the shifts
in demand for skilled and unskilled labor that increased the gap between
the earnings of these two groups.[22] Given two hypotheses, the trade hypothesis and the nonneutral technological hypothesis, the economic ana-
lyst has his work cut out. In brief, that work is to examine the evidence to
determine which of these two hypotheses is more explanatory.

The fact that these two hypotheses have different implications provides
an opportunity to determine which of them is better supported by the evidence. The trade hypothesis relies on *interindustry* shifts in the demand
for different kinds of labor to produce the observed changes in wages for
skilled and unskilled workers. This hypothesis predicts that an increase
in U.S. trade with less-developed countries will induce a change in the
domestic product mix, resulting in a reduction in the demand for unskilled labor in the import-substitute industries and an increase in the demand for skilled labor in the human capital–intensive export industries.
The skill-biased technology hypothesis, in contrast, would predict *intra-
industry* changes in the demand for skilled and unskilled labor. Within industries, a skill-biased change in technology would lead to an increase in
the skilled labor/unskilled labor ratio. Put differently, the technology hypothesis would suggest an across-the-board substitution of skilled labor
for unskilled labor.

In an important study, two University of Michigan economists, George
Johnson and John Bound, constructed a model to determine whether the
observed changes in the U.S. trade structure can be explained by a change
in the pattern of product demand and hence in the domestic product mix.
Their conclusion was that there is little, if any, evidence that changes in
the structure of product demand—that is, the product mix—played a significant role in explaining the change in the wage structure.[23] On the contrary, the evidence strongly supports the hypothesis that nonneutral
changes in technology that were "extremely favorable to certain groups
especially women and the highly educated" and biased against the
young, the inexperienced, and the non–college educated, blue-collar

workers were "the principal cause of the significant wage structure changes in the past decade."[24]

Another test of the relative importance of the technology and the trade hypotheses in explaining changes in wages and income distribution was undertaken by Gary Burtless. He divided U.S. industries into two categories: one that is highly trade-affected and another that is not trade-affected. He hypothesized that if trade was the dominant factor behind the increase in income inequality then inequality should be greater in the sector that is highly trade-affected. This, however, did not prove to be the case. Between 1969 and 1980, wage inequality for males, "calculated as the ratio of annual earnings at the ninetieth percentile of the earnings distribution to earnings at the tenth percentile," increased at identical rates in both sectors, whereas "wage inequality among women [grew] faster in the non-trade industries."[25] Similar results were found for the educational premia. Although these premia have increased since 1969 across the board, they did not rise "any faster in the industries most affected by trade than they have in other industries."[26] Moreover, the evidence does not suggest that the trade-affected industries "shed low wage workers faster than those industries where competitive pressures [came] exclusively from other domestic firms." Indeed, Burtless found that the domestic-oriented industries "cut their use of low skilled workers even faster than trade-affected industries."[27]

There is additional, impressive evidence supporting the hypothesis that nonneutral technology innovations were the major factors responsible for the growth of income inequality in 1980. Among other things, the evidence suggests that across industries there is an inverse relationship between expenditures on R & D and the production worker's share of earnings.[28] As one student noted, "new technology appears not only to be labor saving; it also apparently reduces the demand for less skilled labor";[29] and though there has been a rather steady shift in the demand for more skill-intensive jobs since the 1940s, in recent decades this shift "has been increasingly concentrated among the highest skill level, . . . [and] this change in the nature of skill demand is associated with an accelerated shift in demand toward more skilled workers within, rather than between industries."[30] This is illustrated in Table 5.16, which shows the changes that have occurred across occupations between 1972 and 1992. The largest percentage losers were in the least-skilled occupations, whereas the largest gains were made by higher-skilled professionals, managers, and technicians, whose share of employment increased from 23 percent in 1975 to 30 percent in 1992. By contrast, the "operators" share declined from 21 percent to 14 percent.

TABLE 5.16   Occupational Structure of Employment, 1972–1992 (in percentages)

Occupation	1972	1975	1980	1985	1990	1992
Total	100.0	100.0	100.0	100.0	100.0	100.0
Managers	8.9	9.4	10.3	11.4	12.6	12.6
Professionals	10.8	11.5	11.9	12.7	13.4	13.9
Technicians	2.3	2.5	2.9	3.0	3.3	3.6
Sales	10.4	10.7	10.9	11.8	12.0	11.8
Clerical	16.0	16.2	16.8	16.2	15.8	15.8
Service	13.2	13.5	13.2	13.5	13.4	13.7
Craft	12.6	12.3	12.4	12.4	11.6	11.2
Operators	21.2	19.4	18.2	15.7	15.1	14.4
Farm	4.7	4.4	3.7	3.3	2.9	2.9

Source: U.S. Department of Labor, *Monthly Labor Review* (Nov. 1993): 8.

The conclusion that nonneutral, skill-biased technology is the principal factor responsible for the increase in the dispersion of earnings is not, however, inconsistent with the view that trade did contribute, at least in part, to the disparate earnings profiles of the skilled and the unskilled. To gain a more precise estimate of trade's contribution, a number of economists have placed reliance on factor-content analysis. This analysis attempts to measure the impact of trade on the demand for skilled and unskilled workers by comparing the factor content of a country's product mix after the change in trade with what it was before.

The factor-endowment hypothesis predicts that U.S. exports would consist of skilled labor–intensive goods and imports of unskilled labor–intensive goods. An expansion of U.S. trade with emerging economies should tend, therefore, to tilt the U.S. product mix toward skill-intensive goods and away from the unskilled labor–intensive goods. The factor-content analysis is designed to show how this shift affects the domestic demand for both skilled and unskilled labor. Although the method of estimation is imperfect (see Box 5.1), it does provide some insight regarding the magnitudes involved.

With one exception, studies based on the factor-content analysis conclude that although trade has had some impact on the U.S. wage structure and income distribution, it played a relatively small role. Thus, a study by George Borjas, Richard F. Freeman, and Lawrence K. Katz concluded that trade *and* immigration could account for but 8–15 percent of the increase

---

BOX 5.1 The Factor-Content Methodology

On the assumption that the U.S. trade account is in balance, the factor-content analysis consists of the following steps:

1. Deriving a measure of the quantity of skilled and unskilled labor embodied in U.S. exports;

2. Deriving a measure of the quantity of skilled and unskilled labor that would be required to produce domestically the goods that are being imported into the United States;

3. Determining the impact of trade on U.S. demand for unskilled labor by subtracting the quantity of unskilled labor required to produce exports from the quantity of unskilled labor that would have been necessary to produce domestically the imported goods; the difference between the two is equal to the decline in the demand for unskilled labor as a result of trade; and

4. Determining the impact of trade on U.S. demand for skilled labor by subtracting the quantity of skilled labor required to produce the import substitute goods from the larger quantity of skilled labor required to produce exports; the difference is equal to the increase in the demand for skilled labor as a result of trade.

---

in the income differences between high school and college graduates during the 1980s.[31] Jeffrey Sachs and Howard Schatz used the factor-content approach to examine the impact of trade on jobs in the manufacturing sector and on wages.[32] They concluded that although trade with the developing countries was responsible for a 5.7 percent decline in employment in the manufacturing sector, which was heavily concentrated in the low-skilled industries, it is dubious whether it had a significant impact on wages.[33] They concluded that "since low skill manufacturing employment is such a small proportion of total low skill employment it is difficult to see how the observed effects of trade could be sufficient to account for the bulk of the widening income inequality."[34]

This view is shared by Richard Cooper, whose study focused on the impact of trade on "the least skilled members of the labor force measured by the wage profile," namely, on workers in the U.S. textile, apparel, and leather industries.[35] He concluded that the increase in the unskilled capital–intensive imports can account for only 10 percent of the relative decline of these workers' wages between 1979 and 1990. The major reason for this relatively low impact was the fact that "employment changes in the tradable manufacturing sector were relatively small against the large scale and the large increase of employment in the non-tradable sectors."[36] It should be noted that the manufacturing sector employs only 15 percent of the unskilled workers in the United States. The vast majority of these workers are employed in the service sectors.

Among economists who have employed a factor-content analysis to evaluate the impact of trade on the wage structure, Adrian Wood is the major exception. According to Wood, trade would account for a substantial part of the change in the U.S. wage structure during the 1980s if the factor-content studies were better specified. Wood argued that there are two basic reasons why these studies have been misspecified. The first is the implicit assumption that "the imports in each statistical category—say electrical machinery—are goods of the same type and in particular of the same skill intensity, as the goods produced in the corresponding sector."[37] This, however, is not the case. Manufactured imports from the developing countries consist of low skill–intensive goods, which are not typically produced in the more-developed countries that specialize in the production of skill-intensive manufactures. When, therefore, factor-content analysts use the factors employed to produce the import-substitute good as a proxy for the factors used to produce imports, they inevitably underestimate the unskilled labor content and, hence, "the number of workers, particularly unskilled workers, who would be needed, in the absence of trade, to meet the demand for goods that are now imported."[38] In order to get better estimates it is necessary, according to Wood, to get a measure of the unskilled labor necessary to produce the goods in the low-wage countries.

Wood is aware that this measure would have to be adjusted in two ways before it could be used to estimate the amount of labor necessary to produce these goods in developed countries. The first adjustment would take into account the fact that higher wages in the developed countries would induce firms to use fewer labor-intensive methods than are employed in developing countries. The second adjustment is necessary because the higher prices in developed countries would induce consumers to purchase fewer goods than they otherwise would. Wood concludes that as a result of these two adjustments the estimated displacement of unskilled labor by imports would be smaller than the actual amount of labor embodied in them in less-developed countries, yet they would still be larger than suggested by the conventional factor-content calculations.[39]

Indeed, Wood believes that his method of calculation would roughly double the estimated decline in the demand for labor.

Wood argues that even with these adjustments the impact of trade on employment would be underestimated. His reasoning here is that the competition from less-developed countries would induce firms in developed countries to adopt new, labor-saving technologies to improve their competitive position. And though he acknowledges that there is "no acceptably accurate way, as yet, of quantifying the impact of defensive innovation on labor demand," he asserts that "allowance for them would require something like a doubling of the modified factor content estimate."[40] Moreover, if the analysis were extended to cover the service area as well as the nontraded sector that provide intermediate inputs to the "producers of manufactures and traded services," the estimated impact of trade on labor demand would again roughly double.[41] Taking everything into account, Wood concludes that "trade lowered the economy-wide relative demand for unskilled labor by about 20 percent."[42] Although he could be right, it is difficult to believe that the empirical methods used would meet with the approval of many econometricians.

In attempting to measure the impact of trade on the wage structure, other economists have preferred to emphasize price effects rather than factor content. This approach is based on the Samuelson-Stolper theorem, which, as we note above, states that a decline in the relative price of a good will reduce the returns to the factor that is intensively used in producing the good. Two studies, by R. Lawrence and M. Slaughter and the already-mentioned Sachs and Schatz, address this question.

Lawrence and Slaughter studied changes in the import and export price indexes provided by the U.S. Bureau of Labor Statistics. They correlated changes in these prices with the share of production workers— which they used as a proxy for less-skilled workers—across industries and found (after making appropriate adjustments for total labor productivity changes) that the slight relative decline in the prices of labor-intensive goods could not possibly explain the substantial changes in the U.S. wage structure that occurred during the 1980s.[43]

Using domestic price deflators rather than price indexes, Sachs and Schatz concluded (after adjusting for total labor productivity) that "relative prices of less skill-intensive goods declined after 1978 just as the Heckscher-Ohlin-Samuelson theory would predict." However, "although the results on prices are consistent with the role of trade in squeezing the wages of low skill workers we have not found a large enough relative price effect to account for a significant widening of wage inequalities."[44]

These price studies strengthen the hypothesis that nonneutral technical changes were primarily responsible for growing wage inequality during the 1980s. If, as Sachs and Schatz and Lawrence and Slaughter find, there was a decline—albeit a modest one—in the relative prices of unskilled labor–intensive goods and hence in the wages of unskilled labor, one would expect to find an across-the-board increase in the ratio of unskilled labor to total employment. In fact, however, during the 1980s the ratio of skilled to unskilled labor increased in almost every manufacturing sector. If production workers are used as a proxy for less-skilled labor and nonproduction workers are used as a proxy for skilled labor, then the ratio of skilled workers to total employment increased from 26 percent in 1970 to 31 percent in 1990.

It is clear that the available evidence does not support the hypothesis that trade with developing countries or even the substantial trade deficits of the 1980s had a significant impact on the wage structure. The evidence also indicates that although trade did have an impact on employment in the manufacturing sector, it was not the primary reason for the decline in that sector's importance; its impact largely fell on relatively few industries that were highly labor-intensive.

WAGE STAGNATION REVISITED

We note above that between 1973 and 1996 worker compensation in real terms was virtually unchanged. Some critics attribute this stagnation to the pressures of global competition, which put a damper on firms' willingness to increase wages for fear of losing market shares and on workers' willingness to demand higher wages for fear they would lose jobs. Although these factors undoubtedly played a role in producing the outcome, the decline in the rate of growth of productivity in recent years is the more compelling explanation. Between 1960 and 1973, productivity grew at an annual rate of 3.2 percent. By contrast, between 1973 and 1996 productivity increased at an annual rate of 1.3 percent.[45] Since productivity is the major determinant of wages, the decline in its growth rate was without question the most important factor responsible for wage stagnation. Unfortunately, a definitive explanation for the observed decline in productivity growth has thus far eluded economists.

6

U.S. Foreign Direct Investments Abroad

The increase in foreign direct investments since the 1980s is arguably the most dramatic aspect of globalization. As is the case with trade, this increase, though enabled by technological developments, has for the most part been policy-driven and reflects a basic change in attitudes in developed as well as developing economies. During the early postwar period, foreign direct investment was inhibited not only by the existence of capital controls and currency inconvertibility but also by a basic hostility toward foreign investment on the part of advanced industrial countries and less-developed countries. An influential book by French author J. J. Servan-Schreiber warned of the dangers to Western Europe from what he called *l'américaine défie*, "the American challenge," resulting from U.S. foreign direct investments.[1] Shortly after the publication of this book, Pres. Charles de Gaulle threatened to bring down the international monetary system fashioned at the Bretton Woods conference on the grounds that the widespread use of the dollar as a reserve currency enabled the United States to finance the Vietnam War, which he abhorred, as well as the takeover of European industries.

Even in the United States, despite its large direct investment position abroad, the fear and resentment of foreign ownership of business enterprises was pronounced. A 1970s report that a German company was considering acquiring the twin towers of the World Trade Center in lower Manhattan provoked a hostile response. The recycling of petrodollars by OPEC members during the 1970s induced widespread fear that foreigners were "buying up America" and that there was a clear and present danger that foreign ownership would put at risk U.S. military and technological secrets, farmland, and banks.[2]

The reaction of less-developed countries to foreign direct investments was, if anything, even more severe. They regarded such investments as harbingers of a new era of colonialism and imperialism and as a threat to their recently won independence and sovereignty. Thus, India's government forced IBM to close its Indian affiliate when the company refused to acquiesce to a demand for local majority ownership. Responsibility for the military coup against the Salvador Allende government in Chile was widely attributed to a U.S. corporation with important holdings in that country.

These attitudes underwent a drastic change in the 1980s, reflecting a growing awareness that foreign direct investments can play a crucial role in the growth process by acting as a conduit for the transfer of capital, technology, and organizational and managerial know-how from more advanced industrial countries to emerging economies. Rather than banning foreign direct investments, as they had previously, governments of the emerging economies competed with each other to attract multinational corporations by offering financial incentives in the form of tax rebates and real estate giveaways. More important, to increase their attractiveness to foreign investors, these governments adopted reforms that were long advocated by the investing community but that until recently they had resisted. These reforms included the relaxation of capital controls, privatization of state industries, the easing of regulations pertaining to the remission of earnings, the elimination of performance criteria, the elimination of ownership limits, and the adoption of prudent fiscal and monetary policies.

Although the benefits that host countries derive from foreign direct investments explain the demand, the question as to why foreign firms wish to acquire affiliates despite the high cost involved in acquisition and operation has to be addressed. Economists studying this problem are in general agreement that a sine qua non for foreign direct investments that are motivated by a desire to penetrate host countries' markets is the existence of a firm-specific competitive advantage. This can result from a firm's ownership rights in superior technology or from its superior management, recognized brand name, efficient channel for product distribution, or some other organizational capability.[3] Although a firm-specific competitive advantage is a necessary condition for foreign investments to occur, it is not, however, sufficient in and of itself. Since competitive advantage can probably be exploited in any number of ways, a theory of foreign direct investment must explain why firms choose this route rather than an alternative.

Explanations abound. In some cases the high cost of transportation can make foreign direct investments more attractive than arm's-length exports to penetrate a market. Trade barriers, already in existence or feared, can tip the scales in favor of foreign direct investments. The formation of the European Community—now the European Union—provided a strong incentive for multinational companies to acquire or establish affiliates in any of the member countries, for two reasons. First, the EC regarded the affiliates as European, and so multinationals were able to avoid external tariffs, which would have applied to their goods if they relied on exports. Second, there was a fear that the EC's policies (despite the EC's strong denials) would at some point transform it into a "fortress." Foreign affiliates provided multinational corporations with a degree of insurance: They would be able to retain their market shares within the EC even if this fear was realized.

Although economic considerations are most important in determining whether to penetrate a foreign market through the export route or through foreign direct investments, political factors also play a role. Thus, Japan's foreign direct investments in the United States during the 1980s were strongly motivated by the desire to reduce its current account surplus, which became a source of contention between the U.S. and Japanese governments. To a degree this was also true of Japan's foreign direct investment in the EC and of its investment in the emerging economies of Asia. By producing goods in emerging economies for export to the United States, the Japanese attempted, in effect, to reduce the value of exports identified as Japanese. It should be noted, however, that the lure of cheap labor was also a factor motivating foreign direct investments in those economies.

Despite the enthusiasm many host-country governments currently display toward foreign direct investments, and the alacrity with which many investing firms respond to this demand, the desirability of these investments for the economies involved remains at the center of ongoing, sometimes bitter debates within the sending and receiving countries. Popular attitudes toward these investments depend very much on what motivated them. In general, investments motivated by a firm's desire to ensure continued availability of raw materials have been subject to severe criticism in host countries, where they are frequently viewed as predatory. And investments in emerging economies by multinational corporations to take advantage of low-cost labor have been subject to severe criticism in source countries, on the grounds they lead to an export of jobs. Finally, investments designed to improve access to markets tend to be regarded with suspicion by some in the source countries as well as the host countries for different reasons. In the source countries, critics contend these investments replace exports with foreign production. In the host countries, investments are sometimes condemned on the grounds they displace local firms. The question as to whether these criticisms are justified is the central issue in this chapter and in Chapter 7, where we attempt to evaluate the impact of outward and inward foreign investments on the U.S. economy.

THE GROWTH OF U.S. FOREIGN DIRECT INVESTMENTS

As we note above, foreign direct investments worldwide increased by 540 percent between 1980 and 1994. The United States, the leading player during the 1960s and 1970s, was joined in the 1980s by Japan and the European Community and even by some emerging economies. And though the overall investment activities of newcomers in recent years tended to overshadow those of the United States, the latter was by no means relegated to the sidelines. Indeed, between 1980 and 1996 the value of U.S. foreign direct investment, measured at current costs, increased by almost 250 percent. Even more spectacular, however, was the almost sixfold increase in the value of foreign direct investments in the United States (see Table 6.1).

It was not long before the critics of globalization concluded that the growth of U.S. foreign direct investments shared responsibility, with the expansion of manufactured imports from emerging economies, for the U.S. economic malaise. This conclusion was based upon three propositions: that multinational enterprises (MNEs) were systematically shifting production and employment from home-based parent companies to foreign affiliates; that the raison d'être of foreign affiliates was to enable MNEs to lower their cost of production by utilizing low-wage labor; and finally that affiliate sales to home countries displaced domestically produced import-substitute goods whereas their sales to the host and third countries displaced domestically produced exports. How valid are these propositions?

THE DEPLOYMENT OF PRODUCTION AND EMPLOYMENT BY MNEs

Table 6.2 shows changes in gross product and employment of U.S. MNEs and in their distribution between home-based parents and majority-

---

BOX 6.1   Alternative Valuations of the Foreign Direct Investments
          Positions

Three alternative valuations of the [foreign direct investment] positions are available: Historical cost, current cost, and market value. The historical-cost position measures United States Direct Investment Abroad (USDIA) at its book value, which in most cases is the initial acquisition price. . . . Its analytical usefulness is limited, however, because it reflects prices of various years and thus cannot be interpreted as either a constant or a current-dollar value.

To meet the need for measures that are valued at prices of the current period, the [Bureau of Economic Analysis] has developed current-cost and market-value estimates of the position. The direct investment position at *current cost* revalues that portion of the position that represents U.S. parents' claims on the tangible assets of affiliates (such as plant, equipment and inventories). . . . The direct investment position at *market value* revalues both the tangible and intangible assets on which U.S. parents have claims. . . . The current cost and market value assets are produced only at the global level and not by country or industry.

Note: All country and industry data for USFDIA are available only on an historical-cost basis.

Source: Raymond J. Mataloni Jr., "A Guide to BEA Statistics on U.S. Multinational Companies," *Survey of Current Business* (March 1995): 43.

---

owned foreign affiliates (MOFAs).[4] An examination of this table reveals that between 1982 and 1995 the MOFA share of the aggregate gross product increased slightly, from 22 percent to 25 percent; their share of total multinational corporation employment increased from 21 percent to 24 percent. In the manufacturing sector, the MOFA share of gross product increased somewhat more, from 22 percent to 29 percent, whereas their share of employment increased from 26 percent to 31 percent. Although these data suggest that foreign direct investments might have had some impact on manufacturing employment in the United States, the extent of the impact should not be exaggerated. A closer look at the data reveals that the major factor behind the increase in the MOFA share of employment in the manufacturing sector was a decline in manufacturing employment by the parents and not a substantial increase in MOFA employment. Between 1982 and 1995, the last year for which data are available, total MNE employment in the manufacturing sector declined by 1.2 mil-

TABLE 6.1 U.S. Foreign Direct Investment Position, 1980–1996, at Current Cost (billions of U.S. dollars)

	U.S. Foreign Direct Investment	Foreign Direct Investment in the U.S.	U.S. Net Foreign Direct Investment Position
1980	396	126	270
1981	412	160	252
1982	387	177	210
1983	376	183	193
1984	368	211	157
1985	395	231	164
1986	431	267	164
1987	505	313	192
1988	527	375	152
1989	560	436	124
1990	620	467	153
1991	644	492	152
1992	659	500	159
1993	715	551	164
1994	788	585	253
1995	884	654	230
1996	971	729	242

Source: U.S. Department of Commerce, *Survey of Current Business* (June 1995): 60, and (July 1997): 33.

lion as a result of a 1.5 million decline in parent employment and a meager 300,000 increase in MOFA employment. It would appear that the "massive" loss of jobs resulting from outward foreign direct investments, which plays an important role in the critics' rhetoric, is little more than a statistical illusion.

THE QUEST FOR CHEAP LABOR AS A DETERMINANT OF U.S. FOREIGN DIRECT INVESTMENTS

In the critic's scenario, the lure of cheap labor is, if not the principal determinant of U.S. foreign direct investments, then certainly a leading one. Again, the available evidence fails to support this contention. Table 6.3 shows the geographic distribution of U.S. MOFAs in 1996. If the availability of cheap labor was a major determinant of the location of U.S. foreign

115

TABLE 6.2 Gross Product and Employment of United States MNE Parents and Majority-Owned Affiliates in All Industries and in Manufacturing, 1982 and 1995

	Gross Product (millions of U.S. dollars)				Employment (000)			
	1982	Percentage of Total	1995	Percentage of Total	1982	Percentage of Total	1995	Percentage of Total
All industries	1,018,734	100	1,820,641	100	23,727	100	24,541	100
Parents	796,017	78	1,357,682	75	18,705	79	18,569	76
MOFA	223,717	22	462,959	25	5,022	21	5,972	24
Manufacturing	542,689	100	1,002,764	100	14,247	100	13,040	100
Parents	421,050	78	713,144	71	10,532	74	9,045	69
MOFA	121,639	22	289,620	29	3,714	26	3,995	31

Source: Raymond J. Mataloni Jr., "U.S. Multinational Companies' Operations in 1995," Survey of Current Business (Oct. 1997): 49.

TABLE 6.3   Geographic Distribution of U.S. MOFAs in 1996 at Historical Cost (billions of U.S. dollars and percentages)

	$	%
All countries	796	100
Canada	92	12
Western Europe	400	50
Japan	40	5
Australia	28	3
Latin America and other Western Hemisphere	144	18
Africa	8	1
Middle East	9	1
Emerging Asia and Pacific	72	9
Addendum:		
Advanced industrial countries	560	70
Emerging economies	233	30

Source: Sylvia Bargas, "Direct Investment Position for 1996: Country and Industry Detail," *Survey of Current Business* (July 1997): 36.

direct investment, we would expect to see substantial investment in emerging economies. This, however, is not the case: In 1996 70 percent of all U.S. foreign direct investments at historical cost were located in the advanced industrial countries of Western Europe, Canada, Japan, and Australia, where wage rates are relatively high. In the same year, U.S. foreign direct investments in Latin America accounted for 18 percent of the total, whereas investments in the emerging economies of Asia and the Pacific accounted for 9 percent of the total.

The data in Table 6.4, which show the industrial composition of U.S. foreign direct investments in 1996, provide additional evidence regarding the influence of cheap labor as a determinant. Affiliates motivated by cheap labor are almost always found in the manufacturing sector. Yet in 1996 manufacturing affiliates accounted for only 34 percent of the total, and 75 percent of these were located in advanced industrial countries. Put somewhat differently, only 8.5 percent of total U.S. foreign direct investment was accounted for by manufacturing affiliates in developing economies, where the availability of cheap labor can be—and has been— an important determinant.

TABLE 6.4 Industrial Composition of U.S. Foreign Direct Investments, 1996, at Historical Cost (billions of U.S. dollars)

	All Industries	Petroleum	Manufacturing	Wholesale Trade	Banking	Other Financial	Services	Other Industries
All countries	796	75	273	72	32	257	37	49
Canada	92	11	44	8	–	16	5	7
Western Europe	400	29	134	37	14	146	24	14
Japan	40	5	16	7	0.4	9	0.8	0.5
Australia	28	2	9	2	0.4	4	1	7
Latin America	144	6	41	8	6	69	3	11
Africa	7	4	2	–	–	1	–	–
Middle East	9	3	2	–	–	1	–	–
Emerging Asian Pacific	72	10	24	10	7	11	2	7

Source: Sylvia Bargas, "Direct Investment Position for 1996: Country and Industry Detail," *Survey of Current Business* (July 1997): 36, table 3.

On a more positive note, the data in Table 6.4 indicate that foreign affiliates in petroleum and other extractive industries accounted for 15 percent of the total position, whereas services and service-related industries—wholesale, banking, other finance, and services proper—accounted for approximately 50 percent of the total. The heavy concentration of U.S. foreign direct investments in the service industries, broadly defined, combined with the preponderance of manufacturing affiliates in the more-advanced industrial countries strongly suggest that the major motivation for foreign affiliates was to gain access to foreign markets rather than to secure raw materials or to exploit low wage rates.

U.S. Foreign Direct Investments and the International Production System

Although the availability of cheap labor in emerging economies was not the principal factor motivating U.S. foreign direct investments, it did play a role in the international production strategies of MNEs. As we have already noted, one component of these strategies was to acquire affiliates in emerging economies, to which labor-intensive operations could be sourced. The ability to do so was facilitated by policies adopted by emerging economies as well as more advanced countries that reduced the cost of crossborder movement of intermediate goods. An examination of the maquiladora system in Mexico—a system similar to the export-processing zones in emerging Asia—suggests how this was accomplished.[5]

To expand employment opportunities following the elimination by the United States of the *bracero* program—which permitted the admission of Mexican guest workers to harvest U.S. crops—the Mexican government adopted in 1965 the Border Industrialization Program. The essence of this program was to encourage foreign investors to establish assembly plants near the U.S.-Mexico border by eliminating duties on intermediate goods brought into Mexico for further processing, provided the goods were re-exported to the source countries. To support this initiative the United States amended its tariff schedules and introduced sections 806.30 and 807 of the U.S. Tariff Code, which stipulated that those goods, when re-exported back to the United States, would be subject to a tariff based only on the value added to them in Mexico. In effect, the two governments significantly reduced the tariff on crossborder transactions involving intermediate goods between the two countries, providing by design a fillip for a finer international division of labor.

Despite these efforts, it was not until the 1980s, when as a result of the debt crisis the Mexican government abandoned its import-substitute strategy of development, that the maquiladora program was assigned a high priority. To further stimulate interest in this program, the government in 1983 relaxed regulations applying to the maquiladoras, permitting them to sell up to 20 percent of output to domestic markets. Further liberalization occurred in 1989, when the restriction that maquiladoras had to be located on the border was removed and the proportion of allowable domestic-market sales was increased to 50 percent.

The loosening of the regulations since 1982 resulted in a substantial increase in the number of maquiladoras and in the value of their exports to the United States and in a change in the composition of these exports. Where the early maquiladoras concentrated almost exclusively on the assembly of toys, apparel, and circuit boards, in recent years there has been a pronounced increase in automation and electronic operations. In addition, there has been an increase in the presence of many non-U.S. firms, particularly from Japan, which were established after NAFTA to gain greater access to the U.S. market.

EXPORT PLATFORMS:
THE EXCEPTION OR THE RULE?

The growth of the maquiladora system in Mexico was paralleled by the growth of export-processing zones in the Asian economies. The prominent role that affiliates located in such zones played in selected consumer goods markets contributed to a widespread belief that a major motivation for foreign direct investments was to establish export platforms for the production and sale of goods in the United States. This was not the case, however, as is apparent from an examination of Table 6.5, which shows the destination of MOFA sales. Sales were made to three distinct markets: to host countries, which accounted for two-thirds of the total in 1994; to other countries, which accounted for 23 percent of the total; and to the United States, which accounted for 10 percent of the total. The conclusion to be derived from these data is unambiguous: The major function of MOFAs, taken as a whole, was to contest foreign markets. Indeed, in 1994 MOFA sales to these markets accounted for 72 percent of total MNE sales to foreign countries, whereas parent exports to these countries accounted for only 28 percent. The heavy reliance that the MNEs placed on affiliates as suppliers to foreign markets is a reflection of the advantages that affiliate sales have relative to arm's-length exports to accomplish this task.

TABLE 6.5   Sales by U.S. Nonbank MOFAs, 1995 (billions of U.S. dollars and percentages)

	Total $	% of Area's Total	Sales to U.S.	% of Area's Total	Sales to Host Countries	% of Area's Total	Sales to Other Foreign	% of Area's Total
All countries	1,432	100	150	10	958	66	324	22
Western Europe	795	100	32	4	515	64	248	31
Canada	193	100	55	28	133	69	5	2
Latin America	135	100	25	18	92	68	17	12
Japan	97	100	4	4	88	91	5	5
Emerging Asian Pacific	141	100	25	18	77	55	39	28

Addendum:	Percent of Total U.S. Nonbank MOFA Sales, by Area
All countries	100
Western Europe	55
Canada	13
Latin America	9
Japan	7
Emerging Asian Pacific	10
All other countries	6

Source: Raymond J. Mataloni Jr. and Mahnaz Fahim-Nader, "Operations of United States Multinational Companies: Preliminary Results from the 1994 Benchmark Survey," *Survey of Current Business* (Dec. 1996): 24, table 15.

At the same time, however, the data also clearly reflect the important role that MOFAs located in emerging economies play in the international production system. Although in the aggregate MOFA sales to the United States accounted for only 10 percent of the total, these sales accounted for 18 percent for MOFAs located in the emerging economies of Asia and Latin America. These sales, moreover, were almost exclusively intrafirm and consisted for the most part of intermediate goods shipped by MOFAs to U.S.-based parents. It should be noted that for MOFAs based in specific emerging economies, the proportion of total sales to the United States was even higher than the average. For Singapore- and Mexican-based MOFAs, sales to the United States accounted for 27 percent of the total, and for Malaysian MOFAs they accounted for 21 percent. By contrast, for Western European–

and Japanese-based MOFAs, sales to the United States accounted for only 4 percent of the total. Among advanced industrial countries, Canadian-based MOFAs were the exception; sales to the United States accounted for 28 percent of the total. This relatively high proportion reflected these affiliates' heavy involvement in the international production of vehicles and parts.[6]

We should note that the difference between European-based affiliates and Japanese-based affiliates regarding the degree to which activities were focused on host market is more apparent than real. The data in Table 6.5 suggest that European-based affiliates' sales to host markets accounted for 66 percent of the total, as contrasted with 91 percent for Japanese-based affiliates. This, however, is somewhat misleading in that a very large proportion of the 31 percent of sales to other countries reported by the European-based affiliates were in reality sales to host-country markets. The reason is that with the formation of the EC it was not necessary for multinational companies to establish affiliates in every member country. An affiliate in any one EC country can export its products to all other EC countries duty-free. Since most affiliate sales to other countries were in reality sales to other European countries, they were for all intents and purposes sales to the extended host country.[7]

In light of the evidence, there is little question that access considerations were the major motivation for U.S. foreign direct investments. Despite all the talk about the lure of cheap labor and the inundation of U.S. markets with manufactured imports from "export-platforms," the vast majority of U.S. foreign affiliates are located in advanced industrial countries, and an overwhelmingly large proportion of their output is sold not in the United States but in host-country markets.

THE IMPACT OF U.S. FOREIGN DIRECT INVESTMENT ON EMPLOYMENT

The most severe criticism aimed at the growth of U.S. foreign direct investments is that it has resulted in the displacement of millions of American workers. Although the Ross Perots and Pat Buchanans focus on the "loss" of jobs resulting from the migration of U.S. firms in whole or in part to low-wage emerging economies, other critics include in their indictment even those foreign direct investments located in advanced industrial countries, which, as was already noted, cater for the most part to host countries. These affiliate sales to host countries and third countries, they claim, undermine U.S. exports and in effect shift the demand for labor away from the United States to the host countries.

An early study by Norman Glickman and Douglas Woodward is a case in point. They estimate that foreign direct investments "cost American manufacturing workers more than 2.7 million jobs between 1977 and 1986 . . . a loss resulting from the displacement of 3.3 million jobs by foreign investments compared with only 588,000 jobs being stimulated."[8] To put this conclusion in proper perspective, Glickman and Woodward note that "over the same period there was a net loss of 868,000 manufacturing jobs," suggesting that in the absence of these foreign investments employment in the U.S. manufacturing sector would actually have increased by 1.8 million jobs. Similarly, Barry Bluestone and Bennet Harrison estimated that during the 1970s U.S. foreign direct investment was responsible for the loss of between 450,000 to 650,000 jobs each year, or between 5.4 million and 7.8 million jobs over the decade.[9]

The problem with these and similar estimates is that they are based on assumptions rather than facts. The facts on which all estimates are ultimately based consist of data regarding affiliates' gross product, sales, and employment. What is not known, however—and what in the absence of detailed, firm-by-firm data is basically unknowable—is how these facts relate to domestic employment. The impact of foreign direct investments on the domestic labor market depends on whether affiliate production and sales to host-country and third-country markets replace or supplement U.S. production and exports to these markets; whether U.S. imports from foreign-based affiliates come at the expense of domestic production of import-substitute industries; and whether foreign direct investments induce an increase in U.S. exports of intermediate goods and capital goods to affiliates.[10] Since the available data do not shed any light on these issues, those producing the estimates have no alternative but to make assumptions. Unfortunately, their estimates depend very much on these assumptions. Those who conclude that foreign direct investments have had a significant adverse impact on the demand for domestic labor assume a high rate of substitution between affiliate sales to host-country markets and exports from the United States, and between imports from affiliates and domestic production of the import-substitute industries; they also assume that an increase in affiliate production does not induce a significant increase in U.S. exports of intermediate goods and capital goods to affiliates. In contrast, those who assume low rates of substitution and a significant increase in induced exports of capital and intermediate goods to affiliates conclude that foreign direct investments have not had a significant adverse impact.

There is, moreover, another factor to consider in assessing the impact of foreign direct investments on domestic employment. That is whether investments are not strategically important for the survival of the enterprise undertaking them. To put the matter somewhat more dramatically, it is possible to conceive of situations where, were it not for these investments, the enterprise would have to shut down completely. Under these circumstances, foreign investments could be credited with creating domestic jobs rather than destroying them. Many observers believe this occurred in the U.S. apparel industry.

Badly battered by imports from emerging economies and lacking the resources and opportunities to develop new technologies, firms in the apparel industry resorted during the late 1960s to the practice of sourcing, both to foreign affiliates and to unaffiliated firms. Under the provision of section 807 of the U.S. Tariff Code, sourcing occurs when materials are cut in the United States, sent abroad for assembly, and ultimately reexported to the United States with duties levied only on the value added. Until 1985 the amount that could be reexported to the United States—and hence the amount that could be sourced—was strictly limited by quota. A bilateral agreement with the Caribbean Basin countries signed in 1985 eliminated this quota and allowed unlimited access, provided the material was both produced and cut in the United States. This change not only provided a fillip to the U.S. fabric industry but also to the apparel industry, which gained easier access to low-wage labor for its labor-intensive operations. According to one authority, L. A. Murray,

> many industry leaders—in the American Apparel Manufacturers Association, the United States Department of Commerce, and other organizations and agencies—believe that without the practice of 807 sourcing, the United States apparel manufacturers would go out of business, causing a significant loss of jobs in the industry. Because of these arrangements domestic manufacturers have been able to take advantage of the relatively cheap labor of Mexico and the Caribbean to manufacture products that are more competitively priced compared with East Asian products. For these reasons 807 sourcing may have reduced the demand for imports from Asia protecting the employment of domestic workers who contribute to some parts of the manufacturing process.[11]

If Philip H. Knight, chair and chief executive officer of Nike, Inc., can be believed, the same situation existed in the footwear industry. In a letter to the editor of *The New York Times*, he wrote: "If [Nike] did not produce in the same low-income countries as our competitors, we would be out of business and our more than 10,000 United States employees would be unemployed. In 1984, our last year of United States production, we lost $10 million on United States produced footwear."[12] The experience of Keytronic, a manufacturer of computer keyboards located in Spokane, Washington, provides another possible case in point. Facing heavy competition from Japan, Keytronic dismissed 277 workers and moved some operations to Juarez, Mexico, where wages were 25 percent of those in the United States. As a result of this redeployment, the chief financial officer reported, corporate sales jumped, and since "many of the components used in the keyboards assembled in Juarez come from plants near Spokane, overall employment in the area has actually increased to keep up with the demand."[13]

Needless to say, these examples are not offered to suggest that relying on foreign affiliates and subcontracting never leads to domestic displacement of labor or that affiliates are established to save jobs in the United States. They are cited rather to underline the inherent difficulties of estimating the impact that foreign affiliates have on employment in the source countries and to caution against placing too much confidence in any of the many estimates that have been produced.

Despite this cautionary note, however, there is a high probability that estimates based on assumptions of low or moderate rates of substitution are likely to be somewhat more reliable than those assuming very high rates. The reason is that the high cost of acquiring and operating affiliates would normally bias a corporation against this mode of delivery if alternative modes existed. It is thus not unreasonable to assume that in most cases the decision to locate abroad, particularly in high-wage countries, was undertaken only after the firm concluded that alternative methods of delivery—exports, for example—are not viable. Under these circumstances, the assumption of a high rate of substitution between affiliate sales to host- and third-country markets and U.S. exports is untenable.

The conclusions that emerge from an analysis of U.S. foreign direct investments can be stated briefly. The *major* motivation for U.S. foreign direct investments was the MNEs' desire to expand their shares in foreign markets, not to exploit cheap labor. Hence, the basic function of affiliates in advanced industrial countries, where the vast majority is located, is to cater to the host countries' markets. Although this is also true for affiliates located in emerging economies and in Canada, those affiliates have an additional function as components in the international production system. In this capacity, affiliates engage in a trading network with parents and with other affiliates in intermediate goods. The extensive intrafirm imports and exports that result from these activities attest to the vibrancy of this international production system. The ability to exploit cheap labor in emerging economies does, of course, play a role in motivating these investments, but it is important to note that these investments constitute a very small proportion of the total. Finally, whereas many estimates have been made regarding the impact of U.S. foreign direct investment on U.S. employment, they cannot be taken too seriously. The data necessary to generate reliable estimates simply do not exist, and those estimates that have been made depend very much on the assumptions that underlie them. There is, however, some reason for believing that the lower impact estimates are closer to the mark than the higher ones.

7

FOREIGN DIRECT INVESTMENTS IN THE UNITED STATES

The official U.S. investment policy is consistent with, and broadly similar to, official trade policies. In both areas, the United States is on record as supporting a free and open approach based on the principle of nondiscrimination. The investment policy was enunciated as early as 1979 and has been repeated by every administration since. Before a subcommittee of the Committee on Foreign Affairs, Charles Meissner, at the time an assistant secretary of state, summarized U.S. policy as follows:

> The United States has long believed that flows of trade, finance and investments can make their most effective contribution to long-run steady economic growth in an open climate in which these flows can respond to market forces. Consistent with our belief in such an open system, general United States international investment policy is not to adopt government measures which either promote or discourage inward or outward investment flows. We favor a system which offers the same opportunities to both foreign and domestic investors on a nondiscriminatory basis.[1]

The guarantee of freedom and openness is, as is usually the case, not absolute. Historically, foreign investments in sectors under federal regulation have been prohibited or severely limited. Among the more important of these are the domestic maritime industry and the nuclear production and distribution industries, where foreign investments are completely proscribed. In the telecommunications, broadcasting, and domestic air transport industries, among others, foreign investments have until recently been limited to specified proportions unless otherwise au-

thorized by the responsible federal regulatory agencies. In still other industries, including banking, prior federal agency approval is required.[2]

In addition, in some industries the United States has insisted upon a
reciprocity condition: Foreign firms, for example, are denied leases to
mine certain minerals or fuels on federally owned lands if their home
governments do not grant the same privileges to U.S. firms. Foreign participation in government-subsidized R & D programs is permitted only if
the home governments permit U.S. companies located in their countries
to participate in similar programs that they sponsor and, in some cases,
only if other conditions are satisfied, including effective protection of U.S.
intellectual property rights, the right of establishment, and the granting
of national treatment.

In general these exceptions to the policy of openness have in the past
been relatively unimportant. A potentially greater challenge to this policy
is posed by the Florio-Exon amendments to the Omnibus Trade
Competition Acts of 1982 and 1993, which extended the authority of the
Committee on Foreign Investment in the United States. This committee,
originally established during the 1970s to review foreign direct investment proposals to ensure they did not jeopardize national security, was
now mandated to investigate all foreign proposals to acquire U.S. firms
engaged in the defense sector to ensure that acquisition would not adversely affect U.S. leadership in technology, impede efforts to limit the
proliferation of nuclear, chemical, and biological weapons, or assist countries engaged in terrorist activities. Although there is general agreement
that most of these objectives are admirable, concern has been expressed
that the amendments could represent a first step toward establishing a
screening procedure for proposed investments in the advanced technology sector. It should be noted, however, that as of this writing this fear
has not materialized.

THE EXPANSION OF FOREIGN
DIRECT INVESTMENT IN THE UNITED STATES

From the end of World War II until the 1980s, U.S. involvement with foreign direct investment was basically as a source country. During this period, the United States supplied more than 50 percent of all world foreign
investments and accounted for less than 25 percent of world inward investments. The situation changed drastically, however, during the 1980s
and the first half of the 1990s, when the United States was the recipient of
large foreign direct investment inflows. Indeed, in 1987 the United States

became the world's leading host country. And though the United States remains a net creditor on direct investment accounts, the ratio of the value of foreign direct investments in the United States to the value of U.S. foreign direct investments abroad rose from 32 percent in 1980 to 75 percent in 1996.[3]

The story to be told about inward foreign investments is somewhat less complicated and controversial than that of outward foreign investments. In general, the desire to obtain and maintain access to one of the world's most dynamic and affluent economies was the principal motivation for such investments. The reasons, however, why access was sought through foreign investments rather than through exports varied from case to case. For the service industries (broadly defined), typified by hotels, restaurants, consulting and legal firms, retail and wholesale distribution, and banking, insurance, and finance industries, onsite facilities are a virtual necessity. For other industries, particularly in the manufacturing sector, the desire to avoid high transportation costs, the availability of a pool of highly skilled workers, the desire to gain access to U.S. technology, and the promise of economies of scale provided incentives to acquire U.S. affiliates.

Two specific developments in recent years, however, contributed to the burst of investment activity, particularly between 1985 and 1990. The first was the large depreciation of the dollar beginning in the mid-1980s; the second was a Japanese decision to increase their investment position in the United States. Just as the run-up in the value of the dollar during the early part of the 1980s encouraged imports into the United States and rendered U.S. exports uncompetitive on world markets, the depreciation of the dollar during the latter part of this decade had the opposite effect. By increasing the dollar price of imports into the United States, depreciation had an adverse effect on countries that relied on exports to gain access to U.S. markets. To maintain and, if possible, expand their shares in the U.S. market, foreign corporations increased their acquisitions of U.S. affiliates.

The second development that contributed to the burst of investment activities in the United States was the decision by Japan to increase its presence in the U.S. market. Japan's large and recurrent trade surpluses vis-à-vis the United States not only exposed it to severe bashing but also resulted in threats of retaliatory measures beyond the imposition of "voluntary" export restraints. Japan responded to these threats in two ways: by increasing its foreign direct investments in the United States; and by shifting the production of selected products that it exported to the United States from parent companies located in Japan to affiliates in the emerging Asian economies. Both of these responses were designed to enable

Japanese companies to maintain their market shares in the United States while reducing their increasingly embarrassing export surpluses.[4]

THE U.S. RESPONSE TO
FOREIGN DIRECT INVESTMENTS

The desire by foreigners to increase direct investments in the United States was generally met with favor. As we have already noted, the new jobs these investments promised resulted in the granting of attractive offers to prospective investors. At the same time, the fear that critical U.S. industries were being put at risk by foreign investments receded, at least for the time being. This is not to suggest, however, that these investments met unanimous approval. Spokesmen for U.S. automobile companies, among others, were not overjoyed at the expansion of Japanese production facilities in the United States. Legislators representing industries threatened by the expansion of foreign affiliates demanded the adoption of domestic-content requirements to ensure affiliates did not degenerate into "screwdriver factories" that simply assembled parts that were manufactured in, and imported from, home countries. And, periodically, charges were levied that foreign-owned affiliates were engaged in unfair and discriminatory labor practices, that they paid lower wages than their U.S.-owned counterparts, and that high-level positions were systematically filled by foreigners rather than by Americans. In the remainder of this chapter, we will assess the impact of foreign direct investments on the U.S. economy. A statistical portrait of the geographical origins and industrial composition of foreign direct investments in the United States is followed by an examination of the effects these investments have had on gross product, employment, wages, and productivity.

FOREIGN INVESTORS

In the not-too-distant past, the fear that foreign direct investments in "sensitive industries" would jeopardize U.S. security was not uncommon. However, the definition of *sensitive industry* and the ways in which foreign ownership represented a security risk were never spelled out in detail. Worst-case scenarios were in vogue. At one time, the threat was said to emanate from the potential monopolization by the Japanese of a vital technological component, the absence of which would paralyze the entire defense system. At another time, the thrust focused on a potential foreign takeover of U.S. banks, which could then be used to finance terrorist activities aimed at U.S. interests. Even foreign ownership of real estate—particularly farmland—caused discomfort. In some unspecified manner, these investments were regarded as putting the U.S. food supply at risk. And somehow, Japanese ownership of the landmark Rockefeller Center on New York's prestigious Fifth Avenue was considered an affront. Although these paranoid fears seem, at least for the time being, to have receded, the xenophobia that fueled them has clearly not disappeared. For this reason, it is of some interest to examine both the source of foreign direct investments in the United States and their industrial composition to ascertain whether they constitute any threat to U.S. security or well-being.

The foreign direct investment position in the United States, by area, between 1982 and 1996 on a historical cost basis is shown in Table 7.1. An examination of the table reveals two significant changes in the source of these investments during this period. The most important of these was the increase in the share of Asia and the Pacific area, from 9 percent in 1982 to 21 percent in 1996. This increase was due almost entirely to the expansion of Japan's position. The second was the decline in the share of Latin America and other Western Hemisphere countries. Europe's and Canada's shares remained roughly the same.

On a more disaggregated level, investors from six advanced industrial countries accounted for approximately 80 percent of total foreign direct investments in the United States in 1996. The countries, in order of importance, were the United Kingdom (23 percent); Japan (19 percent); the Netherlands (12 percent); Germany (10 percent); Canada (9 percent); and France (8 percent). The share of OPEC countries, whose investments in the United States during the 1970s and early 1980s were a major source of concern, accounted for less than 0.5 percent of the total.[5]

The fact that virtually all foreign firms operating in the United States are owned by investors from countries with extraordinarily close ties to the United States is no guarantee, of course, that they would not engage in subversive activities. It does suggest, however, that assigning a high priority to this possibility is not very rational.

THE INDUSTRIAL COMPOSITION OF FOREIGN DIRECT INVESTMENTS IN THE UNITED STATES

The industrial composition of foreign-owned affiliates in the United States in 1996 is shown in Table 7.2. The largest single position was in the manufacturing sector, which accounted for approximately one-third of

TABLE 7.1   Foreign Direct Investment Position in the United States on a Historical-Cost Basis, by Major Area, 1982–1996 (millions of U.S. dollars and percentages)

Year	All Areas	Canada	Europe	Latin Amer. and Other Western Hemisphere.	Africa	Middle East	Asia and Pacific
				Millions of U.S. Dollars			
1982	124,677	11,708	83,193	14,229	105	4,401	11,041
1983	137,061	11,434	92,936	15,035	95	4,446	13,115
1984	164,583	15,286	108,211	16,201	194	5,336	19,355
1985	184,615	17,131	121,413	16,826	461	4,954	23,830
1986	220,414	20,318	144,181	16,763	250	4,870	34,032
1987	263,394	24,684	181,006	10,103	521	4,973	42,108
1988	314,754	26,566	208,942	11,243	441	6,570	60,992
1989	368,924	30,370	239,190	16,218	505	7,588	75,053
1990	394,911	29,544	247,320	20,168	505	4,425	92,948
1991	419,108	36,834	256,053	14,546	937	4,864	105,873
1992	427,566	37,843	255,570	17,473	896	4,797	110,987
1993	466,666	40,487	287,940	19,716	1,003	5,220	112,299
1994	502,410	42,133	309,415	25,042	925	5,565	119,331
1995	560,088	46,005	360,762	22,716	936	5,053	124,615
1996	630,045	53,845	410,425	24,627	713	6,177	134,255
				Average Annual Growth Rate (%)			
	11.9	10.4	10.3	3.5	17.0	1.1	19.2
				Percent of Total Position			
1982	100.0	9.4	66.7	11.4	0.1	3.5	8.9
1983	100.0	8.3	67.8	11.0	0.1	3.2	9.6
1984	100.0	9.3	65.7	9.8	0.1	3.2	11.8
1985	100.0	9.3	65.8	9.1	0.2	2.7	12.9
1986	100.0	9.2	65.4	7.6	0.1	2.2	15.4
1987	100.0	9.4	68.7	3.8	0.2	1.9	16.0
1988	100.0	8.4	66.4	3.6	0.1	2.1	19.4
1989	100.0	8.2	64.8	4.4	0.1	2.1	20.3
1990	100.0	7.5	62.6	5.1	0.1	1.1	23.5
1991	100.0	8.8	61.1	3.5	0.2	1.2	25.3
1992	100.0	8.9	59.8	4.1	0.2	1.1	26.0
1993	100.0	8.7	61.7	4.2	0.2	1.1	24.1
1994	100.0	8.4	61.6	5.0	0.2	1.1	23.8
1995	100.0	8.2	64.4	4.1	0.2	0.9	22.2
1996	100.0	8.6	65.0	4.0	–	1.0	21.3

Source: Department of Commerce, *Survey of Current Business* (July 1996): 54; and (July 1997): 39.

TABLE 7.2 Foreign Direct Investment Position in the United States on a Historical-Cost Basis at 1996 Year-End (millions of U.S. dollars)

	All Industries	Petroleum	Manufacturing	Trade	Depository Institutions	Finance, Except Depository Institutions	Insurance	Real Estate	Other Industries
All countries	630,045	42,343	234,323	92,945	31,903	70,185	59,566	30,118	68,661
Canada	53,845	3,577	22,031	4,004	2,296	5,451	7,056	2,487	6,941
Western Europe	410,425	30,560	172,501	43,761	16,909	43,046	46,776	11,456	45,416
Latin America & other Western Hemisphere	24,627	2,241	4,551	3,949	3,715	428	4,697	3,342	1,704
Africa	717	—[a]	258	-48	—[a]	—[a]	0	206	-153
Asia & Pacific	134,255	4,528	34,581	40,544	8,249	20,590	1,034	10,044	14,686
Addenda:									
European Union[b]	372,161	29,685	156,348	39,857	15,782	36,632	40,660	10,520	42,677
OPEC[c]	4,237	1,062	-68	10	563	-7	3	2,564	111
Japan	118,116	128	29,454	38,021	6,816	21,322	771	8,823	12,781

[a] Suppressed to avoid disclosure of data of individual companies.
[b] Austria, Belgium, Denmark, Finland, France, Germany, Greece, Ireland, Italy, Luxembourg, Netherlands, Portugal, Spain, Sweden, and the United Kingdom.
[c] Algeria, Gabon, Indonesia, Iran, Iraq, Kuwait, Libya, Nigeria, Qatar, Saudi Arabia, the United Arab Emirates, and Venezuela.

Source: Department of Commerce, Survey of Current Business (July 1997): 39, table 4.

the total. Aside from the petroleum sector, the remaining foreign investment position was in the service industries, broadly defined. This suggests that the desire to gain access to markets that could not be readily served through traditional exports was a major motivation for these investments.

As with the total investment position, European investors accounted for almost 75 percent of total foreign direct investments in the manufacturing sector: the United Kingdom alone accounted for 25 percent of the total; France, Germany, and the Netherlands each accounted for approximately 10 percent of the total; Japan, a latecomer, accounted for 12 percent of the total. Japanese investments were highly concentrated in the automobile and automobile parts industries and reflected both the voluntary export restraints that constrained Japan's automobile exports to the United States and its desire to ease U.S. pressure as a result of its large and persistent current account surpluses. Japan's largest direct investment position in the United States, however, was in the wholesale trade sector, which accounted for almost one-third of Japan's total position in 1996. These investments were undertaken primarily to facilitate the distribution of Japan's exports, particularly automobiles and automobile parts, to the United States. Japan's activities represent an almost classic example of those that require a physical presence and that cannot be carried out by arm's-length, crossborder trade. One-half of OPEC's very small position in the United States was accounted for by investments in the real estate sector; 25 percent came from the petroleum sector. The hue and cry that greeted OPEC-member investments in the United States during the 1970s and early 1980s is a clear example of how mass hysteria can be generated in any society with xenophobic tendencies.

FOREIGN DIRECT INVESTMENTS
AND U.S. SECURITY

A recent study undertaken by the U.S. Bureau of Economic Analysis and the U.S. Census Bureau sheds new light on the perennial question as to whether any critical U.S. industry is in danger of being dominated by foreign-owned firms. In 1990, the only year for which this information is available, the value added by the 11,900 foreign-owned manufacturing affiliates amounted to $117 billion and accounted for 13 percent of the total value added in the U.S. manufacturing sector. Foreign-owned manufacturing affiliates were highly concentrated in the chemical, food, electronic and electrical equipment, and industrial, mechanical, and equipment industries. These four industrial groups accounted for more than 50 percent of the value added by foreign-owned establishments in the manufacturing sector.[6]

Within these broad industrial groups, foreign-owned establishments existed in 429 of the 459 industries. In 149 industries they accounted for less than 5 percent of the total value added; in 387 industries they accounted for less than 25 percent. In only twenty-two industries did they contribute more than 40 percent, and in only nine industries did they account for more than 50 percent.[7] Moreover, no industry in which foreign firms dominated could be considered critical to the defense or welfare of the United States.

THE IMPACT OF U.S. FOREIGN DIRECT INVESTMENTS ON OUTPUT AND EMPLOYMENT

In recent years, state and local governments actively recruited foreign direct investments by offering generous tax and real estate concessions.[8] They were motivated by the expected increase in tax revenues resulting from expanded output and by the promise of additional jobs. An analysis of the foreign affiliates' operating data sheds some light on the wisdom and success of these activities. Table 7.3 contains data for affiliate gross product and employment in selected years between 1980 and 1995.

Between 1980 and 1995 the gross product of foreign-owned affiliates increased by 460 percent, from $71 billion to $327 billion. This expansion was associated with an increase in the foreign affiliate share of U.S. gross product originating in the private sector, from 3.4 percent to 6 percent. During that same period, the level of employment in U.S.-based affiliates rose from 2,034,000 to 4,928,000.

Although it might appear that foreign direct investments contributed importantly to the expansion of U.S. gross product and employment, that is not necessarily the case. The reason is that a part of the increase in output and employment attributed to affiliates is a replacement for, not an addition to, the output and employment of domestic firms. Foreign investors can increase their stake in the U.S. economy in three distinct ways: by establishing new firms; by expanding already existing firms under their control through capital formation; and by acquiring existing firms from U.S. owners. The first two methods, which are designated as "greenfield" investments, increase the productive capacity of the United States, whereas the acquisition of existing firms does not. Since the increase in gross product attributable to affiliates following the acquisition of exist-

TABLE 7.3 Foreign Affiliate Gross Product and Employment in the United States, 1980–1995

	Gross Product (millions of U.S. dollars)	Employment (000)	Foreign Affiliate Share of Gross Product Originating in Private Sector
1980	70,906	2,034	3.4
1985	134,852	2,862	4.3
1988	190,384	3,844	5.0
1990	239,279	4,734	5.5
1995	326,955	4,928	6.0

Source: Mahnaz Fahim-Nader and William J. Zeile, "Foreign Direct Investments in the United States," *Survey of Current Business* (June 1997): 42, table 1.

ing firms can be completely offset by a decline in gross product attributed to domestically owned firms, the transaction would result in a change in the attribution of gross product rather than a change in its value. Thus, in order to assess the impact of an increase in affiliates' gross product on the U.S. economy, it is important to know the manner in which the expansion of gross product attributable to affiliates occurred.

Between 1988 and 1995, outlays on foreign direct investments in the United States increased by $380 billion. Eighty-three percent of this increase—$316 billion—was due to the acquisition of existing firms, 17 percent—$64 billion—to the establishment of new firms or the enlargement of existing ones (see Table 7.4). During the same period, affiliates' gross product increased by $137 billion, from $190 billion to $327 billion. On the admittedly unrealistic assumptions that the change in ownership of existing firms had no effect on their productivity, and that the efficiency of the new greenfield firms was equal to that of the existing ones, it is estimated that foreign direct investment resulted in a $23 billion increase in U.S. gross product between 1988 and 1995. This estimate is based on the assumption that the increase in gross product is equal to 17 percent of the $137 billion attributed to the foreign affiliates. Even if it is assumed that this underestimates the "true" contribution of the foreign investments by, say, 20 percent, the result would be an increase in gross product due to foreign direct investments of no more than $28 billion.

The same considerations apply to the contribution that foreign direct investments make to employment. As we have already noted, the promise of new jobs was the major reason state and local governments put out the

TABLE 7.4   Investment Outlays (billions of U.S. dollars)

	1988	1989	1990	1991	1992	1993	1994	1995	Total 1988–1995
Investments (total)	72.7	71.2	65.9	25.5	15.3	26.2	45.6	57.2	379.6
U.S. businesses acquired	64.8	59.7	55.3	17.8	10.6	21.8	38.7	47.2	315.9
U.S. businesses established	7.8	11.4	10.6	7.7	4.7	4.5	6.9	10.0	63.6

Source: Mahnaz Fahim-Nader and William J. Zeile, "Foreign Direct Investments in the United States," Survey of Current Business (May 1995): 59, table 2 (for 1988–1989 data); and (June 1997): 45, table 2 (for 1990–1995 data).

welcome mat for foreign investors. Have these hopes been realized? For some areas of the country they clearly have. In South Carolina and other parts of the old Confederacy, foreign investments have helped transform depressed and declining economies into boom areas. Since the early part of this century, many states in the Deep South have placed heavy reliance on the textile industry. With the advent of intense competition from developing economies, state and city officials began aggressively courting outside investors. This campaign paid off handsomely, for example, for South Carolina, with the establishment of BMW, Michelin, Hoechst, and Fuji affiliates. Partially as a result of jobs created by these investments—in early 1996, 9 percent of South Carolina workers were employed by foreign affiliates and many more by firms servicing multinational operations—annual salaries have increased by about 40 percent; unemployment has also declined, from almost 7 percent to just slightly above 5 percent.[9]

Although the experiences of South Carolina and a few other states provide grist for the anecdotal evidence mill, the fact remains that foreign direct investments have created many fewer jobs than commonly believed.[10] The reason, again, is the different impacts on job creation between greenfield investments and foreign investments, which entail nothing more than the transfer of existing firms from domestic to foreign ownership. Between 1988 and 1995, employment by foreign affiliates increased from 3.8 million to 4.9 million.[11] In view of the fact that 83 percent of total foreign investments during this period consisted of takeovers of existing firms, the increase in employment resulting from foreign direct investments is estimated to be closer to 187,000 than to the 1.1 million increase suggested by the data. Again, it is highly unlikely that upward correction of this lower level estimate would increase it by more than 10–20 percent.

FOREIGN DIRECT INVESTMENTS IN THE UNITED STATES AND IMPORTS OF GOODS

The critics of foreign direct investments in the United States have charged that many foreign affiliates are little more than screwdriver plants that were set up to circumvent tariffs and other trade barriers. It is alleged that these plants derive parts and components from foreign-based parent companies and, hence, are instrumental in displacing domestic firms and labor. This concern is fueled by foreign affiliates' heavy involvement in trade and their recurrent trade deficits: In 1995 they accounted for 24 percent of total U.S. exports of goods and for 34 percent of U.S. imports. Affiliates' $118 billion trade deficit in that year accounted for 68 percent of the total U.S. trade deficit.[12]

The picture, however, is more nuanced than critics suggest. An examination of affiliates' exports and imports by industrial sectors, shown in Table 7.5, reveals that the wholesale sector, and not the manufacturing sector, was mainly responsible for both the large value of imports and the large deficit on merchandise accounts. Indeed, in 1995 this sector accounted for 59 percent of total affiliate imports and for 70 percent of the total affiliate merchandise deficit. The manufacturing sector, in contrast, accounted for 32 percent of affiliate imports and for 22 percent of the affiliate merchandise deficit.[13] Since wholesale affiliates were established for the sole purpose of facilitating importation and distribution of parent companies' finished goods, the large value of their imports sheds no light on the import content of affiliates' operations.

A study by Richard Zeile addresses this question directly.[14] To determine whether manufacturing affiliates place heavier reliance on imports than do U.S.-owned corporations, Zeile compared the two groups of companies with respect to the domestic content of gross output, the value-added share of gross output, and the import share of intermediate inputs. The results of these comparisons are shown in Table 7.6.

Although the import share of the affiliates is higher than that of the U.S.-owned corporations in regard to all three measures, the overwhelming importance of domestic content for both groups is indisputable. In 1994, the domestic—that is, American—content of affiliate gross output was 87 percent, and the domestic share of the affiliate intermediate inputs was 81 percent. Even in the motor vehicle and equipment industry, in which the affiliates have been singled out as being heavily dependent on imports, the domestic-content share of affiliate output was 74 percent, compared to 84 percent for U.S.-owned companies, and the domestic share of intermediate

TABLE 7.5 Affiliate Imports and Exports by Industry, 1995 (billions of U.S. dollars)

	U.S. Exports of Goods Shipped by Affiliates	U.S. Imports of Goods Shipped to Affiliates
All industries	138.7	254.9
Manufacturing	55.6	81.8
Wholesale trade	65.5	148.7
Retail trade	1.8	3.7
Financial, insurance, and real estate	—	—
Services	0.5	0.7
Other industries	3.4	0.4

Source: U.S. Department of Commerce, Survey of Current Business (June 1997): 63, table 19.2.

inputs was 68 percent, compared to 76 percent for U.S.-owned corporations. The fact that the affiliate domestic share in all these measures was less than those of the U.S.-owned corporations does not by any means negate the substantial domestic content of these affiliate operations or lend support to the view that they are nothing more than screwdriver plants.

CHARACTERISTICS OF FOREIGN AFFILIATES IN THE MANUFACTURING SECTOR

From time to time critics of foreign direct investments claim that the foreign affiliates are engaged in unfair and discriminatory labor practices, that they pay lower wages than their U.S. counterparts, and that they choose foreigners over Americans for high-level positions. A recent survey of the characteristics of foreign-owned affiliates in the manufacturing sector provides an opportunity to check some of these allegations against the facts.

The basic conclusions that emerge from this survey are that the foreign-owned plants are substantially larger than U.S.-owned establishments; that they tend to be more capital-intensive than U.S.-owned establishments; that labor productivity in foreign-owned plants is higher than that in U.S.-owned establishments; and that the production workers in the foreign-owned plants earn higher wages than in U.S.-owned establishments. It must be emphasized, however, that these differences are due not to foreign ownership per se but rather to differences in the industrial distribution of

TABLE 7.6 Measures of Domestic Content (in percentages)

	1989	1994
Domestic content of affiliates' gross output	88.3	86.9
Domestic content of U.S.-owned firms' gross output	93.3	92.9
Affiliates' value-added shares of gross output	30.6	29.7
U.S.-owned firms' value-added share of gross output	38.2	37.3
Affiliates' import share of intermediate inputs	16.8	18.7
U.S.-owned firms' import share of intermediate inputs	10.8	17.3

Source: William J. Zeile, "The Domestic Orientation of Production and Sales by U.S. Manufacturing Affiliates of Foreign Companies," *Survey of Current Business* (April 1998): 34–36, tables 2–4.

foreign-owned firms and U.S.-owned firms. Thus, foreign-owned firms are more heavily concentrated in capital-intensive industries, in higher wage industries, and in higher productivity industries than are U.S. firms. The observed differences in capital intensities, productivity, and wages reflect these different concentrations rather than differences in ownership.[15]

THE LARGER ROLE OF
FOREIGN DIRECT INVESTMENTS

At the center of the debate concerning the desirability of foreign direct investments, both inward and outward, is their impact on employment. Those opposed to outward investments emphasize the negative effects these investments allegedly have on the domestic demand for labor. Those who court foreign investors and offer incentives of various sorts to induce them to establish affiliates in their political bailiwicks speak glowingly of the positive effects for employment. A close examination of the evidence suggests, however, that these effects have been grossly exaggerated. That "sucking sound" Ross Perot predicted would be heard as U.S. firms headed for Mexico following NAFTA did not materialize, and the number of jobs "created" as a result of the activity of foreign investors in the United States is considerably less than the increase in affiliate employment. Indeed, when all is said and done, the major effects of foreign direct investments—both inward and outward—are similar to those resulting from trade. Like trade, foreign direct investments expand the options available to consumers and reduce the costs of production by exposing firms to more intense competition and by extending the scope of specialization to sectors that cannot, by the nature of the case, rely on the export option.

Even more important than these benefits, however, is the role that foreign direct investments play as conduits for the transmission of technology and managerial and organizational know-how. A fault line in the world economy—potentially a great threat to stability—is the divide in per capita incomes between more affluent and less developed countries. Past attempts to reduce this gap by redistributive schemes have proved to be futile for two basic reasons: First, the affluent countries show little disposition to participate in any significant way; second, the redistribution that did in fact occur more often than not failed to produce any permanent change. Yet when reliance was placed on mechanisms that encouraged or permitted international transmission of technology and managerial and organizational know-how, the results were electrifying.

The rapid recovery of Western European countries after World War II was due in no small part to the transmission of advanced technology developed in the United States during the war, coming largely but not exclusively as a result of U.S. foreign direct investments. One study concluded that between the end of the war and the early 1970s two-thirds of the increase in Europe's output can be attributed to an increase in total factor productivity induced in large part by acquired technology.[16]

The East Asian experience is another example of the significant role foreign direct investment can play in narrowing the income gap. Between 1973 and 1990, the gross domestic product of the East Asian countries increased at an annual rate of 5.6 percent, whereas that of the OECD countries increased at an annual rate of 2.3 percent.[17] The disparate growth rates between these two groups resulted in a significant reduction in the gap between their per capita levels of income. As was the case with regard to Europe and Japan during the early postwar periods, a major factor contributing to East Asia's high growth rates was the transmission of technology and managerial and organizational skills as a result of direct foreign investments by Europe, Japan, and the United States.

Amazingly enough, even this outcome has been assailed by critics of globalization, who perceive the narrowing of the income gap as somehow coming at the expense of the more advanced industrial countries. There is absolutely no basis for this view. A narrowing of the income gap cannot have an adverse impact on more developed countries unless it is associated with a deterioration in the terms of trade, and there is little reason to believe these two developments are related.

PART THREE

A New Beginning?

8

U.S. Trade Policies: From Multilateralism to Bilateralism to Aggressive Unilateralism

Reflecting official government pronouncements, congressional hyperbole, and media accounts, all too many people in the United States are convinced that during the past twenty-five years the United States—a country firmly committed to the principle of a free-trade, open and transparent, and multilateral economic international system—has had to contend with less enlightened trading partners who, though happy to reap the benefits and enjoy the opportunities afforded them by easy access to the world's most affluent market, refuse to open their own markets to U.S. exporters. This image of a vulnerable David in combat with a formidable Goliath has been firmly planted in the American psyche by recurrent references to Japan's undeclared economic war with the United States; by the anguish induced by an increase in manufactured imports from low-wage, less developed countries; by large and recurrent trade deficits; by a seemingly endless series of photographs of U.S. presidents cast in the role of traveling salesmen beseeching foreign statesmen to open their markets to U.S. goods; and by increasingly shrill threats to take retaliatory action against the most blatant offenders in order to level the playing field.

The reality, however, is quite different from the myth. The United States was indeed the foremost advocate of a liberal trade regime during the early post–World War II period and was the principal architect of the GATT system. This policy was broadly supported by industry and organized labor in the United States because of its promise for increasing exports at a time when the European and Asian industries were, owing to the devastation caused by the war, unable to compete either at home or in third-country markets.

With the recovery of Europe and Asia, partially as a result of U.S. aid, disillusionment with U.S. trade policy as well as with the rules of the game embodied in the GATT system set in. Finding that they were no longer able to sell products in the world market at will and feeling the effects of foreign competition at home and abroad, U.S. industry resorted, as it had so many times in the past, to demanding protection of the domestic markets from foreign competition and the adoption of more aggressive policies to achieve greater access to foreign markets. In this campaign they were joined by organized labor, which was particularly distressed by the increase in labor-intensive imports from newly developing economies. These demands were soon reflected in U.S. trade policies. Without abandoning its traditional rhetorical commitment to a rule-based, liberal trading system, the United States began a drift toward protectionism, which in turn has posed a serious challenge to the integrity of the system, indeed, to its very survival.

This chapter focuses on the extent to which U.S. trade policy during the past twenty-five years has undermined the system the United States was largely responsible for creating and how in doing so it has jeopardized the globalization process, which has contributed importantly to the economic welfare of the United States and the rest of the world. It should not be inferred from this focus, however, that the United States alone was responsible for what has been called, by professor Anne Krueger, a "tragedy in the making."[1] Indeed, as we indicate below, similar stories can be told for almost every significant trading country as well. What happened in the United States, however, is particularly important, not only because that country was the bulwark of the postwar trading system but also because of the widely held belief that without the support of a leading country—a hegemony—a liberal trading regime is doomed to failure.

THE MOVE TO ADMINISTRATIVE PROTECTION

In recognizing the need for an "escape hatch" if countries were to agree to reduce tariffs and open markets more widely to imports, GATT provided two avenues of relief. First, it authorized countries to withdraw, temporarily, concessions granted to trading partners in the event the concessions resulted in an unexpected rush of imports that threatened to inflict serious injury to their import-substitute industries. Second, it authorized countries to levy antidumping duties and countervailing duties on imports that were sold at less than fair-market price as a result of their being "dumped" or because their producers were granted subsidies. Even before GATT was established, U.S. trade legislation provided for both types of relief.

Until the early 1970s, U.S. industries seeking relief from the pressures of foreign competition placed almost exclusive reliance on the safeguard clause in the U.S. Trade Act (section 201). This, however, proved to be a slender reed. Not only were the criteria for relief difficult to satisfy, as the petitioning industry had to demonstrate that as a result of a tariff concession imports increased unexpectedly and that this increase in imports caused or threatened to cause serious injury; in addition, the powers vested in the International Trade Commission (ITC), which was designated to hear the complaints, were severely restricted.

Indeed, the ITC was basically an adviser to the president, who remained free to accept or reject its recommendations. Unlike members of Congress, who are prone to press for additional protection whenever local interests are alleged to have been threatened, the president is less inclined to be swayed by protectionist demands, particularly when they conflict with the administration's broader foreign policy objectives. This reality reduced considerably the efficacy of the escape clause as a protectionist instrument. Between 1975 and 1980, only forty-four escape-clause petitions were filed with the ITC. Of these, seventeen were denied relief; only eight of the remaining twenty-seven, which the ITC transmitted to the executive with a positive recommendation, eventuated in higher tariffs or in the imposition of nontariff barriers.[2]

In addition to the "uncertainty of the final determination in view of the discretionary power of the president," a GATT review of U.S. trade policies attributed the decline in the use of section 201 to high legal costs incurred by petitioners seeking relief.[3] More important, perhaps, was the discovery by U.S. industry of much more potent instruments of protection: antidumping tariffs and countervailing duties, which could be levied to offset alleged attempts by foreigners to sell goods in the U.S. market at below-cost prices.

The U.S. antidumping legislation consists of two acts, one passed in 1916, the other in 1921. The 1916 act was essentially an antitrust act rather than one that targeted imports sold at prices below fair-market value. The basic objective was to restrain foreign enterprises from engaging in predatory behavior with the *intent* of monopolizing commerce and injuring U.S. industry. This behavior was characterized as criminal and sub-jected offenders to criminal as well as civil suits. To prove guilt, however, predation was required.

The antitrust orientation of the 1916 act prompted Congress to pass an-other antidumping act in 1921. It specifically targeted the sale of goods at less than fair-market value and authorized the levying of an antidumping duty equal to the difference between fair-market value and the prices charged. The U.S. Treasury was designated as the agency responsible for the administration of this act.

Until the 1970s the 1921 act was no more effective in providing protec-tion than the safeguard clause, for essentially the same reason: the deter-mination of the executive branch to resist pressures for increased protec-tion. Indeed, as World Bank economist J. Michael Finger insightfully notes,

> the function of the United States antidumping and escape clause procedure
> was much more to preserve the openness of the United States markets than
> to restrict foreign access. Particular pressure for protection . . . could be di-
> rected into antidumping or escape clause investigations. As long as the
> United States government could dismiss nine out of ten petitions as unwor-
> thy, the pressure did not block United States participation in the almost con-
> tinuous rounds of GATT tariff negotiation.[4]

The 1974 and 1979 Trade and Tariff Acts, however, effectively trans-formed this relatively benign measure into the weapon of choice for protec-tionists. In 1974, as an expression of its frustration with the executive branch's reluctance to levy additional duties recommended by the ITC, Congress extended the scope of the 1921 antidumping act by redefining *dumping* to include *all* sales at prices below whole costs. Although prior to 1974 the U.S. Treasury had the authority to impose antidumping duties if sales were made below cost, it typically refrained from doing so when price reductions were deemed necessary to remain competitive in depressed markets.[5] The 1974 law thus effectively reduced the executive branch's dis-cretionary power. In addition, the law stipulated a fixed time schedule for the investigation of unfair trade petitions and provided for judicial review when the executive branch rejected the ITC's recommendations.

In 1979, the process of providing teeth to the antidumping and counter-vailing duty provisions was carried one step further. Jurisdiction for the ad-ministration of these provisions was transferred from the U.S. Treasury to the Department of Commerce. This department, ever sensitive to the needs of the business community, was assigned the dual responsibility of con-ducting investigations of dumping charges and of estimating the margin of dumping, which was defined to exist whenever the differential between the fair market value and the actual price was greater than 0.5 percent.

At the same time, the ITC was charged with the responsibility for determining, within forty-five calendar days from the filing of the petition, whether the dumped imports caused material damage to a U.S. industry. In the event both the Department of Commerce and the ITC reported in the affirmative, the levying of an antidumping duty was mandatory.

Before examining the effects of these changes on the use of the antidumping duty, we briefly review the evolution of the use of countervailing duties to offset foreign subsidies. Foreign subsidies on exports have long been a concern to Americans. One of the first protectionists, Alexander Hamilton, singled them out as being "one of the greatest obstacles of all to the successful prosecution of the new branch of industry." Noting that "foreign countries grant subsidies to improve their competitive position," he argued that for fledgling nations like the United States the "interference and aid of their own governments are indispensable." It was not until the Tariff Act of 1897, however, that authorization was granted for the levying of countervailing duties to offset the effects of foreign subsidies. It should be noted, moreover, that this authorization was not constrained by injury considerations; the existence of subsidies per se, whether or not injurious to U.S. industries, sufficed to justify the imposition of countervailing duties.

This act was thus already in effect when GATT authorized the levying of countervailing duties to offset subsidies that caused or threatened to cause material damage. Since the GATT charter contained a grandfather clause, the United States was free, despite the GATT restriction regarding damage, to levy countervailing duties even if no injury was sustained. This had little practical effect, however, before 1974, inasmuch as the U.S. Treasury, which administered the countervailing duties program as well as the antidumping program, was not disposed to offer relief. The Trade and Tariff Act of 1974 ensured that this state of affairs would not continue. It imposed the same discipline regarding cases involving charges of unfair subsidies as it did on those charging dumping. This included establishing a specific time schedule for the review of complaints, providing for judicial review of administrative decisions denying the petitioners relief, and mandatory levying of countervailing duties under certain circumstances. The 1974 law also authorized the levying of countervailing duties on nondutiable goods, which previously had been exempt. For this category of goods, however, Congress stipulated an injury requirement, inasmuch as these goods were not covered by the grandfather clause.

In the Trade and Tariff Act of 1979, Congress basically enacted into U.S. law GATT's "Tokyo Code on Subsidies," including a provision that countervailing duties could be imposed only if it could be demonstrated that the subsidies that enabled the producers to sell their goods at prices below fair market value inflicted a material injury on U.S. firms. This provision was to apply, however, only if the subsidizing countries signed on to the Tokyo Code. Subsidized goods originating in countries that did not sign on to the Tokyo Code could still be countervailed even if no damage was sustained by the import-competing industries.

The Role of Creative Accounting in Administrative Protection

The changes effected by the 1974 and 1979 trade acts as well as the magic of creative accounting transformed what were basically benign laws into potent protectionist instruments. Between 1981 and 1990, 376 antidumping investigations were initiated[6] (see Table 8.1). In 72 percent of the investigations that reached formal determination, the Department of Commerce ruled that dumping had in fact occurred.[7] Creative accounting played an important role in this outcome. By law, *dumping* is defined to exist when the export price is lower than either the price in the home market, or the price in a third country market, or a constructed "fair value" based on the cost of producing the good. It would seem that once the two prices to be compared in order to determine whether dumping has occurred are specified the law is precise enough to prevent the interpretive pitfalls of creative accounting. This, however, is not the case.

To illustrate the powerful role that creative accounting has played in the application of U.S. antidumping laws, consider the following. Assume that the relevant prices are the "home price"—that is, the price in the *exporting* country's market—and the export price, or the price that the importer in the United States paid for the good. Since over a period of time, goods are typically sold in the home market at different prices, to determine *the* home price, it is necessary to rely on an average of these prices. Thus, if within a period of time 100,000 units are sold in the home market at $1 per unit, another 100,000 units at $1.50 per unit, and an additional 100,000 at $2 per unit, the average price in the home market would be $1.50 per unit. Now, assume that during the same period the country exported 300,000 units to three separate U.S. importers. The first paid $1 per unit for 100,000 units, the second $1.50 per unit for 100,000 units, and the third $2 per unit for 100,000 units. Since the average price for these

TABLE 8.1 Escape Clause, Antidumping, Countervailing Duty, and Section 301
Cases by Year and Findings

Section 201 (Escape Clause) Cases		
Year	*Number of Cases*	*Outstanding Affirmative Actions*
1975 to 1980	44	n.a.
1981 to 1985	15	n.a.
1986 to 1990	3	n.a.

Antidumping Actions		
Year	*Number of Cases*	*Outstanding Affirmative Actions*
1981	15	85
1982	51	n.a.
1983	19	52
1984	46	104
1985	61	112
1986	63	122
1987	41	151
1988	31	167
1989	25	198
1990	24	196

Countervailing Duty Cases		
Year	*Number of Cases*	*Outstanding Countervailing Duties*
1981	7	48
1982	75	n.a.
1983	35	53
1984	22	56
1985	60	86
1986	43	76
1987	11	89
1988	13	88
1989	8	91
1990	6	86

Section 301 Cases		
Year	*Number of Cases*	
1980	2	
1981	—	
1982	1	
1983	1	
1984	1	
1985	9	
1986	9	
1987	3	
1988	15	
1989	4	
1990	3	

Source: Patrick Low, *Trading Free: The GATT and United States Trade Policy* (New York: Twentieth Century Fund, 1993), tables 4.4–4.7.

imports is $1.50 per unit, exactly equal to the average price charged in the home market, it would be reasonable to conclude that no dumping had occurred. This, however, is not the way the Department of Commerce saw things. Since any export price below the average home price of $1.50 can be used as evidence of dumping, the Department of Commerce would conclude, based on these data, that the 100,000 units sold at a price of $1 per unit were, in fact, dumped.

But this is just the beginning. The 1974 Trade and Tariff Act opened up additional windows of opportunity by authorizing the Department of Commerce to estimate the cost of producing a good in order to determine "fair value" in the exporting country. The requirement, when using this constructed cost method, was to set the home country's "fair value" at a level high enough to cover the average total cost of production and to regard sales at prices below this level as evidence of dumping. This requirement, however, overlooks the fact that a rational, nonpredatory, profit-maximizing firm would, during the course of a business cycle, charge prices below its average total cost during slack periods and above average total cost during brisk periods. In the Department of Commerce interpretation—insisting on full cost pricing at all times—all goods sold to importers during the slack period at prices below the average total cost of production could be considered evidence of dumping.

Moreover, the very use of the constructed cost method invites the employment of creative accounting when authorities are predisposed to find evidence of dumping. In the United States, constructed "fair values" for the home country—that is, the exporting country—are developed by the Department of Commerce, which frequently relies on the "best available information"—normally not very good and sometimes supplied by domestic competitors—to determine the firm's average variable cost of production. To this estimate are added an amount equal to 10 percent to cover administration, sales, and other costs and an additional amount equal to 8 percent for the profit margin. Quite aside from the fact that the Department of Commerce has enormous leeway in estimating a foreign firm's average variable costs, this method penalizes all firms with low overhead costs and low price margins.[8] As one student of antidumping noted, "A foreign exporter that merely meets the prevailing U.S. price and in the process earns less than 18 percent above his average variable cost, is dumping under the administration of the United States antidumping laws."[9] This is not, moreover, a marginal concern. Although it is generally agreed that the constructed cost method should be used only as a last resort, it has in fact played a major role in recent years. Tracy Murray estimated that this method of computing the home country's "fair value" was used in approximately one-third of the investigations conducted by the Department of Commerce between 1979 and 1986,[10] whereas other investigators claim that it was used in as many as two-thirds of the investigations.[11]

The biased way in which the U.S. government applied antidumping legislation is succinctly summarized by N. David Palmeter in a widely quoted paragraph:

> The standards of the law, the procedures it uses, and the implementation of these standards and procedures by the Department of Commerce increasingly ensure that . . . an exporter determined to have been selling in the United States below fair value has probably been doing no such thing in any meaningful sense of the word "fair." On the contrary, rather than being a price discriminator, a dumper is more likely the victim of an antidumping process that has become a legal and an administrative non-tariff barrier.[12]

This state of affairs led another student to conclude that "a determined antidumping authority could find virtually any . . . injury to have been caused by dumping. . . . If dumping and injury can be shown whenever it suits a government to do so, that government can also increase protection for a domestic industry whenever it suits it to do so."[13] It is no exaggeration to claim that the failure to rein in the widespread use of antidumping and countervailing duties by a country considered to be the foremost advocate of trade liberalization made a mockery of the GATT system and ultimately laid the groundwork for its reform.

The antidumping tariffs and countervailing duties imposed were exceptionally high. One estimate is that by 1992 these duties increased the average of U.S. tariffs in the manufacturing sector from 6 percent to 23 percent.[14] Astonishing as that is, it still does not fully measure the full impact of administrative protection. The process itself imposed significant if unquantifiable costs. As professor Anne Krueger notes, the requirement that foreign firms return, within sixty days, a Department of Commerce questionnaire requesting information on cost and prices at home and abroad; the authority given to the Department of Commerce to "construct costs" in the event that the information supplied by foreign firms is deemed to be unsatisfactory; the requirement that the Department of Commerce provide provisional relief to complainants, even before sufficient evidence has been produced to suggest that unfair trading has occurred; and the requirement that all suspect imports during the investigation period be subject to whatever retaliatory duties are subsequently imposed have all contributed to a high degree of uncertainty and to the potential of a significant increase in costs to both the importers and the exporters.[15]

More significant perhaps is the extent to which the threat of invoking antidumping and countervailing duties motivated many U.S. trading partners to attempt to resolve whatever problems they had in alternative ways, particularly by a "voluntary" restraint on exports. By 1989 the United States negotiated sixty-four export restraint agreements with its trading partners.[16] Dr. Finger notes that many of these negotiations were preceded by U.S. threats to levy antidumping and/or countervailing duties.[17] According to Finger and Murray,

> the unfair trade laws provide the standard against which imports are evalu-
> ated in the 1980s and the rationale by which most import restrictions are jus-
> tified. But antidumping or countervailing duty actions are not always the
> way import restrictions are implemented. Half of the cases undertaken in the
> 1980s have led to negotiated export restraints rather than to antidumping or
> countervailing duties.[18]

The steel industry is a case in point. Threatened by an increase in steel imports from newly built and highly productive steel plants in Europe and Japan, the beleaguered U.S. steel industry filed numerous petitions with the ITC requesting relief. To stay the increase in imports, the United States in 1969 negotiated a voluntary export restraint arrangement with Japan and with the European Community covering the period 1969–1977. These arrangements were then extended for an additional three-year period.

When this agreement lapsed, the steel industry deluged the ITC with 201 antidumping petitions and 149 countervailing duty petitions supported by 3 million pages of documentation as part of a strategy to force foreign governments to negotiate voluntary export restraint agreements. The strategy worked: In 1982 the EC and Japan each agreed to restrict exports to a level not to exceed 5.4 percent of the U.S. market. This, however, proved to be a pyrrhic victory, as Mexico, South Korea, and Brazil rushed in to fill the gap. In 1984 the industry again filed hundreds of petitions, including an escape clause petition submitted by Bethlehem Steel. After reviewing this petition, the ITC recommended that relief be granted. This recommendation was rejected, however, by Pres. Ronald Reagan on the grounds that it was not in the national interest. Instead he requested that the United States Trade Representative (USTR) initiate negotiations for a comprehensive export restraint program.

These negotiations were completed during the early part of 1984. On October 1, 1984, a comprehensive, five-year voluntary restraint program was put into effect that called for a reduction in the share of steel imports from the twenty signatory countries from 25 percent of the market to 18 percent. Two students note that this agreement was the "price the exporting countries paid to settle a massive number of dumping and CVD cases brought by the steel producers."[19]

The experience of the steel industry was not unique. Because of the reluctance of the Reagan administration to raise tariffs, increased reliance was placed on "grey area" measures to protect industries that felt threatened by an increase in imports. The more prominent of the grey area measures were, in addition to voluntary export restraints, orderly marketing arrangements, export forecasts, and discriminatory import systems. These measures were employed to restrict imports for, among other things, machine tools, automobiles and road transport equipment, electronic products, and textiles and clothing.[20]

For several reasons, these voluntary export restraint arrangements were preferred by the United States and its partners over resort to the safeguard clause or antidumping or countervailing duties. For the United States they offered a major advantage, enabling it to restrict imports without having to compensate trading partners for the impairment and nullification of benefits, as it would under the escape clause. As for U.S. trading partners, accepting voluntary export restraints enabled them to avoid the high cost of defending themselves against the charge of unfair trading; permitted them to maintain some control over the reduction of their exports; and gave them the opportunity to reap excess profits generated by the increase in the price thanks to the reduction in the volume of those exports.[21]

FROM MULTILATERALISM TO BILATERALISM AND AGGRESSIVE UNILATERALISM

Resorting to administrative protection—by the United States or any other country—amounted to a direct challenge to the fundamental principles that underpinned the postwar multilateral trading system. This is not only because it enabled countries to raise tariff barriers with one hand while reducing them with the other; or even because it allowed the use of quantitative restrictions that were explicitly prohibited by the GATT charter; or because it made the system less transparent; or because it enabled countries to end-run accepted GATT discipline. Rather, it violated the concepts of multilateralism and the bedrock principle of nondiscrimination upon which the system was based. In the nature of the case, resorting to administrative protection shifts the focus from multilateral to bilateral negotiations and from the principle of nondiscrimination to overt discrimination. An agreement to restrain exports of Japanese automobiles to the United States, for example, is one that can only be arrived at bilaterally and cannot be anything other than discriminatory. Its target is not automobile imports into the United States in general but rather automobile imports from Japan.

As if that was not bad enough, United States soon moved from a bilateral approach in trade negotiations to something even more sinister, what Jagdish Bhagwati calls "aggressive unilateralism."[22] The seeds for this development are to be found in Title 3, chapter 1 (hence section 301) of the Trade and Tariff Act of 1974, which mandates the USTR to seek to redress the actions by foreign governments that violate, in its opinion, the "rights of the United States under . . . any trade agreement" and to discourage all foreign government activity that is "unjustifiable, unreasonable or discriminatory . . . and burdens or restricts United States commerce." The explicit objective of this provision was to gain access for U.S. exports to foreign markets when this access was inhibited by foreign governments in violation of GATT or other treaty obligations. For the most part, this section was consistent with GATT. Indeed, it specifically mandated that the USTR was to refer disputes to the GATT dispute settlement mechanism in the event that negotiations with representatives of offending countries did not lead to a satisfactory resolution. If section 301, as it appeared in the 1974 act, can be faulted at all, it is because it did not prohibit the USTR or the president from taking retaliatory action before this action was authorized by GATT.[23]

Amendments to section 301 in 1979, 1984, and particularly in 1988 fundamentally changed this relatively benign measure into an aggressive, offensive instrument for trade wars. These amendments extended 301's provisions to areas not subject to GATT discipline and to actions by foreign governments that were not GATT-prohibited. In addition, they established rigid time schedules for the USTR to determine whether foreign governments had engaged in activities that impaired U.S. access to foreign markets and, if so, what retaliatory actions were to be taken. All of this was to occur without consultation with the offending parties and without the authorization or consent of its trading partners or GATT.

The most egregious modification of the original section 301, however, resulted from a provision in the Omnibus Trade and Competitiveness Act of 1988, which put into place what were to become known as "Super 301" and "Special 301." Super 301 mandated the USTR to conduct annual investigations to identify unfair trading practices by foreign countries and to publicly cite the worst offenders. The USTR was then required to enter into negotiations with these offenders with the objective of modifying or eliminating the offending practices. In the event these negotiations failed, the USTR was *mandated* to take retaliatory action. The law also established a rigid time schedule in order to avoid a prolonged process that, in the view of some congressional critics, was a basic defect in the GATT dispute resolution mechanism.

Special 301 dealt exclusively with the protection of intellectual property rights. Section 1303 of the 1988 act mandated the USTR to investigate and publicly identify countries that "deny adequate and effective protection of intellectual property rights or deny fair and equitable market access to United States persons that rely on international property protection."

The principle that underlies section 301 informed a new trade strategy, announced by President Reagan on September 23, 1985.[24] This strategy was designed "to level the playing field" by eliminating the trade barriers of other countries. According to a GATT report on U.S. trade policies, the United States,

> while supporting multilateral trade liberalization, has sought through Section 301 to complement it with bilateral or unilateral actions. When multilateral discipline and rules are seen by the United States as inadequate, or where dispute settlement procedures under the GATT do not work as expeditiously as the United States considers that they should, bilateral and unilateral actions have sometimes been taken when they are considered by the administration to be the only available method of defending United States rights and interests.[25]

Between 1975 and 1990, the USTR initiated eighty-two investigations under Section 301. In the first decade under Section 301, investigations were initiated exclusively by private petitions. Between 1985 and 1990, however, seventeen were self-initiated by the USTR. Section 301 cases involved not only trade in manufactures and agriculture but also trade in services, intellectual property rights, and foreign direct investments, which at the time were not subject to GATT discipline. Although most cases were resolved through negotiations or left to linger, the United States took retaliatory action in six cases between 1985 and 1990. In taking these actions, the United States acted unilaterally; it neither requested nor received GATT authorization.[26]

A dispute between the United States and Japan concerning computer chips provides a dramatic illustration of the effectiveness of Section 301 in pressuring U.S. trading partners to acquiesce to U.S. demands.[27] In 1960 Japan's Ministry of International Trade and Industry (MITI) adopted a policy designed to foster growth of the computer chip industry in Japan. This policy entailed, among other things, subsidizing research, extending low-interest loans to nascent chip firms, restraining imports, and banning foreign direct investments. Following protests by the United States—that its share of Japanese computer markets was less than its share in other major markets, evidence that it was being denied access—the Japanese began during the 1970s to dismantle the elaborate support system that they had constructed. When this did not lead to an expected increase in the U.S. market share, U.S. chip firms argued that Japan had done little more than transform an overt protectionist system into a covert one. After the United States initiated a 301 action, the two governments agreed in 1982 to form the High Technology Working Group. This agreement was followed by a MITI-led effort to increase the sale of U.S. chips in the Japanese market, with the result that the U.S. share rose from 10 percent to 14 percent in 1983. A decline in the aggregate demand for chips in the Japanese market during 1984–1985, however, resulted in a 4 point decline in the U.S. market share and a decline in chip prices, which in turn led to U.S. accusations that Japan was not only protecting its domestic markets but was also engaged in dumping activities. Accordingly, in late 1985, the U.S. semiconductor industry brought a number of antidumping charges against Japanese firms and again invoked Section 301, claiming the Japanese government was denying U.S. firms access to its chip market.

The first antidumping suit, which charged that Japanese firms were dumping 64K DRAM chips, resulted in a 1986 Department of Commerce finding that Japan was in fact guilty of unfair trading practices. The United States retaliated by levying an antidumping duty on these chips equal to the dumping margin. By this time, however, the 64K DRAM chip was succeeded by the next generation of chips, the 265K DRAM chip, so that operationally the retaliatory tariff was meaningless inasmuch as few, if any, 64K DRAM chips were imported.

The "guilty" verdict, however, sufficed to alert the Japanese government that the Department of Commerce's attitude was potentially troublesome for two other chips that had been brought to market: the 265K DRAM chip and a chip known as EPROMS, both already subject to pending antidumping suits. To avoid retaliatory penalties on these chips, the Japanese agreed to enter negotiations with the United States. These negotiations concluded with an exchange of letters in September 1986 announcing "An Arrangement Between the Government of Japan and the Government of the United States of America Concerning Trade in Semiconductor Products."

This arrangement addressed three problems raised by U.S. firms: market access, Japanese dumping in the U.S. market, and Japanese dumping in third markets. There is some ambiguity as to terms regarding access. The official document notes only that the United States anticipates substantially improved opportunities reflecting the "competitiveness of the United States industry." Yet a Department of Commerce publication, *Inside U.S. Trade*, published a letter widely regarded as a secret annex to the arrangement, stating that Japan agreed to increase its imports of U.S. chips until they amounted to 20 percent of the total Japanese market.[28]

The antidumping provision of the arrangement was more explicit. In arriving at the dumping margin, the Department of Commerce used the constructed cost method. In an unusually cooperative act, MITI agreed not only to obtain from each Japanese semiconductor firm cost and price data but also to take measures to ensure that Japanese companies did not export any chips at prices less than the companies' specific fair values.

With the signing of this arrangement, the United States permanently suspended the 301 investigation of the semiconductor industry as well as a complaint of unfair practices, thereby temporarily suspending the Department of Commerce's dumping investigation. However, when Japan failed to comply with the access agreement and with the fair market value practice in third countries, the United States in 1987 imposed retaliatory tariffs against Japanese exports valued at $300 million. These tariffs were reduced to apply to Japanese exports valued at only $165 million when the EC complained that U.S. efforts to impose a price floor on Japanese exports to the European market were illegal under GATT.

Four features of this agreement and the events leading up to it are particularly noteworthy and indicate the degree to which GATT rules were violated. The first is an explicit acceptance of the notion that the fact that the U.S. share of a particular market falls short of its shares in other markets is prima facie evidence that U.S. firms are being denied access to that market. The second is the introduction of quantitative criteria to determine whether the parties are in compliance with an agreement. Third, the agreement strongly suggests that the United States, in an attempt to increase market share, was perhaps inadvertently reducing the shares of other countries. (There is no provision in the agreement that the increase in the U.S. share was to be associated with either an increase in total imports or was to be exclusively at the expense of foreign firms. This casts some doubt on the official U.S. position expressed in the *President's Economic Report 1995*[29] that the bilateral negotiations were trade-expanding.) Finally, the U.S. attempt to set a floor for the price of Japanese chips in third markets was clearly a violation of GATT rules, a conclusion concurred in by the GATT panel established to hear the EC's complaint against the United States on this issue.

The semiconductor agreement, which informally set a quantitative target for U.S. exporters amounting to 20 percent of the total Japanese market, was not unique. There is strong evidence that quantitative targets were established in Japanese-U.S. agreements covering, among other things, leather and leather shoes, medical technology, superconductors, auto parts, and telecommunications. In the latter agreement, both sides agreed to "an annual evaluation of progress in value and share of procurement of foreign telecommunication products and services covered by the measures and guidelines to achieve over the medium term a significant increase in access and sales of foreign telecommunication products and services."

Super 301 and Special 301 have been severely criticized by virtually every U.S. trading partner, who perceive them as a blatant attempt by the United States to use its immense market power to forcibly impose its will on sovereign states. They resent the fact that the United States has arrogated to itself the authority to define unfair practices[30] and, in effect, to bring to trial and punish alleged offenders without allowing them the opportunity to defend themselves. From their perspective, the United States is seen as attempting to establish, without their consent, a parallel set of rules that in many respects runs counter to GATT. This view was succinctly stated by GATT:

> The trade policies of the United States have been influenced by the perception that the United States' efforts to keep its markets open have not been matched by corresponding efforts on the part of major trading partners. It is the declared intention of the United States to seek multilateral solutions for difficulties with its trading partners. . . . *However, a major concern of all trading partners remains the question of consistency between its efforts to seek improvements in multilateral rules and disciplines . . . and the bilateral or unilateral initiatives outside the GATT framework to promote the United States trading interests.*[31]

Despite the widespread criticism of Section 301, it has its supporters. Proponents argue that in the absence of a mechanism to ensure access something like Section 301 is necessary to promote GATT objectives. One distinguished legal authority, Robert Hudec, has argued that a distinction should be made between actions taken under Section 301 that represent "justified disobedience" and those that do not. Disobedience is justified if the actions are taken "to prevent a more damaging outcome. It is justified only in those situations where continuing to play by the rules threatens to produce a legal impasse or other legal failure that carries a still greater risk of damage to the legal system."[32] More concretely, Hudec argues that an action is justified if it pushes trading partners to cease and desist from activities that are illegal under GATT.[33] Hence, insofar as Section 301 attempts to counter GATT-prohibited activities by improving access to foreign markets, it is beneficial. Even so, actions taken by the United States because it believes trading partners are engaged in "unreasonable" activities—even if these activities are not illegal under GATT—clearly are not to be condoned.

Although there is some validity to this argument, the basic question is whether the proposed solution is compatible with the maintenance of a rule-based, nondiscriminatory trading system. The Council of Economic Advisors believes that it is. In the *President's Economic Report 1995*, the council argues that

> the American approach [in pursuing liberalization and the promotion of exports] has been that of nondiscrimination: negotiated reductions in trade barriers should apply to all trading nations; individual nations should not cut deals that benefit themselves at the expense of others. . . . Even though nations will seek concessions by others in areas of most immediate interest to themselves, nondiscrimination makes trade liberalization a public good—what is produced by one country in negotiations with another is available to all.[34]

Unfortunately, U.S. performance has not always matched the rhetoric. Certainly the 1986 U.S.-Japan semiconductor agreement was widely regarded by third countries as discriminatory, and despite U.S. insistence that the specified "numerical targets" referred to total imports and not to imports from the United States exclusively, the evidence that the United States cut a deal to promote its own chip industry is strong. It is interesting to note that when the chip agreement came up for renewal in 1996 the Japanese insisted that the provision calling for measuring market shares be eliminated and that the agreement be open to other countries as well. These demands are widely regarded to have been motivated by the EU's complaints that the United States used the original agreement to increase the shares of U.S. companies in the Japanese market at the expense of European companies.[35]

Again, this situation was not unique. In various agreements the United States negotiated with Japan under the aegis of the "Framework for a New Economic Partnership," announced in July 1993, "numerical targets" designed to increase the value of U.S. exports to Japan played a fundamental role. The objectives of the umbrella agreement were to explore Japan's sector-specific trade barriers and to attempt to eliminate them as well as to identify the macroeconomic structural factors that impeded access to Japan's markets. At the outset, four priority sectors were identified: government procurement in medical technology, telecommunications, insurance, and automobiles and automobile parts. Other sectors included flat glass, financial services, and intellectual property rights.

Hanging above these negotiations was Damocles' sword: Section 301. The U.S. strategy was articulated clearly by a high-level but (unfortunately) unidentified trade official, who stated that the United States could not be satisfied "until foreign companies gain the same share of the market for various goods and services in Japan as in other industrial nations."[36] Significantly, he added that if Japan did not agree to accept "numerical targets" the United States was prepared to impose them unilaterally. "We have to measure results," he concluded. "We have to be able to assess results at the end of the day."[37]

The importance of this issue to the United States and Japan is suggested by a last-minute meeting between the Japanese foreign minister and several high-level U.S. officials at the time, including U.S. Secretary of State Warren Christopher, Treasure Secretary Lloyd Bentsen, USTR Mickey Kantor, National Security Adviser Anthony Lake, and President Clinton's counselor, David Gergen. At this meeting Foreign Minister Hata indicated that U.S. insistence on numerical targets could jeopardize "Japan's willingness to cooperate with the United States on Russian aid, Korea and other global issues." Despite this appeal—an implicit threat—the United States persisted in its demand—backed by its own threat to resort if necessary to Section 301—that "Japan agree not only to open its markets but also to accept numerical indicators that would show whether Tokyo was really following through."[38]

The potency of these demands and threats is suggested by the quick agreements reached in the medical technology, telecommunications, insurance, and flat glass sectors. When quick agreements could not be reached, the sectors—which included paper, paperboard, and wood products—were put on the USTR's 301 watch list and thus became prime targets for future investigations.

The U.S. strategy, including resorting to unilateral actions, was very much in evidence during the critical negotiations leading up to the U.S.-Japan automobile and automobile parts agreement. In a joint communiqué following the establishment of the New Economic Partnership, the parties agreed that measures would be adopted in the automobile and automobile parts sectors that would "result in a substantial degree of expanded procurement of foreign-made parts by Japanese companies, both within Japan and at overseas transplants" and that "objective guidelines . . . designed to assess programs in these sectors" would be devised.[39]

Actual negotiations began in October 1993, with the U.S. delegation submitting an initial proposal containing three demands: that Japan increase its imports of U.S.-made parts; that Japan's U.S.-based automobile transplants raise their purchases of U.S.-made parts to a level comparable to that of the Big Three (Ford, General Motors, and Chrysler); and that the number of Japanese dealers handling U.S. vehicles be increased sufficiently to accommodate a large expansion in sales of U.S.-made vehicles. The American Automobile Manufacturing Association suggested that a sales target of 100,000 U.S. vehicles per month was an appropriate figure.[40]

The negotiations collapsed when Japan rejected outright the inclusion of any numerical targets, and they were not resumed until May 1994, when the United States agreed to withdraw its demand for numerical targets. Despite this important concession, the negotiations foundered, and the United States apparently decided to go into threat mode. On September 30, 1994, the United States initiated a 301 investigation of the aftermarket auto parts sector, and on May 16, 1995, it announced its intention to levy a 100 percent punitive tariff on thirteen Japanese luxury vehicles with an import value of $6 billion. At the same time, it initiated a case against Japan in the newly created WTO on the grounds that Japan's automobile inspection regulations discriminated against U.S. manufacturers of car parts. Japan, in turn, retaliated by bringing a WTO countersuit against the United States on the grounds that the threatened punitive tariff would result in an impairment and nullification of benefits.

Rather than proceed beyond the point of no return, the two governments finally reached an agreement on June 28, 1995, the day the punitive tariffs were to go into effect. Considering the sound and fury that preceded it, this agreement was extraordinarily mild and represented a decisive defeat for the U.S. attempt to impose a managed trade regime on Japan. The agreement must have been anticlimactic for the U.S. delegation. In essence, Japan agreed to expand the "voluntary" purchasing plan regarding auto parts, to eliminate the alleged discriminatory regulations on auto parts, and to encourage more dealers to handle U.S. vehicles.

In an attempt to put a bright face on the outcome, the USTR announced that the agreement would result in a $7 billion increase in Japan's U.S.-based output; in a $6 billion increase in U.S. parts exports to Japan; and in an increase in the number of dealers handling U.S. vehicles to accommodate annual sales equal to 30,000 units by the year 2000. The Japanese negotiator responded by stating that these were U.S. "expectations" and not Japanese commitments.[41]

For the record, we should note that the United States has denied that the agreements contain specific targets or commitments regarding market shares. According to *The Economic Report of the President 1995*, the criticisms levied against the agreements reached by the United States under the aegis of the partnership framework are

> disingenuous. None of the agreements set market share targets, either for United States firms or for foreign firms generally. A wide range of objective indicators was suggested and ultimately agreed to, with different indicators for different sectors depending on the characteristics of each sector. Furthermore none of the market access concessions are limited to United States firms; Japanese market-opening measures are available to all on a most favored nations basis.[42]

Since the report does not define *objective indicators*, it is difficult to know whether it is a refutation of the commonly held view that numerical targets were established or is simply another way, perhaps more diplomatic, of confirming that view.

In light of these negotiations, it is difficult to join ranks with those who support Section 301. Although it is undeniable that the threat to use 301 has succeeded in prying open previously inaccessible markets, the method of accomplishing this is inimical to a nondiscriminatory, rule-based system. Precisely because the U.S. market is the world's most affluent, access to it is an issue of highest importance for almost every country. If it is able to arbitrarily deny access to its market, the United States creates an intolerable situation that the framers of GATT, advertently or inadvertently, avoided. In a variety of ways GATT's rules provided insulation from the threat of being barred from this or any other market. Such insulation was provided by the decision to conduct tariff negotiations in a multilateral rather than a bilateral setting; by the binding of tariffs that removed the threat of their being increased in order to gain a bargaining edge; and by compensation offered for any "impairment and nullification" of a trade partner's benefits. U.S. threats to impose antidumping or countervailing duties or to initiate 301 investigations—in order to browbeat partners into accepting voluntary export restraint agreements or to establish quantitative quotas—strips away this insulation.

We should note that by adopting a policy of aggressive unilateralism the United States poses a threat not only to the most vulnerable economies but to all trading partners. At the conclusion of negotiations for the new U.S.-Japan comprehensive chip agreement in August 1996, for example, Japan put the United States on notice that it would no longer engage in one-on-one negotiations. Japan's vice minister of international trade and industry is quoted as saying, "The era of bilateralism is over."[43] *The New York Times* noted hopefully that this new Japanese attitude toward bilateral negotiations "will contribute to the death of America's toughest trade weapon, the ability to impose sanctions under Section 301."[44]

CONCLUSION

This chapter examined the evolution of U.S. trade policy from the early post–World War II period to (roughly) the conclusion of the Uruguay Round. The basic thesis is that the U.S. retreat from early, unconditional support of a rule-based multilateral trading regime has put the GATT system—and by extension the entire globalization process—at risk. It must be emphasized again, however, that the United States is not the only culprit. Indeed, in one way or another administrative protection has characterized the trade policies of most major trading countries. Thus, between 1980 and 1990 the European Community—now the European Union—filed 904 antidumping cases. Of these, 76 percent resulted in some restrictive action.[45] Moreover, since the antidumping program in the EU is influenced more by political discretion than by rules, "antidumping measures can become a pinnacle of fortress Europe."[46]

Likewise, in Canada, "antidumping laws were increasingly focused on protecting domestic producers from foreign competitive pressures." In 1984, largely in response to the widespread use of antidumping and countervailing duties by the United States and the EC, Canadians enacted the Special Import Measures Act (SIMA), broadly similar to the U.S. antidumping and countervailing duty acts and designed to "make Canada's legislation more effective in protecting Canadian producers from dumped or subsidized imports."[47] From the 1984 enactment of SIMA to 1989, 138 dumping cases and four subsidy cases were investigated. Of these, 60 percent resulted in restrictive—that is, price-increasing—actions.[48] Although Japan has refrained from resorting to administrative protection, there is little question that its anticompetitive *keiretsu* system and its distribution system have provided Japan a high degree of protection, which, though not in conflict with the letter of GATT-WTO rules, is certainly not in conformance with their spirit.

The spread of unilateral actions by countries other than the United States is further evidenced in proposals by the EU and Japan to initiate their own 301-like procedures, with specific emphasis on GATT-prohibited activities by the United States. The existence of three 301-like programs—with verbal missiles aimed at the three leading participants of the trading system—cannot but transform a cold trade war into a hot one. Taking our lead from the nuclear disarmament movement, it surely is time to call a halt to what is clearly a self-destructive process.

9

THE URUGUAY ROUND AND BEYOND: A NEW BEGINNING?

After six arduous years, the seventh GATT-sponsored round of multilateral trade negotiations—the so-called Tokyo Round—was brought to a close in 1979. Although this round succeeded in further reducing tariffs, it was on the whole a disappointment. Early hopes—that the round would reverse the drift toward protectionism that was undermining the foundations of the GATT system, that it would address and correct the systemic defects that were becoming increasingly troublesome, and that a consensus could be reached to extend GATT discipline to sectors not then covered—were not realized. Even more discouraging was the degree to which the GATT membership became fractious. In an environment in which it was difficult to attain a consensus on anything, GATT introduced a major departure from past practices by encouraging the drafting of separate treaties—subsequently called codes—which would apply only to those countries that agreed to sign on to them.

Nine codes were eventually drafted. Among the more important were those pertaining to technical barriers to trade, government procurement, subsidies and antidumping duties, and customs valuations. The intent was that countries, though they had a choice as to whether or not to accept the obligations of any code, would, once accepted, apply the rules in a nondiscriminatory manner. The United States as well as some other countries, however, did not agree with this interpretation. In three of the codes that the United States accepted—the technical standards code, the subsidies-countervailing duty code, and the government procurement code—the unconditional MFN principle that it had so vigorously defended in the past was violated: The commitments embodied in these three codes were to apply only to those countries that also signed on to them. Thus, GATT "à la carte" replaced the grand idea of major trading countries marching to the beat of a single drummer, and the integrity of the system was breached.

The sense that the postwar trading system was self-destructing was exacerbated by the developments in the United States we describe in Chapter 8. As we note there, the increase in U.S. trade deficits, particularly with Japan, and the perception that U.S. exports were being refused access to foreign markets while the American market remained open to foreign competition led to increasingly strident demands for the adoption of protectionist policies. During the early 1980s no fewer than three hundred protectionist bills were considered by the U.S. Congress. To forestall these demands and to help shore up the rapidly disintegrating trading system, newly elected Pres. Ronald Reagan urged convening a new GATT-sponsored round to pick up where the Tokyo Round left off, with particular emphasis on unresolved issues of interest to the United States: the elimination of agricultural export subsidies, which were inhibiting U.S. exports; the extension of GATT discipline to trade in services, particularly in the finance area, where the United States had a strong comparative advantage; the protection of intellectual property rights; and the strengthening of GATT's dispute-settlement mechanism.

GATT-weary after the difficult Tokyo Round, few countries were eager to enter into further negotiations. The U.S. government persisted, however, and in September 1986 it achieved success with the launching of a new round of negotiations in Punta del Este, Uruguay. The road to Uruguay, however, was not smooth. The developing countries, led by India and Brazil, raised strenuous opposition to the U.S. proposal to extend GATT's discipline to trade in services, particularly in the financial field, and to any GATT measure against "trade distorting practices arising from inadequate protection of intellectual property."[1] In addition, the United States and the European Community remained at loggerheads concerning a U.S. proposal to eliminate, or at any rate to moderate, export subsidies for European agricultural products. It required five years, many meetings, and U.S. threats to go the regional route before the participating parties agreed to reconvene for yet another round.[2]

If the lag between the initial proposal for a new round of negotiations and its initiation was long, the time spent in negotiations was even longer. The seven years that elapsed between the beginning and conclusion of the negotiations attest to the broad range of issues brought to the table as well as to the difficulties in achieving agreement on a number of them. And though in the end many of these issues remained unresolved, varying degrees of progress were made on a number of fronts. These included a further reduction in tariff and nontariff trade barriers; the freeing of the agriculture and textile sectors from the web of nontariff barriers, which was an affront to the fundamental principles of GATT; a revision of the safeguard measures; the tentative extension of GATT-like discipline to trade in services; the adoption of measures for the protection of intellectual property rights; the acceptance of new rules regarding subsidies and government procurement; the strengthening of the dispute-settlement mechanism; and, last but not least, the replacement of GATT by a new international organization, the World Trade Organization. In one critical area, however, the negotiators failed to achieve more than minimal progress, namely, the curbing of the use of antidumping duties as a way to protect almost any industry determined to avoid competition from abroad.

THE REDUCTION OF TRADE BARRIERS

Although the reduction of trade barriers was not assigned as high a priority in the Uruguay Round as in previous GATT-sponsored rounds, significant progress was made in this area. Not only were tariff rates and other nontariff barriers reduced; the number of participants, particularly from developing countries, increased significantly, as did the number of bound commitments. Tariff rates on manufactures were reduced by an average of 39 percent in developed countries and by an average of 20 percent in developing countries. The value of duty-free imports into developed countries increased from 20 percent of total imports to 44 percent as tariffs were eliminated on a number of important industrial sectors, including pharmaceuticals, steel, medical equipment, and paper. In addition, the proportion of tariffs that were bound by the developing countries increased from 15 percent in the pre-Uruguay Round to 58 percent afterward. This increase in bound tariffs reflects a substantial change in developing countries' attitudes toward GATT in recent years. By the end of the Uruguay Round, the average tariff rate on manufactures was reduced to approximately 6 percent.

In addition to reducing tariff rates, the Uruguay Round struck a blow against nontariff trade barriers by banning the use of quotas to restrict imports, except for balance of payments purposes, and by mandating phase-out over a four-year period of all grey area measures. These measures—which include inter alia voluntary export restrictions, orderly marketing arrangements, so-called export forecasting, and discriminatory import systems—were employed by the United States to restrict the import of steel and steel products, machine tools, electrical products, and textile and clothing imports that were not already constrained by multi-fibre agreements. The one exception to this mandate was a provision in the final text that authorized each country to retain one grey area measure until December 31, 1999.

It is questionable, however, how effective this ban on grey area measures will be. Professor Alan V. Deardorff has argued that since a voluntary export restraint program, for example, requires the consent of both parties it is scarcely likely that either party would acknowledge its existence, let alone lodge a complaint that would be necessary to enforce the ban. In his view, the ban would tend to drive the voluntary export restraint agreements—and possibly other grey area measures as well—underground, thereby reducing the transparency of the system.[3]

The final draft of the Uruguay Round also included agreements regarding sanitary and phytosanitary measures, technical barriers to trade, custom regulations, and rules of origin. By and large, these agreements were designed to prevent a country from establishing disguised trade barriers. The object of the phytosanitary agreement, for example, was to ensure that these standards were not to be used for protective purposes (though each country had the right to set its own standards regarding safety and health). The agreement stipulated that whatever standards were adopted should be scientifically justified and should conform with international standards already in place. In bringing their laws into conformance with the Uruguay agreement, participating countries basically had three options: They could harmonize their regulations by adopting internationally recognized standards; they could place reliance on an "equivalence principle," which states that although the exporting partner's standards differ from those of the importing country they achieve basically equivalent results and, hence, their products are admissible; or they could adopt their own standards without regard to harmonization and equivalence provided they are applied in a nondiscriminatory manner, are scientifically justified, and are based on a realistic assessment of risks. Anticipating that the inherent ambiguities in this agreement would almost certainly lead to disputes, the agreement called for the establishment of a committee on sanitary and phytosanitary measures under the aegis of WTO.

The historical record strongly indicates the need for some kind of discipline in this area if the attempt to liberalize trade in agricultural commodities is not to be reduced to a mockery. The fact that a myriad of uninformed "experts" manage, without a scintilla of scientific evidence, to convince large numbers of people that this or that product is unsafe leaves little doubt that anyone desiring protection will have no difficulty in acquiring allies. A case in point is the refusal of many European countries to accept hormone-fed beef from the United States despite robust scientific evidence that it does not pose a danger to health.[4]

THE UNBINDING OF AGRICULTURE AND TEXTILES

In the agricultural and textile and apparel sectors, however, the Uruguay Round began what would appear to be a prolonged process to remove obstacles to trade and increase the transparency of the trading system. Against all odds, the Uruguay agreement holds out the promise that at some point in the future these sectors will become fully integrated into the GATT system.

The Agriculture Agreement

During the arduous negotiations of the Uruguay Round, no issue was as difficult and contentious as trade in agricultural products. A major reason is that measures responsible for trade distortions in this sector were not enacted for protectionist reasons but rather to increase farmers' incomes. In the United States, these measures took the form of production controls and guaranteed prices, which resulted in deficiency payments to farmers. When market prices fell below guaranteed prices, farmers sold their outputs to the government at the guaranteed prices, and quantitative restrictions were deployed to prevent imports from swelling the surplus.

The EC's agricultural policy relied mainly on the establishment of target prices set at levels higher than those that would prevail in a free market. To prevent an influx of imports, the EC put into place a system of variable duties that automatically adjusted so as to raise the price of potential imports to target-price levels. In addition, export subsidies were granted to facilitate the sale to third-country markets of the agricultural surpluses induced by high target prices. These policies transformed the EC from its historical position as a food importer to a food exporter and inevitably brought the EC into conflict both with the United States and with the so-called Cairnes Group (consisting of fourteen small and medium-sized agricultural exporting countries), whose markets in third countries were threatened. Negotiations during the Uruguay Round regarding agriculture basically centered on reaching an agreement that would satisfy the three major players: the United States, the EC, and the Cairnes Group.

After initial efforts failed to get off the ground, threatening to derail the entire round, the United States in 1986 proposed a ban on all export subsidies on agricultural products, the tariffication of nontariff barriers, and the elimination of price supports for agricultural goods. Although the Cairnes Group supported the U.S. proposal, the proposal was rejected by the EC, which insisted on retaining export subsidies. Five more years of negotiation were required to hammer out an agricultural agreement, which was announced in December 1991 and became, with minor changes, part of the final agreement coming out of Uruguay. This agricultural agreement addressed three major issues: market access, export competition, and domestic supports.

Regarding market access, the agricultural agreement mandated the conversion of existing quantitative restrictions on agriculture to their tariff equivalents—a process dubbed the "tariffication of nontrade barriers"—and the reduction of the resulting tariff rates by 36 percent. We should note in passing, however, that though this provision helped make trade barriers more transparent it did not contribute significantly to liberalization of trade. For a variety of reasons the tariffs that emerged as replacements for quantitative restrictions were so high as to afford almost absolute protection.

In addition to the tariffication of nontariff barriers and the reduction in tariff rates, the agreement called for access commitments for specific products. The most promising of these commitments—because they represented a sharp break with past practice—were those undertaken by Japan and Korea, which opened their markets to rice imports. In exchange for a six-year grace period before tariffication, the Japanese agreed to permit rice imports equal to 4 percent of total domestic consumption at the outset, rising to 8 percent of the total within six years. South Korea committed itself to rice imports equal to 1 percent of domestic consumption at the outset, rising to 4 percent after six years.

The agreement also called for a reduction in export and domestic subsidies. Specifically, advanced industrial countries agreed to reduce budgetary outlays for export subsidies by 36 percent by the year 2000 from levels prevailing during the 1986–1990 period. To ensure this reduction translated into a reduction in the volume of subsidized exports, these countries also agreed to reduce the quantity of subsidized exports by

21 percent. The corresponding reductions for developing countries was 24 percent and 14 percent by the year 2004.

With regard to domestic subsidies, the final draft drew a distinction between support measures that did not distort trade and those that did. The nondistorting measures—the "green box" measures—were exempt from any reduction requirements. Unbelievably, these included two of the largest agricultural subsidy programs: U.S. deficiency payments and the EU's compensation payments. With regard to the trade-distorting measures, advanced industrial countries agreed to reduce outlays on them by an average of 20 percent by the year 2000 from the 1986–1989 level, whereas developing countries committed to a 13 percent reduction from the same level by the year 2004.

Although these reductions were significant, they do not remove subsidies as an important ingredient in agricultural trade. It is estimated that as a result of the Uruguay Round domestic per annum subsidies will decline from $197 billion to $162 billion when the reductions are fully implemented; export subsidies—largely for wheat, beef, coarse grains, dairy products, and sugar—will decline from $22.5 billion to $14.5 billion.

Although there can be no gainsaying the Uruguay Round's achievements in bringing the agricultural sector under GATT discipline and in assuring that countries could no longer pursue agricultural policies without regard to their effects on trade, they fall short in achieving equality with the industrial sector. Banned in the industrial sector, export subsidies remain very much alive in the agricultural sector. And though the tariffication of nontariff barriers has made the existence of trade barriers more transparent, they remain unreasonably high. Likewise—although attempts to distinguish between domestic measures that distort trade and those that do not are certainly commendable—the too-generous definition of what constitutes a green box measure virtually assures that any country intent on pursuing a protectionist agricultural policy will have an adequate arsenal at its disposal.

It would be a mistake, however, to be overly critical here. In light of the inherent difficulties in the agricultural sector and the diverse interests of the major negotiating partners, it would be unrealistic to have expected much more. The agreement cleared away some of the underbrush, and the stage has been set for significant liberalization in the future. Since the Uruguay Round stipulated that a new round of negotiations regarding agricultural trade will be convened in 2000, not too much time has to elapse to determine whether this hope is to be realized.

The Textile and Apparel Sectors Agreement

The Uruguay Round also scored a potentially significant success with regard to trade in textiles and apparel by adopting a schedule to phase out the Multi Fibre Agreement (MFA). This is significant not only because the MFA was in fundamental violation of all the major principles underlying GATT but also because it provided the strongest evidence in support of the widely held view that the GATT system was basically a rich country club with a strong, built-in bias against less-developed countries. A study undertaken by the United Nations Commission for Trade and Development (UNCTAD), for example, concluded that had trade in the textile and clothing sectors not been constrained by the MFA and high tariffs clothing exports from the developing countries would have increased by 135 percent, textile exports by 78 percent over the actual levels.[5] Trela and John Whalley estimated, based on similar assumptions, that imports of clothing and textiles into the United States, Canada, and the EC would have increased by 305 percent, 200 percent, and 190 percent respectively.[6]

The Uruguay agreement calls for full integration of the textile and apparel sectors into the GATT system within a ten-year period. The phase-out of quotas was to occur in four stages: First, 16 percent of quotas was to be eliminated immediately after the implementation of the agreement; this was to be followed by an additional 17 percent after three years, 18 percent after seven years, and the remaining 51 percent at the end of the ten-year period. In addition, industrial countries agreed to reduce their tariff rates in this sector by an average of 20 percent (12 percent for the United States). To ensure that importing countries would not be inundated with a flood of imports during the transition period, safeguard provisions were clearly specified. For instance, imports from multiple sources could be combined to determine whether a domestic industry has been damaged as a result of imports; another provision was designed to avoid the transshipment of goods through countries not covered by MFA quotas.[7]

THE SAFEGUARD AND UNFAIR TRADE CLAUSES REVISITED

Despite the Uruguay Round's significant contribution in lowering trade barriers and in providing greater access, it remains questionable whether the drift toward protectionism—the fundamental problem facing the trading system during the pre-Uruguay period—was adequately ad-

dressed. The focal point of this problem was the system's import contingency provisions, that is, the safeguard clause and the unfair trading
clauses. For a variety of reasons (see Chapters 3 and 8), the safeguard
clause, which was intended to insulate economies from unanticipated
surges in imports, fell into disuse. J. Michael Finger notes that a "GATT
secretarial tabulation of safeguards and safeguard-like actions covering
January 1958 through March 1987 listed only twenty-six cases."[8] In the
United States during the 1980s there were only four safeguard cases per
year, compared to eighty-six unfair trade cases per year.[9] At the same
time, Dr. Finger notes, "complaining about the unfairness of foreigners
has become the most popular way for an industry seeking protection
from imports to make its case to its government."[10] As we have already
noted, threats of levying antidumping duties and the ease in producing
evidence of dumping were the major factors responsible for the voluntary
export restriction agreements and other grey area measures designed to
"manage" trade. Plugging these loopholes was clearly a prerequisite if
the drift toward protectionism was to be stopped. This the Uruguay
Round failed to do. Marginal modifications in the safeguard clause did
little, if anything, to increase its attractiveness to those seeking contingency relief. Indeed, the apposite Uruguay Round requirements—that
countries invoking the safeguard clause provide "objective evidence
[linking] . . . the increase in imports to any serious injury"[11] and that they
commit to progressive liberalization of restrictions after the fourth year
and to complete removal within five years—tend to make the clause even
less attractive. Yet the provision that proscribes countries from suspending equivalent concessions (as compensation for the restraints put on
their exports for the first three years if the safeguard measures were invoked as a result of an absolute and not just a relative increase in imports)
tends to make the clause somewhat more attractive.[12] On balance, however, it is doubtful that this change will have a significant effect, one way
or the other, on the use of the safeguard clause for contingency protection
as long as unfair trading clauses continue to provide protection on demand. There is little evidence, moreover, to suggest that the Uruguay
Round accomplished anything to alter this situation.

The best way to address problems posed by unfair trade clauses is to
limit their use to their original purpose, namely, to curb predatory behavior that threatens to create a monopoly. If that was done, an industry desiring protection would have to demonstrate not only that prices of foreign goods are below fair value but also that the exporter's intention is to
drive out competitors. In the event that it is not possible to limit their use

exclusively to prevent predation, however, a second-best solution would be to change the rules of the game to preclude the use of creative accounting in evaluating whether dumping has occurred; to limit the harassment of foreign firms when an unfair trade charge is levied; and to raise the standards of proof regarding injuries resulting from alleged unfair acts.

Unfortunately, the Uruguay Round's antidumping agreement did not adopt either of these courses of action, although in some respects an attempt was made to curb some of the more egregious abuses.[13] As a result of the Uruguay Round, a country wishing to invoke the antidumping provision is required to conduct open hearings, to give the offending party an opportunity to refute the charges, and to issue a final report explaining how the determination that dumping occurred had been reached. Additional modifications include a restraint on the way in which costs could be constructed; a requirement that the margin of dumping had to be at least 2 percent and not the ridiculously low 0.5 percent of the pre-Uruguay period; and a requirement that the dumped imports had to be equal to at least 3 percent of total imports. When all is said and done, however, the Uruguay agreement did little to stiffen the injury requirement or to discourage creative accounting. Indeed, by specifically authorizing the use of some methodologies employed during the pre-Uruguay period and by cautioning the dispute settlement panels to refrain from rejecting petitions on the grounds panel members did not like the methodology used to prove the existence of dumping, the Uruguay agreement might even have taken a step backward.[14] The failure to curb more effectively the use of the antidumping duty provision leaves the post-Uruguay system vulnerable to protectionist attacks, just as its predecessor had been. Whether the drift toward protectionism will continue in the new world trading system will thus be determined more by national authorities, and their inclinations to provide protection, rather than by any constraints imposed by the new GATT.

In contrast to the dumping issue, the subsidies and countervailing duties agreement gives promise for restricting, to some extent, this set of protectionist weapons.[15] The central features of the agreement increased the transparency of the system, distinguished between different types of subsidies, and established a more effective mechanism to resolve disputes regarding the levying of subsidies and the use of countervailing duties.

Transparency was increased by requiring each country to submit an annual report that lists, among other things, the various subsidies it maintains and the data necessary to evaluate their impact on trade. Subsidies were classified as being either prohibited, actionable, or nonactionable.

Prohibited subsidies include export subsidies and subsidies designed to replace imported inputs with domestic inputs. *Actionable subsidies* are those that inflict injury, whether advertently or not. *Nonactionable subsidies*, which remain completely unconstrained, include those for research, impoverished regions, and environmental projects. Countervailing duties may be applied only against actionable subsidies, and then only if it is demonstrated they have caused injury to domestic industries. Disputes regarding the classification of subsidies and their impacts on other countries, as well the application of the countervailing duty, were to be resolved through the WTO dispute settlement mechanism.

In general this agreement helps resolve many ambiguities in the Tokyo Round's subsidy and countervailing duty codes. Its application should reduce significantly the effectiveness of countervailing duties as an instrument of protection.

THE EXTENSION OF GATT-LIKE DISCIPLINE TO SECTORS NOT PREVIOUSLY COVERED

The emphasis thus far has been on the Uruguay Round provisions that relate to the reduction of trade barriers. Although the agreement's contributions in this area are significant, equally if not more important is the potential for extending GATT-like discipline to sectors not previously covered. Two agreements negotiated during the Uruguay Round—the General Agreement on Trade in Services (GATS) and the General Agreement on Trade Related Investment Measures (TRIMS)—brought to the fore a major problem that (though treated on bilateral and regional levels) has received but scant recognition on the multilateral level: the problem of market access in situations that require establishing a physical presence in a foreign country.

The Birth of the General Agreement on Trade in Services

The U.S. desire to extend GATT-like discipline to the service sector was a major factor motivating the Uruguay Round. Indeed, as we have already noted, the initial negative reaction of India and Brazil to this proposal almost prevented the round from getting under way. Although at the end of the day the United States achieved much less than it had hoped for, the round put trade in services firmly on the agenda. It will surely take many years and, alas, many additional conferences to resolve the thorny issues that liberalization in this sector poses.

Virtually nonexistent under the original GATT, world trade in services has grown to more than $1 trillion per year, 20 percent of total world trade in goods. As we have already noted, the United States has become the world's largest trader in this sector and in 1996 developed a service surplus of $81 billion, 43 percent of its trade deficit in goods that year. It is not surprising, therefore, that the United States insisted that trade in services be given high priority at the Uruguay Round.

What emerged from the negotiations was the General Agreement on Trade and Services, which became an integral component of the newly established WTO. Before examining GATS's provisions, we must explore some of the unique problems in the service sector that made the negotiations so difficult and the outcome somewhat disappointing. Nondiscrimination and national treatment are basic to any attempt to create an orderly multilateral trading system. In the goods sector these objectives are achieved by requiring all participating parties to adhere—with minor exceptions—to the MFN clause and to extend the principle of national treatment to all imports. This virtually guarantees that imports would be treated similarly regardless of the country of origin and that once admitted to the country they would not be subject to more onerous restrictions than those applied to domestically produced goods. This simple formula, which resolved the problem of access as far as goods were concerned, could not be applied to the service sector. The reason is that the mode of delivery in the service sector frequently but not always requires providers to establish a physical presence in markets where they sell. Since border taxes cannot be imposed on such services, the granting of national treatment to service providers would be tantamount to establishing a free trade region for services. Because this was not an acceptable across-the-board solution, negotiations involved seeking out compromises within the bedrock principle of nondiscrimination.

Predictably, compromises resulted in a byzantine arrangement. Each country that subscribed to GATS was required to submit a list of service sectors to be covered. Sectors not included on the list would not be subject to GATS discipline. Yet subscribing countries could exempt some subsectors within listed sectors at the time it joined the agreement.

With regard to the MFN principle, GATS stipulates that each foreign service or service supplier subject to the agreement must be treated no less favorably than other foreign services or service suppliers in this sector. The agreement, however, does not obligate participating countries to extend unconditional MFN privileges; a country may withhold MFN privileges to suppliers from countries that do not reciprocate. These exceptions, however, can be put into effect only at the time that a country becomes a signatory to the agreement. They are limited, moreover, to no more than ten years and are subject to periodic review and negotiations. In commenting on these arrangements, one astute observer notes that "in essence the GATS transforms national treatment from a principle into an object of negotiations. The result is that the GATS at least on this point conforms more closely to a sector-based approach to liberalization than to a principle-based approach."[16] Another commentator notes, "Although national treatment of foreign suppliers and elimination of nondiscriminatory barriers to market access are required by the GATS, these rules apply on a sector by sector, country by country basis."[17]

Despite these limitations, GATS does make a modest contribution toward liberalizing trade in services. Among other things, the agreement prohibits signatories from restricting access to services that are not exempted, placing limitations on the number of suppliers, the value and volume of services they can supply, the total assets of the suppliers, the organization of the enterprise, and the number of employees they can employ. In short, for suppliers covered by this agreement the principles of national treatment and MFN not only ensure nondiscrimination but also provide a free trade regime.

Before the Uruguay Round concluded, it was apparent that a number of countries intended to request exemptions in the telecommunications, financial, and maritime transport sectors. Realizing that excluding these important sectors from GATS would severely impair the value of the agreement and could lead to its unraveling, participants agreed to continue negotiations in these sectors even after GATS went into effect. Members maintained the right to invoke an exception, however, in the event negotiations did not succeed.

Given developing countries' reluctance to open service sectors to foreign competition, and given advanced industrial countries' reluctance to grant access to markets in the absence of sectoral reciprocity, it is impossible to estimate how far GATS will ultimately go toward liberalizing trade in the service sector, although some signs are positive. Some observers note that the situation has been complicated by the fact that under current arrangements the choice facing countries is between free trade in the service sector or no trade at all. They point out that in the goods sector the ability to negotiate a reciprocal reduction in tariffs provides an important incentive to eliminate protective barriers. This consideration leads Professor Deardorff to suggest that "a cue be taken from trade in goods where tariffs have provided the currency for negotiations. Countries should be encouraged to institute something similar to tariffs on trade in services, and then they should use these as both a measure of the departure from national treatment and as the subject for further negotiations."[18] Specifically, Deardorff suggests that all countries should be "permitted . . . to levy a special tax on the operations of foreign producers. . . . And the level of the tax would then become the subject of future negotiations."[19] In addition to providing countries with the chips necessary for successful negotiation, this proposal has, according to Deardorff, the additional advantage of "offering a reasonable chance of bringing all service sectors under the purview of the GATT."[20] It may seem bizarre that countries can be induced to move toward freer trade by imposing additional obstacles, but byzantine structures frequently require byzantine solutions.

General Agreement on Trade Related Investment Measures

The most remarkable aspect of TRIMS is that an agreement was reached at all. Despite the fact that foreign-affiliate sales in host-country markets have become the primary mode of penetrating such markets, developing countries—as well as a few OECD countries—have vigorously opposed eliminating certain practices that would be in conflict with the basic principles underlying GATT if they existed in the goods market. As one student notes,

> There is still a long way to go before there is general acceptance that investment is simply another way of trading. Importance is attached to ownership of companies or assets for both good and bad reasons so that conditions, which if applied to goods pure and simple would be regarded as blatantly protectionist, are attached to investments by even those boasting of the most liberal trade and investment policies.[21]

The liberalization of investment regimes entails addressing two basic problems. The first concerns the terms of access for foreign firms, whereas the second concerns the terms of operation once access is secured. An across-the-board application of the MFN principle and the national treatment principle would ensure equal access to all firms. This, however, would result in a situation comparable to free trade in goods, and for reasons that need not be spelled out here it is unlikely to be acceptable to many countries. One of the major problems in negotiating a treaty on trade-related investment measures is to reach some compromise on this issue. Among the thorny questions that have to be negotiated are the sharing of equity between nationals and foreigners and the designation of the sectors of the economy in which foreigners may and may not invest. It should be noted that even countries with the most liberal investment regimes—the United States, for example—restrict access in certain sectors either on national security grounds or to achieve some social objectives.

After access is secured, the regulations applying to foreign firms sometimes impose serious obstacles. Among the more important are regulations limiting the number of foreigners that affiliates may employ, imposing quotas on inputs that may be derived from abroad, setting targets for exports, and limiting the amount of earnings that can be remitted. Resolving differences on these matters is as difficult as those regarding access.

For these reasons it is not surprising that TRIMS was somewhat short on substance. Ultimately, TRIMS's fundamental objective was to establish that certain practices were in patent conflict with GATT's basic principles. To this end, TRIMS stipulated that national treatment and the elimination of quantitative restrictions were to be considered core principles. For instance, TRIMS listed a number of practices considered to be in violation of these principles. Among them were local-content requirements, limits on the proportion of inputs that foreign affiliates can import, and requirements that a balance between exports and imports be achieved. It should be noted that such restrictions have been a bone of contention between more advanced industrial countries, which maintain the restrictions violate GATT rules, and developing economies, which insist on their sovereign rights to impose them.

Additional TRIMS provisions provide for transitional periods for implementation of the agreement—two years for developed countries, five years for developing countries, and seven years for the least developed countries—call for greater transparency, mandate the use of the WTO dispute settlement mechanism, establish a TRIMS committee, and provide for a review of the agreement after five years. In short, TRIMS did little to develop an investment code comparable to that of GATT for trade in goods. It did, however, succeed in putting trade-related investment measures on the agenda. It should be noted that OECD has begun work on a comprehensive investment code, which was to be released in 1997. Serious disagreements regarding the contents of this code have, however, thrown a monkey wrench into the process.

Agreement on Trade-Related Aspects of Intellectual Property Rights

The importance the United States places on the protection of intellectual property rights is reflected in the Special 301 provision of the Omnibus

Trade and Competitiveness Act of 1988 and in the first USTR report, mandated by that act, which charged that every U.S. trading partner, to one degree or another, violated these rights. During the Uruguay Round the U.S. delegation worked hard and long to bring to fruition an agreement that would protect the rights of owners of intellectual property. The result was the Agreement on Trade Related Aspects of Intellectual Property Rights (TRIPS). Unlike GATT and GATS, the basic objective of this agreement was not to remove obstacles to trade but rather to establish minimum standards designed to protect owners of intellectual property and to provide strong institutional support for them. Until TRIPS, protection of international intellectual property rights was the responsibility of the World Intellectual Property Organization. Unfortunately, many countries—particularly those most prone to violate intellectual property rights—did not belong to this organization and hence were not subject to its discipline. In addition, the International Court of Justice, which was designated to adjudicate disputes in this area, was ineffectual. By transferring responsibility to the newly established WTO, the United States and its allies in this venture hoped to extend international discipline to member countries and to provide a more efficient dispute settlement mechanism than the one it replaced.

The major provisions of this agreement can be quickly summarized. All members are obligated to adhere to general principles of national treatment and MFN one year after the agreement comes into effect. In addition, it stipulates minimal standards for the duration of proprietary rights for trademarks, industrial designs, and layout designs of integrated circuits. Signatories must also agree to adhere to the Paris Convention covering patent rights and to the Berne Convention regarding copyrights, with additional provisions stipulating rental rights, the prohibition of unauthorized recording of live performances, and the recognition (and hence protection) of computer software as literary works. Criminal penalties for commercial piracy are stipulated.

The agreement also stipulates that certain developments are not patentable. These include, among other things, diagnostic tests, surgical methods, and new plants and animals. Participating countries are also authorized to take measures to prevent owners of intellectual property from pursuing actions that unreasonably restrain trade and adversely affect the international transfer of technology[22] and those that have an "adverse effect on competition,"[23] which, unfortunately, is not defined.

Enforcement of TRIPS, as in the case of the other agreements, is the responsibility of each member country. The agreement, however, stipulates that whatever methods are adopted for enforcement be effective, fair, and quick. In the event of disputes, the dispute-settlement mechanism of the WTO must be invoked.

Recognizing difficulties that are likely to ensue, the agreement stipulates a five-year transition period for developing countries and a ten-year period for the least-developed of this group. In addition, TRIPS does not cover patents that have already been granted but have not as yet been cleared for marketing. This was a major concession to developing countries, which feared that applying the agreement to patents already in the pipeline—particularly pharmaceutical patents—would mean that the immediate cost of complying would be too large to undertake. This concession to developing countries, however, has raised some questions as to whether the agreement will in fact come into effect within a foreseeable period of time.

Although the three agreements that attempt to extend GATT discipline to sectors not previously covered—GATS, TRIMS, and TRIPS—leave much to be desired and certainly fall far short of U.S. expectations at the beginning of the Uruguay Round, they should not be dismissed as insignificant. One reason for the growing disaffection with the original GATT, particularly on the part of the United States, was the belief that after the initial surge during the early postwar period it was no longer a reliable agent for promoting a liberal multilateral system. If nothing else, the fact that these partial and highly flawed agreements could be hammered out suggests that with effort and time further progress can be made.

WORLD TRADE ORGANIZATION

Last but by no means least, negotiations during the Uruguay Round forged an agreement establishing the WTO, to which was appended an annex containing a revised GATT and the fifteen agreements that emerged from the negotiations. Even if this organization is regarded as little more than a replacement for GATT, its creation represents an important step forward. Recall that following the failure of the U.S. Senate in 1947 to ratify the treaty establishing the International Trade Organization, GATT was assigned the task of coordinating multilateral trade negotiations, administering rules devised over time by participating parties to govern trade practices, and adjudicating disputes arising from diverse interpretations of those rules. Although there is almost universal consensus that GATT succeeded beyond all expectations in carrying out its mission, the handicaps under which this quasi organization operated—due to the lack of an organizational structure and to inadequate resources—were widely recognized. With the broadening of the trade agenda resulting from the Uruguay Round agreements, it was clear that GATT had to be replaced by an organization with its own budget, secretariat, director-general, and staff.

Professor John Jackson, a leading legal authority on international economic organizations, notes, however, that the WTO should be regarded as more than a replacement for GATT. For though the WTO charter is "minimalist" and is concerned with "institutions and procedural matters rather than with substantive agreements, the establishment of the WTO had a profound substantive impact."[24] Indeed, he doubts that the Uruguay Round agreements could have been implemented in its absence. There are a number of reasons for this. First, he notes that the procedure for amending GATT would have presented insurmountable obstacles to incorporating the changes mandated by the Uruguay Round. This problem was circumvented by the simple expedient of voiding the old GATT and replacing it with a new GATT (1994), which already incorporated the changes resulting from the Uruguay Round. Second, by bringing all the trade agreements under the aegis of the WTO—the new GATT, GATS, TRIMS, and TRIPS—and by requiring all participating parties to access the package in its entirety, the Uruguay Round virtually ended what has been known as a GATT "à la carte." In professor Jackson's words, "No longer will the Tokyo Round approach to side codes resulting in GATT à la carte be the norm."[25] Finally, it would have been extremely difficult to replace GATT's dispute settlement mechanism with a more effective one without the WTO; under those circumstances it is highly questionable whether U.S. approval of the Uruguay Round could have been obtained.

GATT's ineffectual dispute settlement mechanism was frequently cited by the United States as a major reason for resorting to unilateral actions to correct what it perceived as unfair treatment by trading partners. Largely to placate the United States and at the same time to constrain it, an annex was added to the WTO charter, spelling out in some detail procedures for resolving disputes arising from different interpretations of the new GATT as well as GATS, TRIMS, and TRIPS.

These procedures address two major defects of the old GATT mechanism: the inordinate length of time required for the process to run its course; and the inherent ability of the "losing" party to veto the panel's recommendations by simply refusing to accept them. The new procedures establish the right of each party to demand immediate establishment of a dispute panel and to have that panel adhere to a predetermined time schedule covering the entire procedure. Unless one party appeals the panel's ruling, it is considered to be adopted by the WTO, and corrective measures are put into effect. In the event of an appeal the matter is referred to an appeals panel; its ruling is adopted by the WTO unless there is a consensus against such adoption. This virtually ensures that the appellate ruling will in fact be accepted and that the WTO will have the authority to order corrective measures.

This procedure contrasts sharply with that under the original GATT, whereby to become operational a ruling had to be unanimously approved by all participating parties, including the disputants. By granting veto power to the losing party, the original GATT virtually invited powerful participants—the United States, the European Union, and Japan—to resort to extra-GATT legal devices to achieve objectives rather than to work within the GATT framework and face the consequences of seeing a favorable ruling vetoed by the losing party.

This dispute resolution annex was one of three annexes to the WTO charter that had to be accepted in their entirety by all WTO participants. The other two required annexes contained the multilateral trade agreements—the new GATT, GATS, and TRIPS—and the trade policy review mechanism. Twelve side agreements that were appended to GATT 1994 included an agreement on agriculture; an agreement on sanitary and phytosanitary measures; an agreement on textiles and clothing; an agreement on technical barriers to trade; an agreement on trade-related investment measures (TRIMS); an agreement on antidumping; an agreement on custom valuation; an agreement on preshipment inspections; an agreement on rules of origin; an agreement on import licensing; an agreement on subsidies and countervailing duties; and an agreement on safeguards. The fourth annex to the WTO, containing the so-called plurilateral agreements—an agreement on trade in civil aircraft, an agreement on government procurement, an international dairy agreement, and an international meat agreement—was optional.

Predictably, some critics charged that U.S. participation in the WTO would require the United States to surrender economic sovereignty to an international organization. Little evidence exists, however, to support this view. As we have already noted, the WTO charter is concerned exclusively with organizational and procedural matters. The appended annexes contain substantive agreements that were either carried over from the old GATT or were negotiated during the Uruguay Round. Thus, if there is any threat to U.S. sovereignty, it emanates from the substantive agreements rather than from the WTO charter. Regarding the substantive agreements, it is important to note they did not become U.S. law until they were implemented through congressional action. The WTO cannot force Congress to enact a law that it opposes. If that is not enough to convince critics that joining WTO is no threat to U.S. sovereignty, we should note that the charter provides for withdrawal from the WTO six months after posting a notice indicating a desire to do so.

WTO IN OPERATION

Since the Uruguay Round was implemented, two developments give cause for cautious optimism for the future of the multilateral trading system: the successful negotiations of the agreements in some important service sectors under the WTO aegis; and the relatively smooth functioning of the new WTO dispute settlement mechanism.

The decision to continue negotiations in specified service areas after the signing of the Uruguay Round has proved productive. Of the three designated sectors—telecommunications, financial services, and maritime services—agreements were reached in all but the maritime sector. These agreements are significant not only because of the liberalization of those sectors but also because the agreements represent the first fruits of GATS and set a precedent for liberalizing services in additional sectors.

A financial services agreement concluded in December 1997 was signed by 102 WTO member countries. This agreement ultimately calls for an across-the-board liberalization of the banking, securities, insurance, and financial data services sectors. This agreement embodies a conditional reciprocity provision, which states that concessions granted by any country are conditioned upon counterconcessions offered by partner countries.

The telecommunications agreement was reached in February 1997, ten months after the United States rejected an earlier agreement at the last minute. The new agreement, which conforms more closely with original U.S. objectives, commits signatories to opening telecommunication markets to all competitors on an equal footing, dismantling state monopolies that control more than 50 percent of the global markets, relaxing restrictions on telecommunications, including those that limit the share of the domestic industry that could be controlled by foreigners, and reforming regulatory systems that inhibit competition between domestic and foreign-owned companies. Although the United States did not achieve its objective of permitting 100 percent foreign ownership of domestic industries, important concessions were made. Mexico and South Korea, for example, agreed to permit foreign companies to own 49 percent of telephone carriers within their borders. Japan, however, refused to allow foreigners to acquire more than 20 percent of the two companies that dominate the international and domestic telecommunications markets, whereas Canada refused to allow foreign companies to own more than 46.7 percent of any of its telecommunications carriers.[26]

Although not part of the original agenda, an information technology agreement was reached in December 1996. Signed by forty-three countries, it calls for the complete elimination of tariffs on a number of technology information products by 2000. The products included under this agreement are semiconductors, computers and computer equipment, software and telecommunications equipment, office machines, computer diskettes, and CD-ROMs.

Although these agreements represent significant progress in liberalizing trade in specific service sectors, many other sectors remain highly restrictive. The government procurement sector is a case in point. This sector has always been jealously protected by all countries, including the United States. In an effort to reduce barriers that make it virtually impossible for countries to compete for government procurement contracts, OECD countries agreed to adopt the "Code on Government Procurement" in 1979 during the Tokyo Round. This code was renegotiated during the Uruguay Round and today contains provisions designed to increase transparency of procurement processes and to extend national treatment to foreign firms. Unfortunately, only twenty-six countries, mainly from OECD, signed on to this agreement. In order to increase participation, the WTO in 1996 established the Working Group on Transparency in Government Procurement and scheduled negotiations for January 1999.

The second noteworthy development during the post-Uruguay period was the smooth functioning of the new dispute settlement mechanism. Leading up to the Uruguay Round, the United States, disaffected with the impotence of the dispute settlement mechanism, had increasingly relied on aggressive unilateralism to correct perceived wrongs. Early indications are that the adoption of the more effective mechanism has begun to reduce this tendency. During the first three years of the new mechanism's operation, the United States has increasingly relied on it to resolve issues that were previously addressed by 301 investigations. According to the President's Economic Council, "The results of thirty-five complaints filed by the United States suggest that the dispute settlement process has proved very effective."[27] Of course, this conclusion might have been motivated by the additional fact that "the United States [prevailed] in nine out of ten rulings to date."[28] Nothing breeds success like success.

10

INTERNATIONAL TRADE AND LABOR AND ENVIRONMENTAL STANDARDS

In November 1997 the U.S. Congress rejected a request by Pres. Bill Clinton to renew the so-called fast-track provision, which had been a feature of U.S. trade legislation since 1974. The provision authorized the president to negotiate trade agreements with the understanding that upon submission to Congress for approval they would be voted up or down without amendment. The importance of this provision cannot be overstated: In its absence, few if any trading partners would be willing even to negotiate with the United States. Hence, by rejecting the president's request for renewal, Congress in effect put on hold all future trade negotiations and virtually stopped in its tracks the administration's plan to extend NAFTA to Chile and, ultimately, to the rest of the Western Hemisphere.

The driving force behind Congress's rejection was an intense lobbying effort mounted by organized labor and environmental groups. Still smarting from their perceived defeat on NAFTA, these groups demanded prior assurance that all future trade agreements would contain strong, enforceable provisions calling for the upgrading of environmental and labor standards by emerging economies, backed by a mandate to sanction trade in the event of noncompliance. Although the United States has been in the forefront of the campaign to upgrade emerging economies' standards and, in fact, waged a long but ultimately losing battle on this issue during the Uruguay Round, the president was unable to give Congress the assurance it wanted. The reason was that emerging economies were (and are) adamantly opposed to any linkage between trade and environmental-labor standards and to granting jurisdiction over these standards to the

WTO. Since this dispute is not likely to be resolved in the foreseeable future or to go away entirely, it represents a potential danger to the trade system. The objective of this chapter is to explore the issues raised in linking trade to these standards. The first section is devoted to an examination of the trade–labor standards nexus; the second section examines the trade–environmental standards linkage.

LABOR STANDARDS

Efforts to link labor standards and trade are not a new phenomenon. Indeed, proposals to this effect have been advanced for at least 150 years. In an informative essay, professor Virginia Leary notes that these proposals were initially motivated by a realization that any attempt to improve workers' conditions on a national level was doomed to failure because of the "competitive disadvantage [this would produce] in relation to other countries with lower standards." In response to this problem, reformers "urged the adoption of treaties, establishing common labor standards . . . by all European industrialized countries, as well as the establishment of an international organization to supervise these treaties."[1]

At present, major supporters of proposals to harmonize labor standards—the beleaguered import-substitute industries, organized labor, human rights advocates, and some governments, particularly the United States government—advance three major arguments to support their case. Organized labor and industry spokesmen argue that lax standards existing in many developing countries give those countries an *unfair* competitive edge in the production of labor-intensive goods. Second, they contend that pressures exerted by emerging economies on more-advanced countries will inevitably lead to a lowering of the latter's standards, thereby setting off a race to the bottom. Finally, human rights advocates, as well as the U.S. government and its allies, give primacy to the argument that labor standards are a component of universally recognized human rights, which democratic societies have an obligation to ensure are not violated.

Although the motivations of the different advocates vary, all agree that the question of labor standards should be incorporated into trade agreements in one form or another and that these agreements should explicitly authorize levying sanctions against exports of countries that fail to adhere to prescribed standards. Some advocates argue for incorporating a social clause that would establish minimum standards for all participating parties. Others believe that reliance should be placed on GATT Article 16, which authorizes countries to impose countervailing duties to offset advantages foreign exporters enjoy as a result of subsidies. Still others favor placing reliance on GATT Article 23, which authorizes the levying of tariffs by countries whose GATT privileges have been nullified or impaired. Adopting any of these proposals would clearly result in a significant increase in discretionary activities by participating parties and in acceptable GATT-WTO exceptions.

The reaction of developing countries to these proposals was, predictably, highly negative. In the words of one observer, these countries

> feel that developed countries' concerns about working conditions in their countries is due, above all, to their exports' success, and to the growing pressure for protectionism. . . . They consider the social clause proposal to be disguised protectionism [and a stratagem] to deprive them of one of their key comparative advantages: the ability to use low cost labor productively. They object . . . to interference in their domestic affairs and resent the fact that they appear to be asked for reciprocity in social obligations in return for trade concessions.[2]

In light of the strong positions staked out by proponents and opponents of linkage, two questions come to the fore: Who is right and who is wrong? And what can be done to effect a reconciliation so that the dispute does not derail the liberalization process? The answer to the first question is simple: both sides are right and wrong at the same time. The answer to the second question suggests why the first answer is neither wrong nor facetious.

The term *labor standards* covers a broad range of rights and regulations, including, at one end of the spectrum, the prohibition of forced and slave labor and, at the other end, extensive—and probably very expensive—vacation plans for workers. When proponents speak of the need to harmonize labor standards to eliminate practices that lead to unfair trade, what precisely do they have in mind? When opponents reject these proposals out of hand on the grounds that they are protectionist, what precisely do they have in mind? It is clear that in the absence of more precise definitions knee-jerk reactions rather than reasoned ones will prevail and that any effort to reconcile the two views will be doomed from the start.

Labor standards can be classified into two distinct subgroups. The first consists of standards that embrace fundamental human rights and hence transcend time and place and—some even argue—cultures as well. The second consists of standards that are time- and place-specific. The first subgroup has been designated by both the International Labor

Organization (ILO) and the OECD as core standards. The ILO's core includes freedom of association; the right to bargain collectively; prohibition of forced labor; prohibition of discrimination in the workplace; and
equal pay for equal work. The OECD's core tracks that of the ILO and
adds one more element, the prohibition of child labor.

The second subgroup of standards consists of standards that set inter
alia minimum wages, maximum hours, the number of paid holidays,
pension plans, and safety in the workplace. This subgroup is distinguished from core standards in that they are determined by and in turn
reflect a country's level of income and preference. To impose noncore
standards of a high-income country on countries with lower incomes and
different preferences would create a distortion as surely as would a requirement that Angola spend as much money on higher education per
capita as the United States.

Because noncore standards reflect a country's level of income and preference, the competitive edge that low-standard countries derive from
them is not unfair per se; low standards are a legitimate source of comparative advantage for poor countries. Imposing a tax on their exports to
level the playing field is no more justifiable than a tax designed to deprive
the advanced countries' exporters of the competitive edge they derive
from their large endowment of physical and human capital.

The conclusion that emerges is that the case for harmonizing noncore
standards is virtually nonexistent. And so spokesmen for developing
countries are correct when they reject, on protectionist grounds, harmonizing proposals that include such standards. Yet the case for harmonizing core standards remains tenable. Not only are these standards not in-
come-determined, but the evidence strongly suggests that adherence to
them has no impact on trade. An OECD study concludes that "there is no
evidence that low standard countries enjoy a better global performance
than high standard countries" and that "concerns expressed by certain
developing countries that [adhering to] core standards would negatively
affect their economic performance or their international competitive position are unfounded."[3] The study reaches similar conclusions regarding
the impact of core standards on the location of foreign direct investments.
It concludes that "aggregate foreign direct investment data suggest that
core labor standards are not important determinants in the majority of
cases."[4]

Recognizing the basic difference between core standards and noncore
standards opens a window of opportunity. If developed and developing
countries can agree to include a provision in the GATT charter calling for

a harmonization of core standards, it could go a long way toward defusing a potentially disruptive debate. Unfortunately, this is not likely to happen soon. In a communiqué issued after the first WTO ministerial meeting, developing countries emphatically rejected bringing even the question of core standards under the WTO aegis:

> We renew our commitment to the presence of internationally recognized core labor standards. The ILO is the competent body to set and deal with these standards and we affirm our support for its work in promoting them. We believe that economic growth and development fostered by increased trade and further trade liberalization contributes to the promotion of these standards. We reject the use of labor standards for protectionist purposes and agree that the comparative advantage of countries, particularly low wage developing countries, must in no way be put into question. In this regard we note that the WTO and the ILO secretariats will continue their existing collaboration.[5]

The problem with this resolution is that the ILO lacks even the most rudimentary enforcement mechanism. Professor Jagdish Bhagwati attributes the tendency of countries to ratify ILO conventions that affirm each of the core standards, then ignore them, to the absence of any external obligations to comply or any external threat of action for noncompliance.[6] This deficiency, of course, is precisely the reason why advocates of linkage have urged the WTO, with its relatively strong enforcement mechanism, to assume responsibility for core standards.

A skeptic could argue that even if responsibility for core standards was transferred from ILO to WTO it would not make any difference. One such skeptic, Heribert Maier, director-general of ILO, notes that since the WTO tends to act under a consensus principle the transfer of authority from ILO to WTO would result in a tradeoff of "strengthening the means of action at the cost of reducing the sphere of activity."[7]

What Can Be Done?

Given developing countries' opposition to bringing core standards under the aegis of WTO, many advocates conclude that private rather than official action promises are the best way to improve working conditions in emerging economies.[8] By publicizing the inhumane conditions under which some of the better-known American-branded products are manufactured in developing countries, advocates hope that public revulsion—together with a determination not to buy goods made under such conditions—would compel multinational corporations to voluntarily adhere to higher standards. This approach has already borne some fruit. Bowing to pressures exerted by Oxfam, Christian Aid, and UNICEF, among others, the World Federation of Sporting Goods Industries, whose membership includes Reebok, Nike, and Adidas, has agreed to develop a code of conduct to end the abuse of child labor in low-wage factories in Asia.[9] The White House Apparel Industry Partnership, a task force set up by President Clinton that includes representatives from labor unions, industry, and human rights groups, has developed a code of conduct to eliminate apparel sweatshops in emerging economies as well as in the United States.[10] Another component in the campaign to end abuses in emerging economies' workshops is to inform consumers about the conditions under which goods are being produced. The Ford Foundation, for example, has given the American Fair Trade Association a $75,000 grant to publish a directory entitled *Sweatshops or Fair Trade? Now You Have a Choice*. It lists businesses that deal only in goods that are humanely produced.[11] The Fair Trade Movement—not to be confused with those who argue that all trade with low-wage countries is unfair—"seeks to help developing countries sell their goods abroad for as much as they can while also promoting acceptable working conditions."[12] This movement has been quite successful in Western Europe, Australia, and New Zealand but has thus far made few inroads in the United States.

As part of the campaign to keep consumers informed regarding the manner in which goods are produced, companies that adhere to enhanced standards are being offered an opportunity to place designated labels on their products. These seals of approval—"ecotags"—are designed to appeal to consumers willing to pay somewhat higher prices for goods produced in an "acceptable" manner. According to public opinion polls, 85 percent of Americans indicate they would be willing to do so.[13] Finally, a number of organizations, both private and public, have announced their intentions to boycott producers that do not adhere to core standards. Noting that about 200 million school-age children are employed in industries around the world, a UNICEF directive states that "UNICEF should purchase products only from those companies that comply with existing national labor laws and regulations with regard to their employment practices [minimum age of employment, wages, working conditions]."[14]

Following the lead of Duke University, a number of universities and colleges have adopted a policy to license only those producers who agree to adhere to core standards in producing athletic apparel bearing the school's name and logo. The "Duke Code" "bars licensees from using forced labor or child labor and requires them to maintain a safe work-place, pay at least the minimum wage and recognize the right to form unions." To ensure enforcement, the code "requires licensees to identify all factories making products with Duke's name and to allow unimpeded visits by independent monitors."[15]

Even private companies have been forced by public criticism to agree to adhere voluntarily to core standards. Acknowledging that the product of his company "has become synonymous with slave wages, forced overtime and arbitrary abuse," Nike CEO Philip H. Knight announced that his company would refrain from employing new workers below eighteen years of age in its shoe factories and those below sixteen years of age in other companies managed by the corporation. In addition, he com-mitted the company to "tighten air quality controls [in its overseas factories] to insure that the air breathed by workers meets the same stan-dards enforced by the United States Occupational Safety and Health Administration" and that all plants will be open to inspection by labor and human rights groups.[16]

It is difficult to estimate how effective these private efforts will ulti-mately be. One cause for concern is the problem of monitoring and of en-suring compliance with whatever standards are adopted. Another con-cern is to ensure that voluntary programs designed to help the most vulnerable groups in less-developed countries do not end up hurting them further. Thus, though the proposal to raise the minimum age at which children can work, supported by the threat of a boycott, is without question motivated by a strong desire to improve their lot, it can have unanticipated adverse consequences. The assumptions underlying this proposal are that children, freed of the necessity to work, will attend schools for longer periods of time and will mature to adulthood with the skills necessary to escape the poverty trap that initially forced them into the workplace. But how valid are these assumptions? Can it be taken for granted that the schools, teachers, and books needed to achieve these ob-jectives would in fact be available? Can it be assumed with confidence that families, deprived of the incomes that the children earn, would not have to reduce their standards of living even below their current miser-able levels?

Painful as these questions are, posing them serves a useful function; it focuses attention on an aspect of the problem that advocates would rather avoid. The raising of standards—an increase in the school leaving age, for example—entails a cost that many of the poor in emerging economies cannot afford to bear. The United States as a country, and Americans as individuals, have been at the forefront of the struggle to get less-developed countries to raise standards. Although this is commendable, is the U.S. government, World Bank, or the IMF prepared to extend aid and grants to those who would have to bear the costs of this reform? If not, is there any assurance that the attempt to improve the lot of children in less-developed countries will, despite best intentions, not result in further impoverishment?

The situation in Honduras provides a case in point. Many Americans were appalled to learn that apparel workers in Honduras, where the now infamous Cathy Lee Gifford line of clothes is manufactured, earned 40 cents per hour; they are inclined to agree with the sentiments expressed by Charles Kernaghan, executive director of the New York–based National Labor Committee, that the maquiladoras are "monstrous sweatshops of the new world order."[17] Many Hondurans, however, including spokesmen for three leading labor federations, disagree. According to a reporter for The New York Times, the story of one apparel worker, Orellana Vasquez, one of some 450 employees at the Key Star garment assembly plant, which produces beach shorts and other sportswear for the U.S. market, is not unusual. He is quoted as saying: "This has been an enormous advance for me and I give thanks to the maquila for it. My monthly income is seven times what I made in the countryside."[18]

Honduran unions have even opposed the proposal to raise the minimum age at which children may be allowed to work. At present, Honduran children between the ages of fourteen and sixteen can, with the permission of their parents and the Labor Ministry, work six hours per day. To increase the minimum working age would, according to a union labor organizer, create hardships. She is quoted as saying: "Very few Honduran mothers can afford the luxury of feeding children until they are 18 years old without putting them to work."[19] In response to U.S. pressure, maquiladoras, fearing blacklisting, dismissed workers who were less than sixteen years old; the children did not go back to school. Instead they took lower-paying jobs, which were physically more demanding, outside the maquiladora system.[20] Even Kernaghan of the National Labor Committee was forced to admit that his "efforts to end child labor had an unanticipated consequence. Obviously this is not what we wanted to happen."[21] One former teenager summed up the situation as follows: "In eleven years on [a] job [as a fare collector, which he began at the age of thirteen] I worked 14 hours a day, seven days a week, never got a day's vacation, didn't get paid when I was sick, and had to content myself with whatever wage the bus driver felt like paying me. . . . I was a slave with no rights."[22] He now works in a *maquila*. "The work here isn't heavy. There are many benefits and they have to respect your rights. I wish the *maquila* had existed when I started to work. I could have avoided a lot of suffering."[23]

The moral of this story is not that conditions prevailing in the *maquila* are good; they obviously are not. Rather, bad as conditions are, they are often better than most available alternatives, and those people working in the *maquila* are already better off than the 40 percent of Hondurans who remain unemployed. The fact is that in Honduras and elsewhere the expansion of the maquiladora system has increased the demand for labor and has driven up wages.

There is another lesson to be learned, however, from the Honduran experience, one that in many ways is representative of practically all the emerging economies. Raising standards is not costless. If developing countries are to commit to this task, then developed countries should make a commitment to help finance the cost of implementing it.

ENVIRONMENTAL STANDARDS

Among the most avid opponents of the globalization process are a number of major environmental organizations, including Sierra Club, Greenpeace, and Friends of the Earth. These groups waged an unrelenting campaign to defeat NAFTA, to derail the Uruguay Round, and to deny President Clinton's request for fast-track authority. To some degree their opposition reflects the influence of neo-Malthusianism, which was popularized by the Club of Rome during the 1970s. The tenet of this doctrine is that a shortage of natural resources and an impending population explosion have put the planet at risk and that a catastrophe can be avoided only by slowing down the growth process.[24] This thesis has been refuted by technological progress, which has increased the availability of resources manifold, and by the failure of the population to explode, as the Club of Rome expected. Yet the obsessions with growth and its adverse effects on the environment have continued to color, albeit in varying degrees, the perception of many, if not most, environmentalists. For those at the extreme edge of the movement, any activity that promises to stimulate growth is virtually anathema. For others, trade liberalization, which they correctly recognize as an important component of the growth process, has become the bête noir.

Fortunately, the environmental movement is not monolithic. It embodies a large number of devoted environmentalists who, though aware of the potential trade-environment conflict, are also aware that the two groups—one advocating an expansion of trade and the other primarily concerned with the protection of the environment—have much in common and that a cooperative rather than an adversarial approach could lead to mutually satisfactory solutions. This point of view is expressed by Daniel Esty, a prominent environmentalist who represented the Environmental Protection Agency at the NAFTA negotiations and at the Rio de Janeiro Earth Summit in 1992:

> Both sides of the trade and environment debate seek to improve the efficiency of resource use and to add to worldwide social welfare. Both free traders and environmentalists would like to deter one nation from irresponsibly shifting burdens to another or from one generation to the next and both communities face a constant threat from special interests that seek to twist the policy process to their own advantage at the expense of the broader public. Most importantly, policy choices are available that can make trade liberalization and environmental protection mutually compatible and minimize the extent of dispute.[25]

An additional point to emphasize is that the increase in world income that globalization will generate represents the best hope for widespread adoption of more stringent environmental measures, not only in developed countries but in emerging economies as well.

The debate surrounding NAFTA and the Uruguay Round negotiations focused attention, perhaps as never before, on issues that divide environmentalists and trade advocates rather than on those issues that unite them. The proposal to establish a free trade area in North America served as a wakeup call for environmentalists. The lax enforcement of environmental standards in Mexico and the environmentally primitive infrastructure along the U.S.-Mexico border were long regarded as prototypes of what would occur to large portions of the earth if demands for more stringent environmental regulations and standards were not met. A free trade agreement would, in their view, not only exacerbate the infrastructural problems in the border zone but also lead to an outflow of U.S. factories seeking relief from stringent standards in the United States. Ross Perot added fuel to the already raging fire. In his widely circulated book *Save Your Jobs, Save Our Country: Why NAFTA Must Be Stopped*,[26] Perot warned against environmental depredations he was certain would occur if NAFTA was ratified as well as the loss of jobs resulting from the relocation of U.S. firms to Mexico.

It was not only NAFTA, however, that provoked the slings and arrows of the environmentalist attack. Long held in suspicion by the environmental community, GATT now became a target. Two factors were primarily responsible for this. The first was environmentalists' perception that a number of emendations in the GATT charter during the Uruguay Round would create obstacles for countries that wished to adopt more stringent standards than those that were regarded as the norm. The second was a growing perception that GATT rules, as interpreted by the dispute settlement panels, posed a threat to the effective implementation of global agreements dealing with crossborder environmental problems. These perceptions sufficed to verify and to fortify environmentalists' longstanding conviction that GATT's objective and theirs were fundamentally antithetical. The critical question is: How valid are these perceptions?

GATT AND THE ENVIRONMENT

Unlike NAFTA, which has been called "the greenest trade agreement ever negotiated," GATT does not have special provisions or side agreements that directly address environmental concerns. This, however, does not suggest, as many environmentalists claim, that GATT was indifferent to the environment. A fundamental principle underlying GATT was that its obligations would not infringe upon participating parties' sovereign rights to pursue domestic objectives. GATT Articles 20 and 21 were designed to ensure this outcome. As we have already noted, these articles authorized participating parties to waive GATT obligations whenever necessary to enable them to achieve specific domestic objectives, including the protection of human, animal, and plant life and the health of the environment. The only constraints placed on GATT members were that the measures deployed to promote these objectives were to be applied in "a manner which would not constitute a means of arbitrary or unjustifiable discrimination between countries where the same conditions prevail or a disguised restriction of international trade."[27]

The final act of the Uruguay Round agreement confirmed the WTO's sensitivity to both national sovereignty and environmental matters. The preamble to the agreement on technical barriers in trade, which replaced the 1979 standards code, specifically stated that "no country should be prevented from taking measures necessary to ensure the quality of exports, or for the protection of human, animal or plant life or health, of the environment, . . . at levels it considered appropriate." The sanitary and phytosanitary agreements also recognized members' right to take measures they deemed necessary for "the protection of human, animal or plant life and health." These measures included, among other things, food processing and production methods; meat slaughter and inspection rules; rules pertaining to food additives; and the establishment of tolerance levels for pesticides.

Despite these provisions, the Uruguay Round agreements were not well received by environmentalists. They particularly objected to a number of new provisions in the phytosanitary agreement and the technical barriers agreement. Provisions placed the burden of proof on countries wishing to impose more rigorous standards than the existing internationally accepted ones. To receive WTO authorization to impose these more stringent standards, a country would have to demonstrate that the standards can be *scientifically* justified, that they are not disproportionate to the objectives desired, that they are not more trade-restrictive than is necessary to achieve the objectives, and that they do not constitute a barrier to trade.

Although there is some element of truth in the environmentalists' contention that these regulations deter the adoption of more rigorous standards, they are necessary to prevent the trade agenda from being co-opted by protectionists. During the pre-Uruguay period, standards were routinely used as grey area measures to restrict trade. A classic example is the U.S. Corporate Average Fuel Economy Act. Designed to improve automobile fuel efficiency, the act set minimum average fuel economy requirements for the fleets of all companies selling automobiles in the United States. These fleet requirements were not difficult for U.S. manufacturers to satisfy; the poor fuel performance of the gas-guzzling Lincoln Continental could be offset by the excellent fuel performance of the gas-sipping Escort. The act was written in such a way, however, that the superior performance of the small cars produced by foreign manufacturers could not be used to offset the poor performance of their gas-guzzlers. A GATT panel ruled this was unnecessarily discriminatory and hence in violation of GATT rules.

It can be argued, moreover, that modifications in standards agreements that environmentalists took exception to did little more than make explicit what has been implicit all along. The original Article 20 abjured countries from using environmental standards as disguised protection and implicitly subjected them to challenges if they did so. The new requirement that these standards be scientifically justified and that the cost of complying with them be approximately equal to the value they confer is simply a way of spelling out the criteria that must be met if the standards are not to be deployed for protectionist purposes.

The need for some kind of discipline in applying standards is suggested by Pat Buchanan's remarks during his 1996 campaign for the

Republican presidential nomination. In a speech in California, Buchanan criticized a NAFTA provision that would permit the importation of Mexican avocados. Mexican avocados, he argued, endanger domestic crops. He is quoted as saying, "The Mexican avocados are very much infested with a variety of pests from the met fly to the weevil to mites." These pests, he noted, have recently appeared in Californian-grown avocados and "while *it cannot be proven* [italics added] that they came in from Mexico, clearly they came up from San Diego and there is a *general belief* [italics added] that they came in from Mexico." As if that were not enough, during a call-in radio program a few days earlier he responded to a comment by a caller to the effect that the United States should show greater concern about three or four major diseases, by noting: "If we don't close the border with Mexico we are going to suffer. We've got millions of people [i.e., illegal immigrants, who] are not checked for any kind of diseases."[28]

More recently, epidemics of food poisoning caused by fruits and vegetables imported into the United States from Mexico and other Latin American countries have been reported. Predictably, this news occasioned criticisms of WTO rules and led to demands that the United States "regain its sovereign rights" to restrict imports. Unhighlighted in newspaper accounts was the fact that the problem was due not to U.S. inability to keep contaminated imports out but rather to inadequate funding of regulatory agencies and a bureaucratic failure to grant agencies the authority they needed to ban the suspect imports. According to *The New York Times*, "The Food and Drug Administration can stop food at the borders but has no authority to prevent a country with an inferior food-safety system from exporting the food in the first place. The Agriculture Department does have that power, called equivalency, but only for meat and poultry."[29] Granting the necessary authority to the Food and Drug Administration and appropriating funds requested by the Clinton administration could alleviate this problem.

The standards issue, however, is not the only or even the most important concern that environmentalists have with GATT. Another is the perception that GATT has failed to address appropriately the problems arising from environmentally detrimental practices in specific countries where these practices have transborder spillover effects. This issue was brought to the fore by a GATT panel ruling in the now famous—or infamous—tuna-dolphin case brought by Mexico against the United States. The facts of the case can be stated succinctly. In 1988 the Earth Island Institute, a California-based environmental group, sued the Bush administration on the grounds that it was not enforcing the U.S. Mammal Protection Act of 1972. The law was designed to reduce the number of mammals incidentally killed by commercial fishermen. The act not only set a limit on the number of mammals that could be incidentally killed in any given year; it also required the Department of Commerce to certify that foreign governments were initiating measures to reduce the killing and to impose sanctions on the imports of offending countries. The Earth Island Institute's suit charged that the Commerce Department should ban Mexican tuna because Mexican fishermen, using purse-seine nets, were exceeding the kill quota. The plaintiff prevailed in federal court, and the United States imposed a ban on Mexican tuna.

Charging the United States with impairing and nullifying its GATT rights, Mexico brought the issue to GATT for adjudication. The United States argued that it was authorized under GATT Article 20 to levy sanctions since Mexico was endangering the health of animals; the argument was rejected by the panel on two grounds. First, the panel ruled that Article 20 authorized a ban on imports only if the goods, and *not the production process* used to produce these goods, were the source of the problem. Second, the GATT panel ruled that the United States exceeded its jurisdiction inasmuch as the action occurred outside its territorial limits. More recently, the WTO reconfirmed this position, again ruling that a U.S. ban on the importation of shrimp from countries whose shrimpers did not take adequate measures to protect endangered sea turtles was illegal under GATT on the grounds the United States did not have authority "to force other nations to adopt policies to protect endangered species like the turtles."[30]

These rulings were greeted with outrage by the environmentalist community, which regarded them as an infringement of U.S. sovereignty as well as a critical assault on efforts to curb the use of environmentally detrimental methods of production where they have transborder or global effects. In their view the United States should be able to ban the importation of goods from countries that employ methods that violate the Montreal Protocol calling for the ultimate elimination of chlorofluorocarbons (CFCs) and other ozone-damaging chemicals, the Basel Convention restricting the export of hazardous waste materials, the Convention on International Trade in Endangered Species, and the Kyoto Protocol of 1997—all of which depend for their enforcement on the ability to impose sanctions on offending countries' trade.

If these rulings indeed constitute a critical assault on these global treaties, then environmental concerns would be justified. If countries had no way to prevent an offending party from using ozone-destroying methods of production or from burning its forests to clear land for cultivation while polluting the air of neighbors, the efforts to save the planet for future generations would surely be doomed to failure. Fortunately, however, the possibility of this happening is grossly exaggerated. According to Robert Hudec, a leading authority on international law, the import bans authorized by the global environmental treaties are unlikely to be rendered nonoperative by the GATT panel's decisions regarding dolphins and sea turtles. A "GATT member government [that] has signed an international environmental agreement authorizing other signatories to impose trade restrictions against it . . . can quite properly be deemed to have waived its GATT legal rights against such trade restrictions." Hudec further notes that "the waiver concept would be recognized under two rules of international treaty interpretation known as *lex posterior* and *lex specialis*." The former states that when "two agreements signed by the same parties are in conflict, the agreement later in time is presumed to be controlling." The second principle states that "the more specific of two agreements is meant to control even when the more general agreement [in this case GATT] happens to be later in time."[31] The application of these two principles would ensure that the obligations assumed upon becoming signatories to the environmental agreements would override GATT obligations.

We should note in passing that the GATT rulings did not condemn Americans who want to eat tuna or shrimp to being unwilling partners in killing dolphins and sea turtles. Concerned Americans can be spared this role by the use of ecolabeling; companies selling tuna or shrimp in the U.S. market can use such labels to inform consumers that the product was caught in a dolphin-safe and sea turtle–safe manner. This practice, widely used in Europe, would give Americans the opportunity to boycott goods that are produced in an objectionable manner without requiring the United States to violate its GATT obligations.[32]

THE PROBLEM OF DIVERGENT ENVIRONMENTAL STANDARDS

The level of environmental standards and the degree to which they are enforced differ substantially among countries. In general, developed countries' standards are more stringent and more diligently enforced that those in less-developed countries. As a result, developed countries' industry spokesmen argue that their firms are put at a competitive disadvantage, lobby for a reduction in standards, and threaten to relocate if their

demands are not satisfied. To forestall "a race to the bottom," environmentalists have urged amending the GATT charter to require an across-
the-board harmonization of standards; failing that, they favor the right to
impose a countervailing duty to offset what they regard as social dumping or ecodumping.[33] This has in fact already been attempted; a proposed
amendment to the Clean Air bill of 1990 called for a special tax on imports
that were not produced in compliance with the air quality standards prescribed in the bill. This amendment, however, was narrowly defeated.[34]

This proposal has been denounced by spokesmen for developing countries who view it as a not-too-subtle attempt to deny them access to developed countries' markets. Economists also reject it on the grounds that environmental standards, like labor standards, reflect a country's level of
income and preferences and that harmonization would create distortions
inasmuch as it would compel low-income countries to spend more than
they prefer or can afford on pollution abatement and, hence, less than
they prefer on other goods and services.[35]

The attempt to harmonize standards also ignores the fact that values
assigned to different environmental objectives vary from one country to
the next. In some countries, air pollution represents a more significant
problem than water pollution, whereas the reverse may be true for others.
The first group of countries would want to allocate a larger proportion of
their environmental budgets to clean up their air, whereas the second
group would want to spend a larger proportion of their budgets to clean
up the water. Harmonization leads to a loss of flexibility in areas where
flexibility is of the utmost importance.

The irony in debating how to redress "unfairness" caused by diversity
in standards is that the empirical evidence strongly suggests there is not
much of an impact to redress. After reviewing the entire body of empirical literature dealing with the impact of divergence, A. B. Jaffe et al.
conclude that

> overall there is relatively little evidence to support the hypothesis that envi-
> ronmental regulations have had a large adverse effect on competitiveness,
> however that elusive term is defined. . . . Studies attempting to measure the
> influence of environmental regulation on net exports, overall trade flows and
> plant location decisions have produced estimates that are either small, statis-
> tically insignificant, or not robust to tests of model specification.[36]

In another study, Arik Levinson concludes that there is "only a limited
amount of empirical evidence that industrial flight [induced by the diversity of environmental standards] exists."[37] One study by OECD, however,

did report some evidence of industrial flight in industries that are highly pollution-intensive and where the cost of compliance is high; yet the same study emphasized that sectors where firms may be more prone to industrial flight "are the exception rather than the rule."[38]

A number of reasons have been advanced to explain why diversity in standards has apparently had such a small impact on trade and investment patterns and on the location of industry. Among the more important of these are the relative unimportance of the cost of compliance; the slight difference between the high standards in the United States, which are considered the most stringent in the world, and those in other advanced countries; the fact that most multinational corporations are "reluctant to build less than state-of-the-art plants in foreign countries"; and that "plants built by indigenous firms typically embody more pollution control . . . than is required."[39]

Despite the empirical evidence, environmentalists' concern regarding the impact of divergent standards has not abated. They argue that whatever the data show the political impact of the divergence remains potent. Threats by multinational corporations to relocate operations to countries with less stringent standards have, they argue, sufficed to prevent the adoption of more stringent standards than those already in existence. According to Esty,

> environmentalists worry about the political drag created by the low environmental standards in trading partners. Specifically they fear that lax environmental regulations elsewhere give credence to business' arguments about competitive disadvantage and can be significant in debates over the rigor of new environmental laws, leading to weakened support for strong environmental standards.[40]

A revisionist hypothesis regarding the impact of divergent environmental standards, advanced by Michael Porter, challenges the conventional wisdom by postulating that more stringent environmental standards not only do *not* impose a burden on the country's firms but rather stimulate growth and improve the economy's productivity.[41] This could happen if new stringent regulations create incentives for firms to discover ways to produce in a less polluting manner. To the extent that this occurs, the cost of compliance with the more stringent standards could be more than offset by a reduction in the cost of production due to the innovations induced by these new standards.

This hypothesis was recently tested by two economists who studied the impact of stringent environmental regulations on three Norwegian industries. The questions they addressed were whether "firms under strict environmental regulations have a higher tendency to exit from the industry and a lower tendency to increase employment than firms under weak or no environmental regulations."[42] They found that although environmental regulations did not have a significant impact on the basic industrial chemicals industry, they did have a significant impact on the iron, steel, and ferrous alloy industries and on the paper and paperboard industry. Firms subject to stringent environmental regulations in these industries had a higher tendency to *increase* employment and a *lower* tendency to exit than firms that were not subject to strict regulation. The authors conclude that the results support the Porter hypothesis that there is no conflict between environmental policies and economic competitiveness.

There is reason to believe, moreover, that the "Porter effect" will become even more pronounced with the implementation of the polluter pay principle and with a change in the basic approach toward environmental control. The polluter pay principle, which was adopted at the 1992 Earth Summit in Rio de Janeiro, calls for the internalization of environmental costs. If rigorously adhered to—and this cannot be taken for granted—a corporation engaged in pollution-creating activities will have to bear the costs resulting from them rather than passing them on to society. In making polluting activities more costly to the company, the principle creates incentives to adopt methods of production that lessen pollution.

This tendency can be further promoted by a movement away from the traditional "end of the pipe" treatment approach to one that emphasizes prevention. This too would create incentives to develop technologies that promise to prevent pollution at a lower cost to corporations than the current cleanup costs corporations must incur after the damage has already been done. Esty and other environmental advocates carry this line of argument one step farther, suggesting that subsidies be granted to firms using environmentally benign technologies and production processes as a way to raise the relative cost of pollution-intensive technology and production processes.

CONCLUSION

There is no way to fully reconcile the differences between those who assign the highest priority to labor and environmental matters and those who assign the highest priority to trade matters. Nevertheless, as this chapter we hope has shown, the points of conflict in the trade, environmental, and labor debate are not insurmountable. Moreover, it should not be overlooked—although unfortunately it frequently is—that the vast majority of those who advocate trade liberalization are *not* insensitive to the welfare of labor and to the urgent need to prevent and correct environmental depredations. Their commitment to trade liberalization is based on pragmatic, not ideological grounds. Should a point be reached where further liberalization becomes a clear and present danger to the greater welfare, most of those who advocate the expansion of trade will be prepared to do the right thing.

11

REGIONAL AND PREFERENTIAL TRADE AGREEMENTS

In recent years, preferential trade arrangements or, as they are sometimes called, regional trade arrangements, have proliferated. In 1996 at least seventy-six such arrangements were in effect, and the vast majority of WTO members are simultaneously members of at least one such arrangement. The significance of this proliferation of preferential (regional) trade arrangements to the globalization process in general and to the multilateral system in particular has been the subject of heated debate. Proponents of preferential trade arrangements maintain there is no inherent conflict between globalization and preferential trade arrangements and, moreover, that they actually extend the globalization process by expanding the economic space within which free trade exists.

Opponents of preferential arrangements, however, contend such proliferation represents a setback to the globalization process and a potential threat to the integrity of the postwar GATT-WTO trade regime. In their worst-case scenario, proliferation of preferential trade agreements could ultimately fragment the system into a number of competing trade blocs.

To complicate matters, the dominant actors in WTO—the United States and the European Union—are also the most prominent promoters of preferential trade agreements. The EU is, of course, the most complete and the most integrated preferential arrangement in existence. For its part, the United States has not only forged NAFTA but also is committed to forming the Free Trade Area of the Americas, which would link all thirty-four Western Hemisphere countries in a free trade area by 2005, and to transforming the eighteen-member Asia Pacific Economic Cooperation group (APEC) into a free trade area by 2020. This dual allegiance of the two most dominant actors in the world economy raises critical questions regarding the future of the globalization process. Can these two systems—one based on nondiscrimination and the other one on overt discrimination—coexist? Do preferential agreements expand the economic space within which free trade is practiced, as adherents of the view that they are building blocks toward a global free trade regime maintain? Or are they stumbling blocks to the attainment of this goal, as critics allege? The remainder of this chapter will address these questions.

PREFERENTIAL TRADING ARRANGEMENTS DEFINED

Preferential trading arrangements assume two forms: customs unions and free trade areas. In either case, they consist of a group of countries agreeing to eliminate tariffs on goods produced within the area while maintaining tariffs on imports derived from countries outside the area. Although these groups can differ in many ways, including the degree to which they are integrated, the basic difference that distinguishes customs unions from free trade areas is that the former agree to adopt a common external tariff schedule and common customs procedures, whereas in the latter each country retains its own tariff schedule and customs procedures. Within the rubric of free trade areas, two types can be distinguished: open free trade areas and closed free trade areas. As the names suggest, an *open free trade area* is one in which all countries that agree to comply with the rules of the arrangement can gain entry; a *closed free trade area* can exclude countries, even those willing to comply with all the rules of the group.

Customs unions and free trade areas are inherently discriminatory. Such arrangements are preferential precisely because they discriminate in favor of members' exports and against nonmember countries' exports. This feature accounts for the long-standing U.S. opposition to these arrangements and explains why the United States insisted on making the unconditional most favored nation principle the cornerstone of the postwar trading system.[1] With some departures, this opposition continued until the 1980s, when a change in U.S. rhetoric and policy occurred. This shift was heralded by Pres. Ronald Reagan during his campaign to initiate a new round of GATT-sponsored negotiations. In remarks to representatives of the business community and to members of the Export Council Advisory Committee for Trade Negotiations, the president noted:

> To reduce the impediments to free markets, we will accelerate our efforts to launch a new GATT negotiating round with our trading partners, and we

hope that the GATT members will see fit to reduce [trade] barriers. . . . But if these
negotiations are not initiated or if insignificant progress is made, I am instructing
our trade negotiators to explore regional and bilateral agreements with other na-
tions.[2]

Implicit in this statement is the view that the two systems—one based on multilateralism and the unconditional MFN principle, the other on regionalism and preferences—represent two separate routes to achieve the desired objective of liberalizing world trade. The statement, however, leaves little doubt that the president preferred the former to the latter. The regional alternative is to be pursued only if multilateral negotiations fail. A decade later this distinction is blurred. In reporting on the trade policies of Pres. Bill Clinton's administration, the Council of Economic Advisors noted that it "has embraced an outward oriented pro-trade, pro-growth economic strategy. . . . We are using all the tools available to us—multilateral, regional and bilateral—to advance our pro-trade agenda. . . . The Administration has promoted the creation of regional trade agreements as stepping stones toward global free trade."[3]

This shift in U.S. policy—from strong opposition to preferential trade agreements to open-arms acceptance of them—signaled a bursting forth of such arrangements. Before examining the factors responsible for this development, it is important to note that these agreements, although discriminatory by nature and hence in violation of the MFN principle, were not GATT-illegal. As we note above, GATT sanctioned the formation of preferential trade agreements provided the criteria specified in Article 24 were satisfied. The more important of these criteria were that the participating parties eliminate trade barriers on "substantially all the trade between the constituent territories"; that in the case of customs unions, where a system of *common* external tariffs and customs regulations replaces the individual national systems, it shall not "on the whole be higher or more restrictive than the general incidence of the duties and regulations" in effect before the union was established; that a proposal to establish a free trade area or a customs union include a "plan and schedule for [its] formation . . . within a reasonable length of time"; and that the GATT signatories be notified of the intention to establish a preferential arrangement. GATT approval, however, was not required. Rather, each GATT signatory was given an opportunity to recommend changes before the agreement went into effect. If no recommendations were forthcoming, as was almost always the case, the agreement was considered accepted.[4] It is interesting to note that neither GATT nor WTO ever rejected a proposed agreement.

FACTORS UNDERLYING THE FORMATION
OF PREFERENTIAL TRADING ARRANGEMENTS

With the important exception of the European Economic Community, which was politically motivated, few preferential trade agreements were implemented during the early postwar period.[5] Those that were implemented consisted for the most part of small, less-developed countries—mainly in Latin America—which, having adopted import-substitution strategies of development, hoped preferential trade arrangements would enlarge their markets and enable them to reap economies of scale that were unattainable in their small local markets.[6] It soon became apparent, however, that this route provided no solution to their problems; indeed, its major legacy was that inefficient industries increasingly relied on protectionist policies to survive. It was no surprise, therefore, that the first wave of regionalism—as it has come to be called—ended not with a bang but a whimper.

Preferential agreements did not become a prominent item on the trade agenda until the mid-1980s. That development reflected a growing skepticism by emerging and developed countries as to GATT's ability to protect and promote their interests. Developing economies, which had relied heavily on the MFN clause to ensure continued access to world markets, had second thoughts regarding its effectiveness in light of growing administered protection. The developed countries' widespread resort to anti-dumping and countervailing duties reduced the insurance value of the MFN clause and increased the attractiveness of regional preferential agreements. Although such agreements did not guarantee continued access to world markets, they did provide a safe haven in their most important markets. In addition, several students single out the importance of membership in preferential arrangements as a way to secure domestic policy reforms and to ensure against backsliding. John Whalley, for example, notes that "binding the country to the masthead of an international trade agreement, [makes] any future reversal of domestic policy reform . . . more difficult to implement."[7]

Developed countries embraced such arrangements in large part because of a growing belief that GATT membership had become too unwieldy and too fractious to effect the changes they felt necessary if the GATT-WTO regime was to lead to further liberalization. Working with a smaller, more eager, more tractable group of countries would, they believed, enable them to achieve objectives they were no longer able to obtain in the larger multilateral setting. Thus, in exchange for providing trading partners a safe haven, developed countries hoped to obtain commitments to open service sectors, provide adequate protection for intellectual property rights, adopt more rigorous labor and environmental standards, remove structural impediments to trade, adhere to a code of conduct for foreign direct investments, and adopt more effective dispute settlement mechanisms.

In addition, such arrangements helped mitigate the burgeoning free-rider problem that resulted from GATT's MFN principle. Since adherence to the MFN principle ensured that all GATT members would receive equal treatment, countries were under no obligation to reciprocate when they became beneficiaries of concessions negotiated by others. The elimination of tariffs on intra-area trade within the preferential arrangement precluded free riding.

Preferential trade agreements were also at times fueled by noneconomic considerations. As we have already noted, the major motivation for forming the EC was political; although economic means were employed, its objective was to forge a new political entity—a federation of European states. Likewise, the desire to gain Mexico's cooperation in curbing illegal immigration and drug smuggling played a prominent role in the U.S. decision to create NAFTA. Strategic reasons apparently also played a role. According to the Council of Economic Advisors, "The passage of NAFTA [combined with the upgrading of APEC negotiation to a high-profile leaders' meeting in Seattle, Washington] sent a strong signal to the Europeans that the United States had serious regional alternatives should the Uruguay Round of negotiations fall apart." The council also reported that this strategy worked: "German policy makers have . . . stated that this [signal] was part of their motivation for prevailing on their European Union partners to make certain concessions that allowed the GATT negotiations to be successful."[8]

THE NORTH AMERICAN
FREE TRADE AGREEMENT

NAFTA is a textbook illustration of the reasons behind the growing popularity of regional trade agreements. NAFTA, which built on the existing U.S.-Canadian free trade agreement, was driven in large part by Mexico's desire to ensure continued access to its most important market and to lock in the trade reforms that it instituted following the severe debt crisis it experienced in 1982. These reforms included, among other things, a significant unilateral reduction in Mexican tariffs and membership in GATT.[9]

For the United States, the benefits of a preferential agreement with Mexico and Canada—aside from the noneconomic considerations already mentioned—included an anticipated increase in U.S. exports resulting from a further reduction in Mexican and Canadian tariffs, access to the Mexican service markets that had previously been closed to U.S. firms, as well as increased security for its investments, a more effective dispute-settlement mechanism, and a commitment by Mexico to upgrade its labor and environmental standards.

Although NAFTA did not call for an immediate abolition of all tariffs and trade barriers, it did conform with GATT's requirements that a reasonable time schedule be included to achieve this objective. The three countries agreed to phase out all tariffs and most of the existing nontariff barriers in the industrial goods sector within a ten-year period. Recognizing the added difficulties of eliminating trade barriers in the agricultural sector, the phaseout period was extended to fifteen years. These provisions were widely criticized by NAFTA's critics on both sides of the border. Mexican critics argued that since U.S. tariffs were initially lower than Mexican tariffs Mexico was, by agreeing to a complete phase-out, in effect extending more concessions to the United States than it was receiving from the United States. U.S. critics, focusing almost entirely on the promised reduction in U.S. tariffs, bemoaned the expected increase in U.S. imports of labor-intensive goods. Although these criticisms add little light to the question of the desirability of preferential tariff agreements, they do offer additional evidence of the persistence and depth of mercantilistic thinking in developed and less-developed countries.

Although the reduction in intraregional tariffs presumably represented a step toward further liberalization of trade, the adoption of stringent country-of-origin rules and domestic-content requirements had the opposite effect. These rules and regulations are necessary in free trade areas, where each country retains the right to impose its own tariff rates. In their absence, external exporters can sell goods in the free trade area country with the lowest tariff rates with the intention of subsequently reexporting them—free of additional duties—to countries in the free trade area with higher tariff rates.

Rules of origin refer to regulations that determine where a particular good has been produced and hence determine whether a good can be sent from one country in a free trade area to another country duty-free. The International Convention for the Simplification and Standardization of Customs Formalities, signed in Kyoto, Japan, in May 1973, established two criteria to determine a product's national origin. The first refers to goods that are wholly produced in a single country, whereas the second deals with the origin of goods, parts of which are produced in different countries. The identification of goods in the first category poses no problem. For a good in the second category to be considered as originating in a country, the convention requires that that country be the site where the good underwent a "substantial transformation." Unfortunately, the convention is silent regarding the definition of *substantial transformation*; hence during any negotiation regarding national origin negotiators were given wide leeway to define the term as they saw fit.

NAFTA provides three different ways for classifying a good as having been produced in the region. The most obvious is when the good is produced entirely in one or another of the regional countries. Second, goods produced with materials derived from countries outside the region can still be classified as regionally produced if material inputs undergo a change in tariff classifications as a result of operations performed upon them within the region. Finally, goods produced with materials derived from outside the region, even though they do not undergo a change in tariff classifications as a result of operations performed on them within the region, can still be classified as regionally produced if the value added within the region is equal to or exceeds 60 percent of the transaction value or 50 percent of the net cost. Upon U.S. insistence, the domestic-content requirement for motor vehicles was increased from 50 percent of national content at the outset to 56 percent in 1998 (and to 62.5 percent by the year 2002). Special rules were also designed for the textile and clothing industries. To be defined as *regionally produced*, cotton yarn or thread had to be made exclusively with regionally produced cotton, and regionally produced garments had to contain only regionally produced fabric.

These stringent domestic-content requirements obviously provide additional protection for the region's producers of inputs. In addition, however, they inhibit outside foreign direct investors. Japanese automobile transplants in Mexico, for example, tend to place heavy reliance on Japanese-made parts. If these automobiles do not qualify as having been produced in the region because they cannot meet the domestic-content requirement, and hence cannot be sold duty-free in the United States and Canada, a major incentive for establishing assembly plants in Mexico will have disappeared. In the absence of empirical analysis on a case-to-case basis, it is not possible to determine whether the protectionist impact of the rules-of-origin and domestic-content requirements is greater than or less than the liberalizing effect resulting from the reduction in intra-area tariffs.

From the U.S. vantage point, the opening of important Mexican service markets was arguably even more significant than the reduction in Mexican tariffs and trade barriers. Prior to NAFTA, Mexico denied many foreign service vendors access to its markets. To remedy the situation the United States insisted that Mexico extend to U.S. firms in the finance, land transportation, and telecommunication sectors the right of establishment and national treatment. As with the removal of tariffs, provisions were made for a transitional period. In this case the provisions assumed the form of numerical quotas. Specifically, NAFTA provides that the share of Mexican markets controlled by U.S. banks may not exceed 15 percent of the total by the year 2000 or 25 percent of the total by the year 2004. After that date, however, market forces would determine the extent of the U.S. share. For brokerages, the U.S. share was not to exceed 30 percent by the year 2000, after which the market again would be free to determine the outcome. In the land transportation sector, the parties agreed to allow truckers of all three countries to drive their vehicles anywhere in the region by the year 2000. In addition, U.S. and Canadian trucking companies were granted authorization to acquire majority ownership in Mexican firms by the year 2000.

NAFTA is also noteworthy for developing a comprehensive investment code of behavior. GATT's inability to agree to an investment code was a leading factor in the perception that the multilateral trading system could no longer be relied upon to solve increasingly difficult problems. Indeed, the code embodied in NAFTA has been widely hailed as a prototype for a more general code, which is currently being developed under the aegis of OECD. In essence, NAFTA's investment code calls for the right of establishment, the extension of national treatment to foreign investors, the elimination of all performance requirements, the right to repatriate both capital and earnings, the prohibition of confiscation of foreign properties without appropriate remuneration, and respect for intellectual property rights. In addition, the three countries agreed to refer all disputes arising in the investment sector to the dispute settlement mechanism established in NAFTA and to accept binding arbitration by the adjudicating panels.

In addition to liberalizing trade in the goods and service sectors, NAFTA broke new ground by addressing two issues that are rapidly becoming priority items on the trade agenda, namely, the relationship between trade and the environment and that between trade and labor standards (see discussion in Chapter 10).[10] Although it would not be quite correct to suggest that these issues dominated the negotiations, they did play important roles during the actual negotiations and during the process of selling the agreement to the U.S. Congress and public. Organized labor and environmental groups were among NAFTA's strongest opponents. Labor's opposition reflected the fear that NAFTA would open the gates to labor-intensive imports (thereby adversely affecting U.S. wages) and that U.S. firms, seduced by cheap Mexican labor, would relocate south of the border. Environmentalists feared that increased competition with Mexico would lead to a "race to the bottom" insofar as environmental standards were concerned. They also expressed the fear that the anticipated expansion of the maquiladora system resulting from the adoption of NAFTA would lead to further contamination of rivers and water supplies on both sides of the border and to an increase in infectious diseases.

To placate these two powerful interest groups and to moderate their criticism—even if their support for the agreement could not be obtained—U.S. negotiators insisted on addressing these problems in the agreement proper as well as in side agreements addressing labor and environmental standards. Thus, the preamble to NAFTA urges signatories to adopt measures that would raise environmental standards. Signatories affirm that in the event of a conflict between obligations undertaken by signing on to outside environmental agreements—including the Montreal Protocol, the Basel Convention, and the Convention of International Trade and Endangered Species—and those they assumed by signing NAFTA, the former would take precedence over the latter. In various NAFTA articles, environmental concerns were specifically cited. Thus, in the sanitary and phytosanitary provisions of the agreement, participating countries are given the right to exceed international standards, even if trade is constrained. In the investment section of NAFTA, countries retain the right to impose whatever standards they deem necessary regardless of the impact higher standards might have on trade and investments.

The side agreement on the environment calls for the establishment of the North American Commission for Environmental Cooperation, headed by a council of top environmental officers from each country. The major function of the commission is to ensure that the three countries rigorously enforce their *own* environmental laws and that the public be included in the monitoring process. In addition, two institutions, the North American Development Bank and the United States–Mexican Border Environmental Cooperative Commission, were established to identify and help fund environmental infrastructural projects on both sides of the border. And though the side agreement does not adopt minimum standards as urged by U.S. environmentalists, it does prohibit lowering environmental standards in order to lure foreign investors.

Short of mandating a large increase in Mexican wages and imposing labor standards as stringent as those existing in the United States, organized labor's disaffection with NAFTA could not be overcome. Although labor's demands could not be satisfied, a second side agreement did attempt to ameliorate some of the worst fears. The agreement calls for the establishment of a commission for labor cooperation, the governing body of which would be a council consisting of three cabinet-level officers, one from each country, as well as the establishment of national administrative offices in each country. These institutions are responsible for ensuring that labor laws and regulations in each country are rigorously enforced. In the event of a persistent failure to enforce such laws and regulations, the side agreement authorizes sanctioning the imports of the offending party. The labor laws and regulations to be enforced consist of, in addition to the ILO's core rights (i.e., freedom of association, the right to organize, the right to bargain collectively, the right to strike, and the prohibition of forced labor), the protection of children, minimum employment standards, the principle of equal pay for equal work, minimum safety standards in the work place, compensation for occupational illness and injuries, and the protection of migrant workers. (The question whether more advanced countries should impose more rigorous environmental and labor standards on less-developed partners is examined in greater detail in Chapter 10.)

A third side agreement addresses transitional problems. A safeguard-like provision authorizes each country to temporarily reinstate trade barriers if an unexpected surge in imports causes or threatens to cause injury to domestic industries. In addition, the United States established a transitional adjustment assistance fund to help workers who, as a result of an increase in imports from Mexico or of the relocation of U.S. firms to Mexico, either lose their jobs or are reduced to part-time status.

In summary, NAFTA broke new ground in the service, investment, labor, and environmental areas. The agreements could not have been reached in a multilateral setting. In a multilateral framework, Mexico would have been required to extend the negotiated concessions to all GATT members without receiving anything of value in return. The MFN principle, after all, already ostensibly gave Mexico access to the U.S. market and to most other world markets as well. What Mexico gained in return for these concessions was *continued assured access* to the U.S. market and, presumably, a degree of immunity from antidumping and countervailing suits and 301 actions initiated by the United States. Unless the United States had been prepared to cease using those instruments of protection across the board, which of course it was not and is not willing to do, Mexico could not have obtained counterconcessions in a multilateral setting.

However, these were not the aspects of NAFTA that the Clinton administration chose to emphasize. Rather, it went to pains to emphasize that this exercise in bloc-building was just the beginning and that NAFTA should be regarded as a "complement rather than an alternative to United States multilateral efforts."[11] NAFTA was described as an example of "open regionalism" that set the foundations for a world with "several overlapping open pluralistic arrangements with the United States playing a leadership role in North America, Asia and Latin America."[12] To achieve these objectives, as we note above, the United States committed to creating a free trade area embracing the Americas by the year 2005 and to joining in the effort to eliminate trade and investment barriers in the Asia-Pacific by the year 2020.

THE COMPATIBILITY OF PREFERENTIAL AGREEMENTS AND A MULTILATERAL TRADING SYSTEM

Despite the Clinton administration's assurance that regional trade agreements are fully compatible with a multilateral trading system, doubts remain. For instance, there is no way of knowing a priori whether a specific agreement will promote or impede movement toward global free trade. On a general level, the most that can be done is to specify the more important factors that will influence the outcome. Heading the list is the factor featured by professor Jacob Viner in a pioneering study that appeared in 1950.[13] Viner's major conclusion is that a preferential trade agreement has a positive impact if it results, on balance, in trade creation; it has a negative impact if it results, on balance, in trade diversion. *Trade creation* occurs when, as a result of the formation of a preferential trade area, participating countries shift demand from less efficient to more efficient sources of supply. In contrast, *trade diversion* occurs when the formation of a free trade area results in a shift of demand from more efficient to less efficient sources of supply.

To illustrate how the formation of a free trade area can lead to trade creation, we assume a world of three countries: Country A, Country B, and Country C. Of the three, Country A is assumed to be the least efficient producer of widgets; its cost of production exceeds Country B's by 15 percent and Country C's by 20 percent. To protect its inefficient industry from foreign competition, Country A levies a 25 percent tariff on all widgets and relies on its inefficient producer for all its widget needs. Now, assume that Country A and Country B form a free trade area and that the 25 percent external tariff remains in effect. Since Country B is a more efficient producer of widgets than Country A, and since its widgets are no longer subject to the tariff, Country A's consumers will now shift their demand away from the inefficient domestic producers and toward Country B's more efficient producers. The formation of a free trade area has thus resulted in a shift away from a less efficient source, Country A's producers, to a more efficient source, Country B's producers. This is *trade creation*, and Country A's economic welfare will have been increased as a result. Note, however, that had the tariff reduction been extended to Country C's products as well, Country A's economic welfare would have increased by even more.

To illustrate how the formation of a free trade area can lead to trade diversion, consider the following. Prior to the formation of a free trade area, Country A does not produce widgets, whereas Country B and Country C do. Country A purchases all its widgets from Country C, whose producers can sell their widgets on world markets at a price 5 percent lower than can the producers of Country B. Although Country A is not a widget producer, it does impose a 10 percent tariff on widgets for the purpose of raising revenue. Now, assume that Country A and Country B form a free trade area. Although Country C can still sell its widgets on *world* markets at a price 5 percent lower than Country B, Country A will now divert its demand for widgets from Country C, the more efficient producer, to Country B, the less efficient producer. The reasons for this should be obvious: Country C's 5 percent efficiency margin over Country B is more than wiped out by the 10 percent tariff that is still imposed on Country C's widgets yet no longer imposed on Country B's widgets. The formation of a free trade area in this example leads to *trade diversion* and to a reduction in Country A's economic welfare.

The Vinerian conclusion—that welfare would be enhanced if trade creation outweighs trade diversion—is unambiguous. Yet the difficulties in predicting the outcome are severe and become even more so when the assumptions underlying the exercise are changed so that the three-country world becomes a multicountry world and that countries excluded from the original preferential group can join up to form their own preferential groups. And though economists have developed so-called gravity models to determine the degree to which the formation of a preferential trade area enhances intraregional trade beyond that which would occur on proximity and income grounds, and hence provide the basis for estimating whether diversion has occurred, the ability to predict the outcome of a regional agreement, or even to estimate its effects after the event, remain precarious.[14]

The fundamental question under these circumstances, as posed by Jagdish Bhagwati, is this: "Will regionalism lead to non-discriminatory free trade for all through continued expansion of the regional blocs until universal free trade is realized, or will it fragment the world economy?"[15] Slightly rephrased, the question is this: Can a rule-based, nondiscriminatory trading system develop in the absence of the MFN principle?

We gain some insight into this question by comparing the trading system that emerged at the end of the nineteenth century, which lasted until the outbreak of World War I, with that of the interwar period. In a brilliant essay, professor Douglas A. Irwin demonstrates that the choice of the *approach* to trade liberalization—multilateralism or bilateralism—is less significant than whether or not trade is governed by the MFN principle. In the late nineteenth century, he argues, "a network of treaties containing the most favored nations clause spurred major tariff reductions in Europe and around the world. These treaties ushered in a harmonious period of multilateral free trade that compares favorably with, and in certain respects was superior to, the recent GATT era."[16] In contrast, the erosion of the MFN principle during the interwar period, which led to "discriminatory trade blocs and protectionist bilateral agreements," occurred despite the existence of "multilateral institutions and negotiations," which in some cases actually discouraged bilateral attempts at trade reform.[17]

Viewed in this way, the fundamental question is whether there is a way to preserve the *dominance* of the MFN principle while also allowing countries to pursue preferential free trade arrangements. Some students believe we can achieve the best of both worlds. Robert Hudec has argued that with a well-established multilateral system—as exemplified by GATT and its successor, the WTO—some violations of the MFN principle can be tolerated. He contrasts the significance of the MFN principle in a system where trade relations are entirely bilateral with that in a world of multilateral trade relationships:

> When relations are entirely bilateral one's trading partners will always have a network of their own bilateral relations with the rest of the world, and thus will constantly be engaged in entirely separate negotiations with other countries—negotiations that can undermine the commercial value of one's own existing agreement with them. That is what happened during the 1930s when the world got caught up in a continually expanding series of preferential bilateral deals. When bilateralism reigns the only way to avert such

breakdowns is to have a vigorous most favored nations guarantee covering the entire interlocking network of bilateral trade relationships. The GATT created a different world. It was a world of multilateral trade relationships where everyone dealt with everyone else at the same time, and all agreements were locked in to a set of permanent rules applicable to all. In this setting, it was possible to make discrimination less destructive. The key was to define the extent of discrimination in advance and to impose reliable controls against severe changes. To the extent that this can be done, discrimination becomes essentially just another form of protection, no more dangerous than a high tariff. The key is to establish multilateral controls that remove— or at least limit—its unpredictability.[18]

J. Michael Finger, though criticizing GATT's formal reactions to discriminatory free trade agreements—in his view GATT never met a regional trade agreement it did not like—nevertheless tends to agree with Hudec's assessment. For Finger—and possibly for Hudec as well—the importance of WTO-GATT, at least with regard to preferential trade agreements, is less in the formal role assigned to it than in providing countries the opportunity to seek redress in the event they sustain injury as a result of being excluded from a free trade area. According to Finger, "The value of market access that countries have bargained for is a powerful motivation for GATT's procedures. The instinct of countries when the value of the markets it has bargained for is compromised, is to bargain that value back again. Mercantilistic self-interest has proved to be an effective guard against the abuse of discrimination."[19] Given these circumstances, Finger concludes that "the international community can thus take a relaxed attitude toward regional arrangements. Any arrangement that clearly removes trade restrictions deserves the benefit of the doubt. But countries that negotiate regional arrangements must be prepared to negotiate the discriminatory arrangements with their outside trading partners."[20]

The case for regional free trade agreements is further bolstered by two considerations. The first, as we have already noted, is that with 126 members in the WTO, each with its own set of preferences and priorities, it may be impossible—as the United States has argued in recent years—to reach agreement on anything, let alone *further* progress toward an open economy. In these circumstances, the regional approach may be the best available alternative. The second consideration, as professor Anne Krueger notes, is that the available empirical evidence suggests preferential trade areas "have, on balance, more likely been trade creating [rather] than trade diverting"[21] and that the proliferation of preferential trade areas have, at least to the present, not come at the expense of multilateralism.

These considerations, however, have done little to alleviate the disquiet of those who believe the ultimate outcome of proliferating regional agreements will be a tripolar world dominated by three power centers: the European Union, North America, and East Asia. Underlying their disquiet is the belief that these regions are intrinsically antagonistic and that power parity will inevitably lead to economic warfare. Although there is certainly the possibility that this will occur, an alternative scenario can be imagined. The emergence of three centers, each as powerful as the others, could create a more open, less discriminatory system than was ever envisaged by the original signatories of GATT at the dawn of the postwar period or by the 126 members of the World Trade Organization.

12

CONCLUSION:
IS THE GLOBALIZATION PROCESS IN
THE WINTER OF ITS DISCONTENT?

At least since 1973, the globalization process has been held responsible for a wide variety of ills—both real and imagined—confronting the U.S. economy. An examination of the available evidence, however, fails to support allegations that globalization has been the primary factor responsible for the stagnation of wages, the increase in income inequality, the relative decline of employment in the manufacturing sector, and the decline in the rate of growth of productivity. Neither does the evidence suggest that the removal of trade and investment barriers has led to a mass exodus of U.S. firms to low-wage emerging economies, deprived the United States of much needed capital, and put at risk rigorous U.S. environmental and labor standards. Finally, it would be difficult to find support for the often repeated argument that U.S. membership in GATT, or in its successor, the WTO, has in any way infringed upon U.S. sovereignty and exposed the United States to the machinations of its trading partners.

Globalization has resulted in some job displacement, particularly in the unskilled labor–intensive import-substitute industries, which were particularly hard-hit by the expansion of manufactured imports from emerging economies. This, however, has been more than offset both by an expansion of employment opportunities in the service sector—at wages not substantially less than the displaced workers earned in previous positions, at times even at a somewhat higher wage level—and by an increase in the number of jobs in the expanding export industries. The Council of

Economic Advisors recently estimated that one-third of new jobs created between 1992 and 1997 was due to the expansion of exports.

The gains accruing to the United States as a result of the globalization process were not achieved at the expense of their trading partners. Globalization increased the economic welfare of virtually every participating country. This was particularly true for emerging economies, for whom the expansion of trade and of foreign direct investments provided opportunities never before available. Indeed, by mid-1997, just before the Asian economic crisis erupted, the level of per capita income of a number of these countries rose almost to that of some of the more-developed economies.

Despite this impressive record, the future progress of globalization is by no means assured. The major reason is that the process, as we indicate in the Introduction, is policy-driven. Globalization occurred in large part because the major participating countries and their firms, each pursuing their own national and corporate interests, wanted it to occur and adopted policies that together with technological developments enabled it to occur. Understanding this is crucial in evaluating the future of the globalization process. If this process was driven by technology, as many in fact argue, the outcome would be more or less determined. Contrary to this deterministic view, however, the argument presented here is that the future of globalization depends very much on whether participating countries and corporations continue to believe that it promotes their interests.

In democratic societies, perceptions as to what constitutes national interest and how best to promote it are greatly influenced by the relative strengths of different interest groups. In the United States, for example, the fate of proposals that would result in closer integration of the U.S. economy with the world economy will be determined in large part by the relative strengths—measured in units of voting power—of those supporting these proposals and those opposing them. In authoritarian societies, in contrast, particularly where corruption is rampant, national interest is more clearly linked to the interests of the ruling clique. A case in point is former Indonesian Pres. Suharto's last-minute proposal to establish a currency board that would "decree" an increase in the value of the rupia, a proposal that was widely regarded as an attempt to enhance and preserve his family's fortune despite the potentially devastating effect on the Indonesian economy. This would suggest that any effort to evaluate prospects for the future of the globalization process should place greater emphasis on an assessment of the forces supporting and opposing the process than on the historical record of its effects. The remainder of this Conclusion attempts to do precisely that.

OPPOSITION TO GLOBALIZATION
IN THE UNITED STATES

In general, support for the continuation of the globalization process would appear to be more robust in the United States than in almost any other country. The major reason is that the continuation of this process is not likely to impose on the U.S. economy difficult transformational imperatives. The United States has already taken important steps toward rationalizing and deregulating its industries. As a result, it entered the last decade of the twentieth century as the most competitive country in the world. In addition, its highly flexible labor markets have, at the present, enabled economic growth to be translated into new jobs. At the end of 1997, 122 million Americans were employed, and the rate of unemployment was reduced to less than 5 percent of the labor force.

Because of the success of the U.S. economy in recent years, major opposition to the globalization process has come mainly from nativists, organized labor, some environmental groups, and import-sensitive industries. Acting alone, none of these groups can significantly influence U.S. trade policy; together, they have succeeded in mounting formidable opposition to attempts to extend the globalization process. This is demonstrated by the narrow margins by which Congress ratified both NAFTA and the Uruguay Round agreements, the rejection of Pres. Bill Clinton's request to extend fast-track authorization, and the resistance to the proposal to increase the financial resources available to the IMF. In general, however, it is widely conceded that at present the influence of the opposition groups, though not negligible, is limited and will not likely be able to reverse the globalization process. However, if the U.S. economy stumbled into a recession, or if the remarkable job-creating machine sputtered, the ranks of those opposed to globalization would almost certainly increase. Accordingly, the possibility that they would then be able to stay the liberalization process, if not actually to reverse it, cannot be dismissed out of hand.

It is important to note, however, that U.S. support for this process remains strong. For one thing, during the entire postwar period the executive branch, whether controlled by the Democrats or the Republicans, acted as a bulwark against congressional demands for increased protection. More important, the increased integration of the U.S. economy with the world economy has created a new pressure group that acts as a powerful counterweight against the old established one that traditionally has lobbied for protectionism. This new group, comprising industrial firms with heavy global involvement—whether exporters of finished goods, importers of intermediate inputs, or owners of foreign-based affiliates—has lobbied against the imposition of protectionist measures as vigorously as the traditional import-sensitive industries, organized labor, and some environmental groups have lobbied in favor of them.[1]

OPPOSITION TO GLOBALIZATION IN WESTERN EUROPE

The prospects for the future of globalization in some other countries—both advanced and emerging—are, if anything, murkier. Unlike the situation in the United States, in Western Europe the globalization process is likely to be a transformational phenomenon for many countries. As such, it poses a direct challenge to the established order. The basic question is whether their institutions can adapt to meet the imperatives of globalization without stirring up massive opposition from those who will, in the process, be adversely affected.

The conflict between the imperatives of globalization and the welfare states, which has existed in Western Europe since the end of World War II, is a case in point. The highly commendable basic objective of the welfare state was to produce a more equitable society. Minimum wages were set at high levels, and numerous social funds financed by employers were established to provide a variety of fringe benefits, including inter alia generous pension schemes, medical insurance plans, paid vacation plans, day care plans, funeral plans, and, of course, extremely generous unemployment benefit plans. In addition, the politically powerful unions—particularly in, but not limited to, France—succeeded in imposing other regulations that further increased the costs of hire and made it extremely difficult, if not impossible, to discharge redundant workers.

These policies had two adverse impacts on European economies. First, the high level of wages and the taxes levied on corporations to finance social funds drove up the costs of hire as well as prices for European-produced goods. The increase in the costs of hire discouraged firms from employing as many workers as they would have had such costs been lower, whereas the increase in prices reduced competitiveness on world markets. Second, the difficulty in discharging redundant workers acted as a deterrent to the introduction of labor-saving technologies that would have increased factor productivity. The net effect of these policies was to produce high unemployment whenever the growth rate was insufficient to absorb the growing labor force. At the end of 1997, for example, unemployment was 13.2 percent in Belgium, 12.4 percent in France, 11.9 percent in Germany, 12.2 percent in Italy, and 20.6 percent in Spain.

It is clear that the globalization process poses a threat to the continued existence of the welfare state. To compete in a global market, firms have to be as efficient as their competitors. They must be able to introduce new technology, even if that means displacing workers. They will not be able to finance the social funds, which form the backbone of the welfare state, if that drives up prices to a level that makes those firms uncompetitive. At present, Western European countries are at a crossroad. Decisions must be made whether to maintain the welfare state in its present form or to deregulate and rationalize their economies to enable them to compete successfully on the world market and to eliminate the high rates of unemployment. To some extent this issue has already been joined in Western Europe, but it has not by any means been resolved. During the 1977 campaign leading up to the parliamentary elections in France, for example, the Socialist Party program called for an *extension* of the welfare state by proposing a reduction in the length of the working week, from thirty-nine hours to thirty-five hours, without a reduction in wages as well as the creation of 350,000 additional jobs in the state sector. The Socialist Party platform denounced the pressures of the global economy as "a return to the cruelty of nineteenth-century capitalism."[2] De Gaullist politicians, in contrast, broke away, at least temporarily, from their long-held position of denouncing the so-called Anglo-American economic model—their pejorative name for the global economy—by advocating an increase in privatization, a reduction in taxes, and increased deregulation in order to "insert France in a world on the move."[3] Even France's vaunted minimum-wage policy was attacked by France's Senate president, M. Monory, who during the campaign asked whether it was better to have 1 million young people unemployed due to the high level of the minimum wage or to reduce the minimum wage, from 6,000 francs to 4,500 francs per month, in order to generate jobs for them.[4] The future course of globalization—not only in France but elsewhere in Western Europe—will depend in large part on the outcome of this debate.

And that outcome is still not predictable. On the one hand, French leftist parties won the 1997 parliamentary elections, indicating the public's preference for a continuation of the welfare state and a rejection of the Anglo-American model. On the other hand, the new French government, once empowered, embraced—despite strong public protest—the stringent fiscal and monetary policies of the previous administration in order to qualify for admission to the European Union's single currency program. Does this suggest that there is a hidden agenda behind the single currency program? And if it does, is this agenda designed to wean member countries away from the welfare state and make them more competitive players in the global economy, as many believe? Or is it designed to achieve a greater degree of integration to enable the EU to limit its participation in the global marketplace in order to preserve welfare states?

GLOBALIZATION AND THE LESS-DEVELOPED COUNTRIES

The greatest challenge to the globalization process at the present time, however, comes from the emerging economies, the erstwhile highflying Asian Tigers. Until recently, few would have challenged the statements that these economies were major beneficiaries of the globalization process or that their commitment to the continuation of the process was ensured. As a result of the crisis, however, which was signaled by the collapse of Thailand's baht in the summer of 1997 and which subsequently engulfed Indonesia, Malaysia, South Korea, Hong Kong, and, outside of Asia, Russia and Brazil, the future of the globalization process has been called into question. Two countries, Malaysia and Russia, have already reimposed capital controls, and a number of prominent economists who are among the foremost supporters of the globalization process have suggested, in the words of Professor Bhagwati, that "the notion that the optimum world is one characterized by free capital flows will have to be relinquished" and that the system will have to be rethought "in a big way."[5]

Because there is always the danger in times of crisis that the baby will be thrown away with the bathwater, it is important to emphasize that although the increased exposure of the Asian economies to external economic forces unquestionably contributed to and exacerbated the crisis, it was not the primary cause for it. It is true that the crisis was triggered by a huge withdrawal of funds by foreign lenders, investors, and speculators and that these withdrawals induced the severe currency devaluations that drove many banks and corporations with large foreign currency–denominated debt into bankruptcy, but it is also true that before these withdrawals occurred internal developments eroded the fundamental underpinning of the economies and put them at risk. Indeed, it can be argued that this erosion was one of the reasons, but certainly not the only one, for the massive withdrawal of funds.

Although it is beyond the scope of this study to examine the genesis and evolution of the Asian crisis in depth, the major underlying internal factors are clearly discernible. They include rampant speculation fueled by bank loans that drove the prices of real estate and equities to astronomical levels; the decimation of the banks' capital base when the value of the collateral on their loans collapsed after the speculative bubble burst; the tendency of the banks and corporations to place heavy reliance on short-term debt denominated in foreign currencies to finance their operations, which made them extremely vulnerable when their currencies were devalued; the large and increasing current account and budgetary deficits that were financed by short-term loans denominated in foreign currencies; the pervasiveness of crony capitalism, which ensured that those politically well connected would get financing, no matter how dubious their proposals, not only resulting in a misallocation of the available capital but also exposing banks to additional risks when these loans went bad; rampant corruption; the failure of government to provide accurate information regarding the state of their economies, which reduced the ability of lenders and creditors to properly assess risks; the failure of the banks' regulatory agencies to do their job; and the reliance on accounting methods that did not meet international standards and did not reveal accurately the financial positions of banks and corporations until it was too late.

In light of all this, it is clear that even in the absence of adverse external developments the emerging economies were in trouble. But unfortunately, adverse external developments added to their travails. Two of the more important of these were the profound Japanese depression that reduced the value of exports that these economies could sell in their most important external market and impacted the operations of the Japanese foreign affiliates located in the emerging economies; and the huge amounts of speculative funds—"hot money"—that can, with the click of a mouse, be shifted from one market to another. Of the two, the second is the more significant. In time, Japan will get its house in order and resume its role as the second largest global economy. What can be done about the footloose speculative funds is more problematic.

On any given day, currencies valued at hundred of billions of dollars are shifted from one form of currency into another. The owners of these funds are not interested in long-term investments but rather quick profits either through arbitrage—that is, taking advantage of slight differences in the cross-currency values in different markets—or by anticipating changes in the currency's value. Although normally these funds have little effect, on occasion they can roil the currency markets. This can occur when the speculators take a position against a currency, as they did against the British pound in 1992, against the Thai baht and other Asian emerging economies' currencies in 1997, and against Russia and Brazil in 1998. If, as is often the case, the beleaguered country does not have sufficient international reserves to ward off these attacks, the country will be forced to devalue its currency, with devastating impact on the real economy.

Since these flows serve no significant social function, an attempt to curb them by creating disincentives—through taxing these transactions or setting time limits on how long these currencies must be held before they can be sold—would undoubtedly strengthen the global economy, and it is hoped that measures to achieve this will be put into effect as quickly as possible. It is important, however, that the methods used to curb these hot money flows do not end up posing more problems than they resolve, as would be the case if they had an adverse effect on those crossborder flows that do, in fact, serve a very important function particularly for the emerging economies.

With the crisis still unresolved, however, we are left to ponder a number of questions that it has brought to the fore. To what extent has the disclosure of the emerging economies' vulnerability influenced their attitude toward the globalization process? Will these economies be willing in the future to further open their markets to imports and foreign direct investments within a multilateral setting, or will they seek the safe haven of preferential arrangements? Will foreign investors be prepared to return again to the region? Does the global economy require a new architecture, as suggested by a number of economists, and if so, what form should this architecture assume? In view of the hostility that some emerging economies have displayed toward the IMF, are other institutions required to oversee the necessary reforms and to provide a degree of stability in times of crisis? It is well beyond the scope of this study to explore these questions. Indeed, they are raised here largely to emphasize the policy-driven nature of the globalization process and to stress that its continued existence, despite the positive impact this process has had on world economic welfare, cannot be taken for granted.

NOTES

CHAPTER 1

1. See, for example, Robert Kuttner, *The End of Laissez-Faire: National Purpose and the Global Economy After the Cold War* (New York: Alfred Knopf, 1991).

2. International Monetary Fund (hereinafter IMF), *International Financial Statistics* (monthly), various issues.

3. Ibid. It should be noted that exports from the Soviet bloc lagged behind industrial and developing economies. Between 1970 and 1990, the Soviet bloc's share of world exports declined from 10 percent to 5 percent. See United Nations (hereinafter UN), *Handbook of International Trade* (Geneva: UN, 1993).

4. Derived from data in IMF, *International Financial Statistics*, various issues.

5. UN, *Handbook of International Trade*.

6. Organization for Economic Cooperation and Development (hereinafter OECD), *International Capital Markets Statistics, 1950–1995* (Paris: OECD, 1997), pp. 14–16.

7. See Chapters 4 and 12.

8. United Nations Conference on Trade and Development (hereinafter UNCTAD), *World Investment Report 1996: Investment, Trade, and International Policy Arrangements* (New York and Geneva, 1996), pp. 8–9.

9. Ibid., p. 98.

10. Ibid., p. 17.

11. Ibid., p. 37.

12. Andrew W. Wyckoff, "The International Expansion of Productive Networks," in *OECD Observer* 180 (Feb.-March 1993): 8.

13. Ibid., p. 9.

14. UNCTAD, *World Investment Report 1995: Transnational Corporations and Competitiveness* (New York and Geneva, 1995), p. 38. The UN estimates that "worldwide sales by foreign affiliates plus sales associated with worldwide licensing . . . as a percentage of world exports (goods and non-factor services) were 108 percent in 1992," p. 38.

CHAPTER 2

1. See Sebastian Edwards, "Openness, Productivity, and Growth: What Do We Really Know?" *Economic Journal* 108 (March 1998): 383–398; James Harrigan, "Openness to Trade in Manufactures in the OECD," *Journal of International Economics* 44 (1996): 23–38; World Bank, *World Development Report 1987* (Washington: World Bank, 1987).

2. See Moses Abramowitz, *Resource and Output Trends in the United States Since 1870* (Occasional Paper No. 52) (New York: National Bureau of Economic Research, 1956); Robert Solow, "Technical Progress, Capital Formation, and Economic Growth," *American Economics Review* 52 (May 1962): 76–86; Edward F. Denison, *The Sources of Economic Growth in the United States and the Alternatives Before Us* (New York: Committee for Economic Development, 1962), and *Why Growth Rates Differ* (Washington, D.C.: Brookings Institution, 1967).

3. Bronislaw Kasper Malinowski, *Argonauts of the Western Pacific: An Account of Native Enterprise and Adventure in the Archipelagoes of Melanisian New Guinea* (New York: Dutton, 1961).

4. David Ricardo, *The Principles of Political Economy and Taxation* (London: J. M. Dent and Sons, 1911; orig. publ. 1817), chap. 7.

5. For a history of the comparative cost principle and of the concept of free trade, see Douglas A. Irwin, *Against the Tide: An Intellectual History of Free Trade* (Princeton: Princeton University Press, 1996).

6. See Eli Hecksher, "The Effect of Foreign Trade on the Distribution of Income," *Ekonomick Tidscrift* 21 (1919): 447–512, reprinted in American Economic Association, *Readings in the Theory of International Trade* (Philadelphia: Blakiston, 1949), chap. 13; and Bertril Ohlin, *Interregional and International Trade* (Cambridge: Harvard University Press, 1933).

7. Gary Becker, *Human Capital: A Theoretical and Empirical Analysis* (New York: Bureau of Economic Research, 1964).

8. Dilip K. Das, "Changing Comparative Advantage and the Changing Composition of Asian Exports," *World Economy* 21:1 (Jan. 1998): 121–140.

9. See Paul Krugman, "Increasing Returns, Monopolistic Competition, and International Trade," *Journal of International Economics* 9 (Nov. 1979): 469–479; also see David Greenway and Chris Milner, *The Economics of Intra-Industry Trade* (Oxford: Blackwell, 1986), chaps. 2–3; and Elhanan Helpman and Paul Krugman, *Market Structure and Foreign Trade* (Cambridge: MIT Press, 1985).

10. Joseph Schumpeter, *Capitalism, Socialism, and Democracy*, 3d ed. (New York: Harper and Brothers, 1950), pp. 84–85.

11. McKinsey Global Institute, *Manufacturing Productivity* (Washington, D.C.: Oct. 1993).

12. Martin Baily and Hans Gerbach, "Efficiency in Manufacturing and the Need for Global Competition," *Brookings Papers: Microeconomics* (1995): 346.

13. Ibid., p. 308.

14. Editorial, *The New York Times*, August 18, 1997.

15. See Jagdish Bhagwati and V. K. Ramaswami, "Domestic Distortions, Tariffs, and the Theory of Optimum Subsidy," *Journal of Political Economy* 71 (Feb. 1963).

16. See Gene M. Grossman, ed., *Imperfect Competition and International Trade* (Cambridge: MIT Press, 1992); Paul Krugman, ed., *Strategic Trade Policy and the New International Economics* (Cambridge: MIT Press, 1986), chaps. 2–4.

17. We should note that the increase in economic welfare resulting from the capture of the monopoly rents could be more than offset by a reduction in welfare due to the adverse redistributional effects.

18. See Paul Krugman, "Strategic Sectors and International Competition," in Robert Stern, ed., *U.S. Trade Policies in a Changing World* (Cambridge: MIT Press, 1987), pp. 207–243.

19. See Mancur Olson, *The Logic of Collective Action: Public Goods and the Theory of Groups* (Cambridge: Harvard University Press, 1965).

20. See Helen Milner, *Resisting Protectionism: Global Industries and the Politics of International Trade* (Princeton: Princeton University Press, 1988).

21. Stephen Engelberg with Martin Tolchin, "Foreigners Find New Ally in U.S. Industry," *The New York Times*, November 2, 1993, p. 1.

22. Gary C. Hufbauer and Kimberly Ann Elliot, *Measuring the Costs of Protection in the United States* (Washington, D.C.: Institute for International Economics, 1994).

23. Council of Economic Advisors, *President's Economic Report 1995* (Washington, D.C.: U.S. Government Printing Office, 1995), p. 252.

Chapter 3

1. See John Jackson, *The World Trading System: Law and Policy of International Economic Relations* (Cambridge: MIT Press, 1992).

2. According to Irwin, the failure to bind tariffs was a major reason for the disintegration of the nineteenth-century free trade system, which permitted countries to backslide toward greater protection after 1879. See Douglas Irwin, "Multilateral and Bilateral Trade Policies in the World Trading Systems: An Historical Perspective," in Jaime De Melo and Arvind Panagariya, eds., *New Dimensions in Regional Integration* (Cambridge: Cambridge University Press, 1993), p. 100.

3. GATT Article 3, ¶¶ 1–7.

4. *The New York Times*, July 18, 1996.

5. GATT Article 20.

6. GATT Article 24.

7. See Jagdish Bhagwati, "Regionalism and Multilateralism: An Overview," in De Melo and Panagariya, *New Dimensions in Regional Integration*, p. 26.

8. Jackson, *World Trading System*, p. 278.

9. Ibid., p. 279.

10. GATT Article 19.

11. Jackson, *The World Trading System*, p. 166.

12. Brian Hindley, "Safeguards, Voluntary Export Restraints, and Anti Dumping Action," in Organization for Economic Cooperation and Development, *The New World Trading System: Readings* (Paris: OECD, 1994), p. 91.

13. GATT Articles 6 (Dumping) and 16 (Subsidies).

14. Jacob Viner, *Dumping: A Problem in International Trade* (Chicago: University of Chicago Press, 1923).

15. This theorem—known as third degree discrimination—demonstrates that a firm confronted with two demand curves of different elasticities—one domestic and one foreign—can maximize its profits by charging a higher price in the market with the less elastic demand than in the other market.

16. GATT Article 6.

17. Although the term *material injury* is not defined, it has been interpreted to be a lesser injury than the *serious injury* specified in the escape clause. See Jackson, *World Trading System*, p. 237.

18. See GATT Article 16, ¶¶ 2–5.

19. GATT Article 16, ¶ 4.

20. GATT Article 16, ¶ 3.

21. See Chapter 9.

22. See Jackson, *World Trading System*, p. 95.

23. L. A. Murray, "Unraveling Employment Trends in Textiles and Apparel," *Monthly Labor Review* (August 1995): p. 72, n. 24; also see GATT, *Textiles and Clothing in the World Economy* (Geneva: GATT, 1984).

24. Thomas L. Friedman, "Roll Over Hawks and Doves," *The New York Times*, February 2, 1997, editorial page.

CHAPTER 4

1. For a history of the Bretton Woods negotiations, see Richard Gardner, *Sterling-Dollar Diplomacy: Anglo-American Collaboration in the Reconstruction of Multilateral Trade* (Oxford: Oxford at the Clarendon Press, 1956).

2. The term *residents* includes persons, businesses, and governments whose home base is in the country designated.

3. We should note that not all changes in the value of foreign-owned assets are due to transactions recorded on the capital account. The value of these assets can increase or decline because of changes in their valuations rather than as a result of acquisitions or sales of assets.

4. See Barry Bluestone and Bennet Harrison, *The Great U Turn: Corporate Restructuring and the Polarization of America* (New York: Basic Books, 1988).

5. See Paul Kennedy, *The Rise and Fall of the Great Powers: Economic Change and Military Conflict from 1500 to 2000* (New York: Random House, 1987).

6. For a defense of a managed, fair trade policy, see Robert Kuttner, *The End of Laissez-Faire: National Purpose and the Global Economy After the Cold War* (New York: Alfred Knopf, 1991), pp. 122–157.

7. International Monetary Fund, *International Financial Statistics* (monthly).

8. See Paul Krugman, "The Myth of Asia's Miracle," *Foreign Affairs* 73:6 (Nov.-Dec. 1994): 62–78.

9. "A Survey on East Asian Economies: Special Insert," *The Economist* (March 7–13, 1998): 1–18.

10. See Chapter 12.

11. See, e.g., Robert Triffin, *Gold and the Dollar Crisis* (New Haven: Yale University Press, 1960).

12. The net investment position is based on the valuation of foreign direct investments at current prices. Evaluated at market prices, the U.S. net investment position became negative in 1980 and amounted to minus $831 billion in 1996.

CHAPTER 5

1. J. Warnke, "Computer Manufacturing: Changes and Competition," *Monthly Labor Review* (Aug. 1996): 26.

2. U.S. Department of Commerce, *U.S. Direct Investments Abroad* (Washington: Department of Commerce, October 1997).

3. José Campa and Linda S. Goldberg, "The Evolving External Orientation of Manufacturing: A Profile of Four Countries," *Federal Reserve Bank of New York: Economic Policy Review* 3:2 (July 1997): 53–81.

4. Ibid., p. 54.

5. See Louis P. Wells Jr., "Mobile Exporters: New Foreign Investors in East Asia," in K. A. Froot, ed., *Foreign Direct Investment* (Chicago: University of Chicago Press, 1993), pp. 175–195.

6. See M. A. Mann, D. J. Atherton, and L. L. Brokenbaugh, "United States International Sales and Purchases of Private Services," *Survey of Current Business* (Nov. 1996): 110.

7. Letter to the editor, *The New York Times*, March 30, 1997.

8. Wages are used here to denote the total cost of labor, which in addition to wages—in the literal sense—includes fringe benefits and taxes levied on payments to finance a variety of social benefits. The difference between wages and the total compensation of labor can be substantial. In 1994, for example, wages accounted for 80–85 percent of the costs of hire in Denmark and New Zealand; for 70–75 percent in the United States, Canada, Australia, Ireland, and the United Kingdom; for 60 percent in Japan; and for 50–60 percent in France, Germany, and Italy. In the same year, expenditures by employers on social insurance and other taxes levied on payrolls accounted for 30 percent of total compensation costs in Italy and France, for 23 percent in the United States, and for 15 percent in the emerging Asian economies. See Janet Kmitch, Pedro Labory, and Sarah Van Damme, "International Comparisons of Manufacturing Compensation," *Monthly Labor Review* (Oct. 1995): 7–10.

9. See Chinhui Juhn and Kevin M. Murphy, "Inequality in Labor Market Outcomes: Contrasting the 1980s and Earlier Decades,"*Federal Reserve Bank of New York: Economic Policy Review* (Jan. 1995): 30.

10. Robert Bednarzik, "An Analysis of U.S. Industries Sensitive to Foreign Trade, 1982–1987," *Monthly Labor Review* (Feb. 1993): 17.

11. Ibid., p. 21, table 2.

12. Excluding workers who were employed in the fur goods industries, in which hourly wages were $10.80. Derived from ibid., pp. 21–22, table 2.

13. Ibid., p. 25.

14. It should be noted that the view incorporated in the Federal Trade Adjustment Assistance Act, i.e., that workers displaced by imports suffer more severe problems than those who are displaced for other reasons, is not supported by the evidence, which suggests they are not disadvantaged relative to workers displaced for other reasons. See J. T. Addison, D. A. Fox, and G. J. Ruhm, "Trade and Displacement in Manufacturing," *Monthly Labor Review* (April 1995): 58.

15. Ibid., p. 65.

16. Frank Levy and Richard Murname, "U.S. Earnings Levels and Earnings Inequality: A Review of Recent Trends and Proposed Explanations," *Journal of Economic Literature* 30 (Sept. 1992): 1371.

17. Ibid., p. 1371.

18. Ibid., p. 1356.

19. Ibid.

20. Paul Samuelson, "International Factor-Price Equalization Once Again," *Economic Journal* 59 (June 1949): 181–197.

21. Paul Samuelson and Wolfgang Stolper, "Protection and Real Wages," *Review of Economic Studies* 9 (Nov. 1941): 58–73.

22. See Jacob Mincer, "Economic Development, Growth of Human Capital, and the Dynamics of Wage Structure," *Journal of Economic Growth* 1 (March 1995): 29–48; Jacob Mincer, "Human Capital, Technology, and the Wage Structure," in Jacob Mincer, ed., *Studies in Human Capital: Collected Essays of Jacob Mincer*, vol. 1 (Aldershot, England: Edward Elgar, 1993), pp. 366–405; Jacob Mincer, "Human Capital Responses to Technical Change," National Bureau of Economic Research (hereinafter NBER) Working Paper No. 3207. Also see Robert Topel, "Regional and Labor Mixes and the Determinants of Wage Inequality," *American Economic Review* 84 (May 1994): 17–22; and Richard Nelson and Edwin Phelps, "Investments in Humans, Technological Diffusion, and Economic Growth," *American Economic Review* 56 (May 1966): 69–75.

23. John Bound and George Johnson, "Changes in the Structure of Wages in the 1980s: An Evaluation of Alternative Explanations," *American Economic Review* 82 (June 1992): 380–382.

24. Ibid., p. 381.

25. Gary Burtless, "Worsening of American Income Inequality: Is World Trade to Blame?" *The Brookings Review* (Spring 1996): 29.

26. Ibid., p. 30.

27. Ibid., p. 30.

28. E. Berman, J. Bound, and Z. Griliches, "Changes in the Demand for Skilled Labor Within Manufacturing Industries: Evidence from the Annual Survey of Manufacturing," NBER Working Paper No. 4255, January 1993.

29. Marvin H. Kosters, "An Overview of Changing Wage Patterns in the Labor Market," in J. Bhagwati and M. H. Kosters, eds., *Trade and Wages: Leveling Wages Down?* (Washington, D.C.: AEI Press, 1994), p. 29.

30. Juhn and Murphy, "Inequality in Labor Market Outcomes," p. 27.

31. G. Borjas, R. Freeman, and L. Katz, "On the Labor Market Effects of Immigration and Trade," in G. Borjas and R. Freeman, eds., *Immigration and the Work Force* (Chicago: University of Chicago Press and NBER, 1992).

32. Jeffrey Sachs and Howard Schatz, "Trade and Jobs in United States Manufacturing," *Brookings Papers on Economic Activity* 1 (Washington, D.C.: Brookings Institution, 1994).

33. Ibid., p. 29.

34. Ibid., p. 34.

35. R. Cooper, "Discussion of Paul Krugman's *Growing World Trade: Causes and Consequences*," *Brookings Papers on Economic Activity* 1 (Washington, D.C.: Brookings Institution, 1995), p. 366; also see Richard Cooper, "Foreign Trade Wages and Unemployment," Discussion Paper 1701, Harvard Institute of Economic Research, Nov. 1994.

36. Cooper, "Discussion of Paul Krugman's *Growing World Trade*," p. 367.

37. A. Wood, "How Trade Hurt Unskilled Workers," *Journal of Economic Perspectives* (Summer 1995): 65.

38. Ibid.

39. Ibid.

40. Ibid., p. 67.

41. Ibid., p. 68.

42. Ibid.

43. R. Lawrence and M. Slaughter, "Trade and United States Wages: Great Sucking Sound or Small Hiccup?" in *Brookings Papers on Economic Activity* 2 (Microeconomics) (Washington, D.C.: Brookings Institution, 1993).

44. Sachs and Schatz, "Trade and Jobs in United States Manufacturing," pp. 39–40.

45. *Monthly Labor Review*, various issues.

CHAPTER 6

1. J. J. Servan-Schreiber, *The American Challenge* (New York: Atheneum, 1968).

2. See Elliot Zupnick, *Foreign Direct Investments in the U.S.* (New York: Foreign Policy Association, 1980).

3. See Rachel McCulloch, "New Perspectives on Foreign Direct Investment," in Kenneth A. Froot, ed. *Foreign Direct Investments* (Chicago: University of Chicago Press, 1993), pp. 37–58.

4. A *majority-owned foreign affiliate* is one in which a resident of the United States owns more than 50 percent of the affiliate's equity. MOFA data, rather than those relating to all affiliates, are used because gross product data are not available except for MOFAs. It should be noted, however, that even if this was not the case, the use of MOFA data rather than total affiliate data is desired on conceptual grounds. This is so because U.S. parents are in complete control over them, whereas only a 10 percent equity stake is required for a foreign company to be considered a U.S. affiliate. We should further note that in 1994 89 percent of all U.S. affiliates were majority-owned, and 80 percent of all affiliates were wholly-owned. See Raymond J. Mataloni Jr. and Mahnaz Fahim-Nader, "Operation of U.S. Multinational Companies: Preliminary Results from the 1994 Benchmark Survey," *Survey of Current Business* (Dec. 1996): 16.

5. For a discussion of the maquiladora system, see Jeffrey A. Hart, "Maquiladorization as a Global Process," in Steven Chan, ed., *Foreign Direct Investment in a Changing Global Economy* (New York: St. Martin's Press, 1993), pp. 25–37.

6. The relatively large U.S. content in the output of the affiliates located in emerging economies is another indication of the importance of the role these affiliates have played in the international production system. For MOFAs as a whole the imports from U.S.-based parents accounted for approximately 8 percent of the value of affiliate sales. For those affiliates located in emerging Asia, the ratio was 12 percent; for those in Latin America, 13 percent; and for those in Canada, 23 percent. Mahnaz Fahim-Nader and William Zeile, "Foreign Direct Investment in the United States: New Investments in 1996, Affiliate Operations in 1995," *Survey of Current Business* (June 1997): 62.

7. Mataloni and Fahim-Nader, "Operation of U.S. Multinational Companies," p. 25.

8. Norman Glickman and Douglas Woodward, *The New Competitors: How Foreign Investors Are Changing the United States* (New York: Basic Books, 1989), p. 176.

9. Cited in ibid., p. 177.

10. See United Nations Conference on Trade and Development (UNCTAD), *World Investment Report 1996: Investment, Trade, and International Policy Arrangements* (New York and Geneva, 1996), pp. 79–80.

11. L. A. Murray, "Unraveling Employment Trends in Textiles and Apparel," *Monthly Labor Review* (Aug. 1995): 67.

12. Letter to the Editor, *The New York Times*, June 21, 1996.

13. *The New York Times*, October 9, 1996, p. A-1.

CHAPTER 7

1. Cited in Elliot Zupnick, *Foreign Investment in the United States: Costs and Benefits* (New York: Foreign Policy Association, 1980), p. 7.

2. See Edward M. Graham and Paul Krugman, *Foreign Direct Investment in the United States*, 3d ed. (Washington: Institute for International Economics, 1995). We should note that some of these restrictions have been lifted as a result of negotiations during the post-Uruguay period. See Chapter 9.

3. In 1996, the value of U.S. foreign direct investments abroad (USFDIA) exceeded the value of foreign direct investments in the United States (FDIUS) by $242 billion measured at current costs.

4. See Louis T. Wells Jr., "Mobile Exporters: New Foreign Investors in East Asia," in Kenneth A. Froot, ed., *Foreign Direct Investments* (Chicago: University of Chicago Press, 1993); see also Kit Machado, "Japanese Foreign Direct Investments in East Asia," in Steven Chan, ed., *Foreign Direct Investments in a Changing Global Economy* (New York: St. Martin's Press, 1993), pp. 39–66.

5. Derived from data in *Survey of Current Business* (July 1997): 39, table 4.

6. Ned G. Howenstine and William Zeile, "Characteristics of Foreign-Owned U.S. Manufacturing Establishments," *Survey of Current Business* (Jan. 1994): 37, table 2.

7. Ibid., p. 37, table 3.

8. A celebrated case illustrates the ludicrous extremes to which this process was pushed. To win out against the competitive bids of a dozen states, Alabama offered the German producers of Mercedes-Benz automobiles subsidies and tax breaks equal in value to $300 million to induce them to locate a plant in Alabama. Even on the highly inflated estimates of the number of new jobs this project would create, the cost to the citizens of Alabama for each new job was $200,000. See Allen R. Myerson, "O Governor, Won't You Buy Me a Mercedes Plant," *The New York Times*, September 1, 1996, p. A-1.

9. *Wall Street Journal*, February 28, 1996, p. 1.

10. For a breakdown of foreign affiliate employment by states for 1994, see "Foreign Direct Investment in the United States," *Survey of Current Business* (July 1996): 130, table 23.2.

11. *Survey of Current Business* (June 1997): 48.

12. *Survey of Current Business* (June 1997): 63; and *Survey of Current Business* (Feb. 1998): D-57.

13. Mahnaz Fahim-Nader and William Zeile, "Foreign Direct Investment in the United States: New Investments in 1996, Affiliate Operations in 1995," *Survey of Current Business* (June 1997): 63, table 19.2.

14. William J. Zeile, "The Domestic Orientation of Production and Sales by U.S. Manufacturing Affiliates of Foreign Companies," *Survey of Current Business* (April 1998): 29–50.

15. Ned G. Howenstine and William Zeile, "Characteristics of Foreign-Owned U.S. Manufacturing Establishments," *Survey of Current Business* (Jan. 1994): 34–50; and Ned G. Howenstine and William Zeile, "Differences in Foreign-Owned U.S. Manufacturing Establishments by Country of Owner," *Survey of Current Business* (March 1996): 43–56.

16. David Dollar and Edward N. Wolff, *Competitiveness, Convergence, and International Specialization* (Cambridge: MIT Press, 1993), pp. 83–88.

17. World Bank, *World Development Report 1991* (Washington, D.C.: Oxford University Press, 1991).

CHAPTER 8

1. Anne O. Krueger, *American Trade Policy: A Tragedy in the Making* (Washington, D.C.: AEI Press, 1995).

2. Ibid., pp. 39–40.

3. GATT, *Trade Policy Review: The United States of America, 1989* (Geneva: GATT, 1990), p. 181.

4. J. Michael Finger, ed., *Antidumping: How It Works and Who Gets Hurt* (Ann Arbor: University of Michigan Press, 1993), p. 26.

5. Ibid., pp. 27–28.

6. GATT, *Trade Policy Review 1989*, pp. 190 and 191.

7. J. Michael Finger and Tracy Murray, "Antidumping and Countervailing Duty Enforcement in the United States," in Finger, *Antidumping*, p. 245.

8. See Tracy Murray, "The Administration of the Antidumping Duty Law by the Department of Commerce," in Richard Boltuck and Robert E. Litan, eds., *Down in the Dumps* (Washington, D.C.: Brookings Institution, 1991), p. 49.

9. Richard Clarida, "Dumping in Theory, Policy, and in Practice," in Jagdish Bhagwati and Robert Hudec, eds., *Fair Trade and Harmonization*, vol. 1 (Cambridge: MIT Press, 1996), p. 378.

10. Murray, "The Administration of the Antidumping Duty Law," in Boltuck and Litan, *Down in the Dumps*, pp. 45–49.

11. See also James Bovard, *The Fair Trade Fraud* (New York: St. Martin's Press, 1991), chap. 5, pp. 105–168; and Clarida, "Dumping in Theory," in Bhagwati and Hudec, *Fair Trade and Harmonization*, vol. 1, pp. 357–390.

12. N. David Palmeter, "The Antidumping Law: A Legal and Administrative Nontariff Barrier," in Boltuck and Litan, eds., *Down in the Dumps*, p. 66.

13. Brian Hindley, "Safeguards, Voluntary Export Restraints and Antidumping Actions," in *OECD Documents on New World Trade System* (Paris: OECD, 1994), p. 96.

14. See *Financial Times*, December 15, 1992, as quoted in Krueger, *American Trade Policy*, p. 41.

15. Ibid., pp. 42 et seq.; also see Jagdish Bhagwati, *Protectionism* (Cambridge: MIT Press, 1986); and Richard Boltuck and Robert E. Litan, "America's 'Unfair Trade Laws,'" in Boltuck and Litan, eds., *Down in the Dumps*, p. 17.

16. GATT, *Trade Policy Review 1989*, p. 195.

17. J. Michael Finger, H. K. Hall, and D. R. Nelson, "The Political Economy of Administrative Protection," *American Economic Review* 72 (June 1982): 452–466.

18. Finger and Murray, "Antidumping and Countervailing Duty Enforcement," in Finger, *Antidumping*, p. 241.

19. Boltuck and Litan, "America's 'Unfair Trade Laws'" in Boltuck and Litan, *Down in the Dumps*, p. 3.

20. GATT, *Trade Policy Review 1989*, pp. 194, 195.

21. See Robert Feenstra, "Voluntary Export Restraint in U.S. Autos, 1980–1981," reprinted in Jagdish Bhagwati, ed., *International Trade: Selected Reading* (Cambridge: MIT Press, 1987), pp. 203–230.

22. Jagdish Bhagwati, "Aggressive Unilateralism: An Overview," in Jagdish Bhagwati and Hugh Patrick, eds., *Aggressive Unilateralism: America's 301 Trade Policy and the World Trading System* (Ann Arbor: University of Michigan Press, 1990), pp. 1–45.

23. See Robert Hudec, "Thinking about the New Section 301: Beyond Good and Evil," in Bhagwati and Patrick, *Aggressive Unilateralism*, p. 120.

24. See United States Trade Representative, *Annual Report of the President of the United States on the Trade Agreement Proposal, 1984–1988* (Washington: D.C.: Office of United States Trade Representative, 1988).

25. GATT, *Trade Policy Review 1989*, p. 155.

26. Ibid., p. 262; see also Patrick Low, *Trading Free: The GATT and United States Trade Policy* (New York: Twentieth Century Fund, 1993).

27. This account of the semiconductor dispute is based largely on Richard Baldwin, "The Impact of the 1986 U.S.-Japan Semiconductor Agreement," *Japan and the World Economy* 6 (June 1994): 129–152.

28. Cited in ibid., p. 141.

29. Council of Economic Advisors, *President's Economic Report 1995*, (Washington, D.C.: Government Printing Office, 1995).

30. The United States at one time proposed using the criterion of permanent surpluses as an indication of unfair trading practices.

31. GATT, *Trade Policy Review 1989*, p. 280 (emphasis added).

32. Hudec, "Thinking about the New Section 301," in Bhagwati and Patrick, *Aggressive Unilateralism*, p. 131.

33. Ibid., p. 137.

34. Council of Economic Advisers, *President's Economic Report 1995*, p. 204.

35. Andrew Pollack, "Japan's New Tack on Trade: No More 1-on–1 with the U.S.," *The New York Times*, July 30, 1996, p. D-1.

36. Andrew Pollack, "Japan Is Urged to Insure Foreigners' Trade Share," *The New York Times*, October 14, 1993.

37. Ibid.

38. Thomas L. Friedman, "U.S. Says Visit by Japanese Leader Could Turn into a Confrontation," *The New York Times*, February 11, 1994, p. A-8.

39. *The New York Times*, July 11, 1993.

40. See Stanton D. Anderson and Thomas P. Steindler, "The U.S.-Japan Auto Trade Accord: Blueprint for Conflict," *Journal of Japanese Trade and Industry*, no. 1 (1996): 17.

41. Ibid., pp. 16–18.

42. Council of Economic Advisers, *President's Economic Report 1995*, p. 234.

43. Pollack, "Japan's New Tack on Trade."

44. Ibid.

45. Angelika Eymann and Ludger Schuknecht, "Antidumping Enforcement in the European Community," in Finger, *Antidumping*, p. 226, table 12.3.

46. Ibid., p. 238.

47. Mark A. Dutz, "Enforcement of Canadian Trade Remedy Laws: The Case for Competition Policies as an Antidote for Protection," in Finger, *Antidumping*, p. 204.

48. Ibid., p. 213, table 11.2.

CHAPTER 9

1. United States Trade Representative, "Statement on the Protection of United States Intellectual Properties Abroad," April 7, 1986, p. 4.

2. Pres. Ronald Reagan, quoted in Ernst H. Preeg, *Traders in a Brave New World* (Chicago: University of Chicago Press, 1995), p. 51.

3. Alan V. Deardorff, "Market Access," in Organization for Economic Cooperation and Development (hereinafter OECD), *OECD Documents: The New World Trading System* (Paris: OECD, 1994), p. 80.

4. Edmund L. Andrews, "In Victory for U.S., Europe Ban On Treated Beef Is Ruled Illegal," *The New York Times*, May 9, 1997, p. A-1.

5. United Nations Commission for Trade and Development, *Protectionism and Structural Adjustment* (New York: United Nations, 1986).

6. Cited in John Whalley, "Agreement on Textiles and Clothing," in OECD, *The New World Trading System*, p. 73.

7. Ibid., p. 75.

8. J. Michael Finger, ed., *Antidumping: How It Works and Who Gets Hurt* (Ann Arbor: University of Michigan Press, 1993), p. 3.

9. Ibid., p. 250.

10. Ibid., p. 3.

11. GATT Article 4, ¶ 2b.

12. GATT Article 8, ¶ 3.

13. Brian Hindley, "Safeguards, Voluntary Export Restraints, and Antidumping Action," in OECD, *The New World Trading System*, pp. 96–100.

14. Ibid., p. 98.

15. J. Michael Finger, "Subsidies and Countervailing Measures and Anti-Dumping Agreements," in OECD, *The New World Trading System*, p. 109.

16. Patrick Lowe, "Market Presence: A Look at the Issues," in OECD, *OECD: New Dimensions of Market Access in a Globalizing World Economy* (Paris: OECD, 1995), p. 51.

17. Bernard Hoekman, "Services and Intellectual Property Rights," in S. M. Collins and D. P. Bosworth, eds., *The New GATT* (Washington, D.C.: Brookings Institution, 1994), p. 92.

18. Alan V. Deardorff, "Market Access," in OECD, *The New World Trading System*, p. 61.

19. Ibid., pp. 61–62.

20. Ibid., p. 62.

21. J. Startup, "An Agenda for International Investment," in OECD, *The New World Trading System*, p. 190.

22. GATT Article 13:2.

23. GATT Article 40:2.

24. John Jackson, "The World Trade Organization: Dispute Settlement and Codes of Conduct," in Collins and Bosworth, *The New GATT*, pp. 65–68.

25. Ibid., p. 56.

26. *The New York Times*, February 16, 1997, p. 1.

27. Council of Economic Advisors, *President's Economic Report 1998* (Washington, D.C.: Government Printing Office, 1998), p. 230.

28. Ibid., p. 223.

CHAPTER 10

1. Virginia A. Leary, "Workers' Rights and International Trade: The Social Clause (GATT, ILO, NAFTA, U.S. Laws)," in Jagdish Bhagwati and Robert E. Hudec, eds. *Fair Trade and Harmonization: Prerequisites for Free Trade?* vol. 2. (Cambridge: MIT Press, 1996), p. 183.

2. Gijsbert van Liemt, "Minimum Labor Standards and International Trade: Would a Social Clause Work?" *International Labor Review* 4 (1989): 128.

3. OECD, *Trade, Employment, and Labor Standards: A Study of Core Workers' Rights and International Trade* (Paris: OECD, 1996), pp. 12–13; see also Mita Aggarwal, "International Trade, Labor Standards, and Labor Market Conditions: An Evaluation of the Linkages," U.S. International Trade Commission, Office of Economics, Working Paper No. 95-06-C, Washington, D.C., June 1995, p. 7; and Dani Rodrik, "Labor Standards in International Trade: Do They Matter and What Do We Do About Them?" in Robert Lawrence, Dani Rodrik, and John Whalley, eds., *Emerging Agenda for Global Trade: High Stakes for Developing Countries* (Washington, D.C.: Overseas Development Council, 1996), p. 22.

4. OECD, *Trade, Employment, and Labor Standards*, p. 13.

5. Communiqué of the World Trade Organization, Singapore, Ministerial Declaration adopted December 13, 1996.

6. Cited in Kenneth A. Swinnerton and Gregory K. Schoepfle, "Labor Standards in the Context of a Global Economy: A Symposium," *Monthly Labor Review* 117:9 (Sept. 1994): 56.

7. Ibid., p. 96.

8. See Richard Freeman, "A Hardheaded Look at Labor Standards," in U.S. Department of Labor, Bureau of International Labor Affairs, *International Labor Standards and Global Economic Integration: Proceedings of a Symposium* (Washington, D.C.: Department of Labor, 1994).

9. Paul Lewis, "Amid New Wealth of Trade, a Humanizing Movement," *The New York Times*, December 25, 1996, p. D-3.

10. Steven Greenhouse, "Voluntary Rules on Apparel Labor Prove Hard to Set," *The New York Times*, February 1, 1997, p. 1.

11. Lewis, "Amid New Wealth."

12. Ibid.

13. Greenhouse, "Voluntary Rules on Apparel Labor."

14. Barbara Crosette, "UNICEF Vows Not to Buy from Companies That Exploit Children," *The New York Times*, May 25, 1995, p. A-15. We should note that even though many emerging economies have signed on to the 1989 Convention on the Rights of the Child, which forbids exploitation of children, enforcement practice procedures are frequently lax or nonexistent).

15. Steven Greenhouse, "Duke to Adopt a Code to Prevent Apparel from Being Made in Sweatshops," *The New York Times*, March 8, 1998, p. A-16.

16. John H. Cushman Jr., "Nike Pledges to End Child Labor and Apply U.S. Rules Abroad," *The New York Times*, May 13, 1998, p. D-1.

17. Larry Rohter, "Hondurans in Sweatshops See Opportunity," *The New York Times*, July 18, 1996, p. 1.

18. Ibid.

19. Ibid.

20. Ibid.

21. Ibid.

22. Ibid.

23. Ibid.

24. See J. Forrester and B. Meadows, *Limits to Growth* (Rome: Club of Rome, 1972).

25. Daniel Esty, *Greening the GATT: Trade, Environment, and the Future* (Washington, D.C.: Institute for International Economics, 1994), p. 223.

26. Ross Perot, *Save Your Jobs, Save Our Country: Why NAFTA Must Be Stopped* (New York: Hyperion Press, 1992).

27. GATT Article 20.

28. *The New York Times*, March 25, 1996.

29. Marian Burros, "President to Push for Food Safety," *The New York Times*, July 4, 1998, p. A-1.

30. John H. Cushman Jr., "Trade Group Strikes Blow at U.S. Environmental Law," *The New York Times*, April 7, 1998, p. D-1.

31. Robert Hudec, "GATT Legal Restraints on the Use of Trade Measures Against Foreign Environmental Practices," in Bhagwati and Hudec, *Fair Trade and Harmonization*, p. 121.

32. See James Salzman, *Environment Labeling in OECD Countries* (Paris: OECD, 1991).

33. See Charles Arden-Clarke, "Environment, Competitiveness, and Countervailing Measures," in OECD, *OECD Papers on Competitiveness* (Paris: OECD, 1993).

34. See Esty, *Greening the GATT*, p. 164.

35. See Jagdish Bhagwati and T. N. Srinivasan, "Trade and the Environment: Does Environmental Diversity Detract from the Case for Free Trade?" in Bhagwati and Hudec, *Fair Trade and Harmonization*, p. 168.

36. See A. B. Jaffe, S. R. Peterson, P. R. Portney, and R. N. Stavins, "Environmental Regulations and the Competitiveness of United States Manufacturing: What Does the Evidence Tell Us," *Journal of Economic Literature* 33 (March 1995): 157.

37. Arik Levinson, "Environmental Regulations and Industry Location: International and Domestic Evidence," in Bhagwati and Hudec, eds., *Fair Trade and Harmonization*, vol. 1, p. 433.

38. OECD, *OECD Observer* 183 (Aug.-Sept. 1993): 24.

39. See Jaffe et al., "Environmental Regulations," p. 157.

40. Esty, *Greening the GATT*, p. 23.

41. Michael Porter, "America's Green Strategy," *Scientific American* (April 1991): 96.

42. K. R. Golombek and A. Rakrenud, "Do Environmental Standards Hurt Manufacturing?" *The Scandinavian Journal of Economics* 99:1 (1997): 31.

CHAPTER 11

1. See Richard N. Gardner, *Sterling-Dollar Diplomacy: Anglo-American Collaboration in the Reconstruction of Multilateral Trade* (Oxford: Oxford at the Clarendon Press, 1956).

2. Cited in John Jackson, *The World Trading System: Law and Policy of International Economic Relations* (Cambridge: MIT Press, 1992), p. 147 (emphasis added).

3. Council of Economic Advisors, *The Economic Report of the President 1996* (Washington, D.C.: Government Printing Office, 1996), pp. 231 ff.

4. GATT Article 24.

5. From the initial formation of the Coal and Steel Community, the seed from which the European Union ultimately emerged, to the most recent creating of a common currency, the not-so-hidden agenda guiding this regional arrangement was the forging of a new political entity, a federation of European states. Although economic instruments were used to achieve this objective, when economic and political considerations conflicted, the highest priority was invariably assigned to the political.

6. The Latin American Free Trade Association (LAFTA), established in 1960, is an example of these early preferential trade arrangements.

7. John Whalley, "Regional Trade Agreements in North America: CUFTA and NAFTA," in Jaime De Melo and Arvind Panagariya, eds., *New Dimensions in Regional Integration* (Cambridge: Cambridge University Press, 1993), p. 357; see also John Whalley, "Why Do Countries Seek Trade Agreements?" in Jeffrey A. Frankel, ed., *The Regionalization of the World Economy* (Chicago: Chicago University Press, 1998), p. 71.

8. Council of Economic Advisors, *President's Economic Report, 1998* (Washington, D.C.: Government Printing Office, 1998), p. 230.

9. See Whalley, "Regional Trade Agreement in North America," in De Melo and Panagariya, *New Dimensions in Regional Integration*, p. 357.

10. See Chapter 10 for a fuller discussion of the issues regarding these standards.

11. Council of Economic Advisors, *President's Economic Report, 1996* (Washington, D.C.: Government Printing Office, 1996), p. 219.

12. Ibid., p. 220.

13. Jacob Viner, *The Customs Union Issue* (New York: Carnegie Endowment for International Peace, 1950).

14. For a discussion of gravity models, see Alan V. Deardorff, "Determinants of Bilateral Trade: Does Gravity Work in a Neoclassical World?" in Frankel, *The Regionalization of the World Economy*, pp. 7–21; see also Jeffrey H. Bergstrand, "The Gravity Equation in International Trade: Some Microeconomic Foundations and Empirical Evidence," *Review of Economics and Statistics* 67 (Aug. 1985): 474–481.

15. Jagdish Bhagwati, "Regionalism and Multilateralism: An Overview," in De Melo and Panagariya, *New Dimensions in Regional Integration*, p. 32.

16. Douglas A. Irwin, "Multilateral and Bilateral Trade Policies in the World Trading System: An Historical Perspective," in De Melo and Panagariya, *New Dimensions in Regional Integration*, p. 91.

17. Ibid.

18. Robert Hudec, "Discussion of J. Michael Finger's 'GATT's Influence on Regional Arrangements,'" in De Melo and Panagariya, *New Dimensions in Regional Integration*, p. 154.

19. J. Michael Finger, "GATT's Influence on Regional Arrangements," in De Melo and Panagariya, *New Dimensions in Regional Integration*, p. 145.

20. Ibid., p. 148.

21. Anne O. Krueger, "Overview," in Frankel, *The Regionalization of the World Economy*, p. 273.

CHAPTER 12

1. See Helen Milner, *Resisting Protectionism: Global Industries and the Politics of International Trade* (Princeton: Princeton University Press, 1988); and Helen Milner, "Trading Places: Industry for Free Trade," in John S. Odell and Thomas D. Willett, eds., *International Trade Policies: Gains from Exchange Between Economics and Political Science* (Ann Arbor: University of Michigan Press, 1990), pp. 141–172.

2. *The New York Times*, May 15, 1997, p. A-12.

3. Ibid.

4. Ibid.

5. Nicholas D. Kristof, "Experts Question Roving Flow of Global Capital," *New York Times*, 20 September 1998, p. 18.

BIBLIOGRAPHY

"A Survey on East Asian Economies: Special Insert." *The Economist* (March 7–13, 1998): 1–18.

Abbott, Kenneth W. "Defensive Unfairness: The Normative Structure of Section 301." In *Fair Trade and Harmonization: Prerequisites for Free Trade?* edited by Jagdish N. Bhagwati and Robert E. Hudec, vol. 2, 415–472. Cambridge: MIT Press, 1996.

Abramowitz, Moses. *Resource and Output Trends in the United States Since 1970.* Occasional Paper No. 52. New York: National Bureau of Economic Research, 1956.

Addison, J. T., D. A. Fox, and C. J. Ruhm. "Trade and Displacement in Manufacturing." *Monthly Labor Review* (April 1995): 58–67.

Aggarwal, Mita. "International Trade, Labor Standards, and Labor Market Conditions: An Evaluation of the Linkages." U.S. International Trade Commission, Office of Economics Working Paper no. 95-06-C. Washington, D.C., June 1995.

Anderson, Kym. "Social Policy Dimensions of Economic Integration: Environmental and Labor Standards." In *Regionalism Versus Multilateral Trade Arrangements*, edited by Takatoshi Ito and Anne O. Krueger, 57–90. Chicago: University of Chicago Press, 1997.

Anderson, Kym, and R. Blackhurst, eds. *The Greening of World Trade Issues.* London: Harvester-Wheatsheaf, 1992.

Anderson, Stanton D., and Thomas P. Steindler. "The U.S.-Japan Auto Trade Accord: Blueprint for Conflict." *Journal of Japanese Trade and Industry* 1 (1996): 16–18.

Andrews, Edmund L. "In Victory for U.S., Europe Ban On Treated Beef Is Ruled Illegal." *The New York Times*, 9 May 1997, p. A-1.

Arden-Clarke, Charles. "Environment, Competitiveness, and Countervailing Measures." In *OECD Papers on Competitiveness.* Paris: OECD, 1993.

Baily, Martin, and Hans Gerbach. "Efficiency in Manufacturing and the Need for Global Competition." *Brookings Papers: Microeconomics.* Washington, D.C.: Brookings Institution, 1995.

Baldwin, Richard. "The Impact of the 1986 U.S.-Japan Semiconductor Agreement." *Japan and the World Economy* 6 (June 1994): 129–152.

Baldwin, Robert E. *The Political Economy of U.S. Import Policy.* Cambridge: MIT Press, 1985.

———. *Trade Policy in a Changing World Economy.* Chicago: University of Chicago Press, 1988.

Baldwin, Robert E., and Anne O. Krueger, eds. *The Structure and Evolution of Recent U.S. Trade Policies.* Chicago: University of Chicago Press, 1984.

Bargas, S. E. "Direct Investment Position for 1996." *Survey of Current Business* (July 1997): 34–41.

Becker, Gary. *Human Capital: A Theoretical and Empirical Analysis.* New York: Bureau of Economic Research, 1964.

Bednarzik, Robert. "An Analysis of U.S. Industries Sensitive to Foreign Trade, 1982–1987." *Monthly Labor Review* (Feb. 1993): 15–31.

Bergstrand, Jeffrey H. "The Gravity Equation in International Trade: Some Microeconomic Foundations and Empirical Evidence." *Review of Economics and Statistics* 67 (Aug. 1985): 474–481.

Berman, Eli, John Bound, and Zvi Griliches. "Changes in the Demand for Skilled Labor Within Manufacturing Industries: Evidence from the Annual Survey of Manufacturing." National Bureau of Economic Research Working Paper no. 4255. Jan. 1993.

Bernard, Andrew, and J. Bradford Jensen. "Exporters, Jobs, and Wages in United States Manufacturing: 1976–1987." *Brookings Papers: Microeconomics.* Washington, D.C.: Brookings Institution, 1995.

Bhagwati, Jagdish N. "Aggressive Unilateralism: An Overview." In *Aggressive Unilateralism: America's 301 Trade Policy and the World Trading System,* edited by Jagdish N. Bhagwati and Hugh T. Patrick, 1–45. Ann Arbor: University of Michigan Press, 1990.

———. "The Demands to Reduce Domestic Diversity Among Trading Nations." In *Fair Trade and Harmonization: Prerequisites for Free Trade?* edited by Jagdish N. Bhagwati and Robert E. Hudec, vol. 1, 9–40. Cambridge: MIT Press, 1996.

———. "Free Traders and Free Immigrationists: Strangers or Friends?" Russell Sage Foundation Working Paper no. 20, 1991.

———. "The Generalized Theory of Distortions and Welfare." In *Selected Readings in International Trade,* edited by Jagdish N. Bhagwati, 265–289. Cambridge: MIT Press, 1987.

———. *Protectionism.* Cambridge: MIT Press, 1986.

———. "Regionalism and Multilateralism: An Overview." In *New Dimensions in Regional Integration,* edited by Jaime De Melo and Arvind Panagariya, 22–50. Cambridge: Cambridge University Press, 1993.

———. "Trade and the Environment: The False Conflict?" Bradley lecture. Washington, D.C.: American Enterprise Institute, 1993.

Bhagwati, Jagdish N., ed. *Selected Readings in International Trade.* 2d ed. Cambridge: MIT Press, 1987.

Bhagwati, Jagdish N., and Robert E. Hudec, eds. *Fair Trade and Harmonization: Prerequisites for Free Trade?* Vols. 1 and 2. Cambridge: MIT Press, 1996.

Bhagwati, Jagdish N., and Marvin H. Kosters, eds. *Trade and Wages: Levelling Wages Down?* Washington, D.C.: AEI Press, 1994.

Bhagwati, Jagdish N., and Hugh T. Patrick, eds. *Aggressive Unilateralism: America's 301 Trade Policy and the World Trading System.* Ann Arbor: University of Michigan Press, 1990.

Bhagwati, Jagdish N., and V. K. Ramaswami. "Domestic Distortions, Tariffs, and the Theory of Optimum Subsidy." *Journal of Political Economy* 71:1 (Feb. 1963): 44–50.

Bhagwati, Jagdish N., and T. N. Srinivasan. "Trade and the Environment: Does Environmental Diversity Detract from the Case for Free Trade?" In *Fair Trade and Harmonization: Prerequisites for Free Trade?* edited by Jagdish N. Bhagwati and Robert E. Hudec, vol. 1, 159–224. Cambridge: MIT Press, 1996.

Bluestone, Barry, and Bennet Harrison. *The Great U Turn: Corporate Restructuring and the Polarization of America.* New York: Basic Books, 1988.

Boltuck, Richard, and Robert E. Litan. "America's 'Unfair Trade Laws.'" In *Down in the Dumps,* edited by Richard Boltuck and Robert E. Litan, 1–21. Washington, D.C.: Brookings Institution, 1991.

Boltuck, Richard, and Robert E. Litan, eds. *Down in the Dumps: Administration of the Unfair Trade Laws.* Washington, D.C.: Brookings Institution, 1991.

Borjas, George J., and Valerie A. Ramey. "Foreign Competition, Market Power, and Wage Inequality: Theory and Evidence." National Bureau of Economic Research Working Paper no. 4556. 1993.

Borjas, George J., Richard Freeman, and Lawrence F. Katz. "On the Labor Market Effects of Immigration and Trade." Harvard University, Harvard Institute of Economic Research Discussion Paper no. 1556. 1991.

_____. "On the Labor Market Effects of Immigration and Trade." In *Immigration and the Work Force,* edited by G. Borjas and R. Freeman, 213–214. Chicago: University of Chicago Press and NBER, 1992.

Bound, John, and George Johnson. "Changes in the Structure of Wages in the 1980s: An Evaluation of Alternative Explanations." *American Economic Review* 82 (June 1992): 380–382.

Bovard, James. *The Fair Trade Fraud.* New York: St. Martin's Press, 1991.

Brown, Drusilla K., Alan V. Deardorff, and Robert M. Stern. "International Labor Standards and Trade: A Theoretical Analysis." In *Fair Trade and Harmonization: Prerequisites for Free Trade?* edited by Jagdish N. Bhagwati and Robert E. Hudec, vol. 1, 227–280. Cambridge: MIT Press, 1996.

Burros, Marian. "President to Push for Food Safety." *The New York Times,* 4 July 1998, p. A-1.

Burtless, Gary. "Worsening of American Income Inequality: Is World Trade to Blame?" *The Brookings Review* (Spring 1996): 23–35.

Campa, José, and Linda S. Goldberg. "The Evolving External Orientation of Manufacturing: A Profile of Four Countries." *Federal Reserve Bank of New York: Economic Policy Review* 3:2 (July 1997): 53–81.

Casella, Alessandra. "Free Trade and Evolving Standards." In *Fair Trade and Harmonization: Prerequisites for Free Trade?* edited by Jagdish N. Bhagwati and Robert E. Hudec, vol. 1, 119–156. Cambridge: MIT Press, 1996.

Cass, Ronald A., and Richard D. Boltuck. "Antidumping and Countervailing-Duty Law: The Mirage of Equitable International Competition." In *Fair Trade and Harmonization: Prerequisites for Free Trade?* edited by Jagdish N. Bhagwati and Robert E. Hudec, vol. 2, 351–414. Cambridge: MIT Press, 1996.

Chan, Steven, ed. *Foreign Direct Investment in a Changing Global Economy.* New York: St. Martin's Press, 1993.

Charnovitz, Steve. "Exploring the Environmental Exceptions in GATT Article XX." *Journal of World Trade* 25:5 (1991): 37–55.

_____. "GATT and the Environment: Examining the Issues." *International Environmental Affairs* 4:3 (1992): 203–233.

_____. "The Influence of International Labor Standards on the World Trading Regime: A Historical Review." *International Labor Review* 126:5 (1987): 565–584.

Clarida, Richard. "Dumping: In Theory, in Policy and in Practice." In *Fair Trade and Harmonization: Prerequisites for Free Trade?* edited by Jagdish N. Bhagwati and Robert E. Hudec, vol. 1, 357–390. Cambridge: MIT Press, 1996.

Clark, Colin. *The Conditions of Economic Progress.* London: MacMillan, 1935.

Cooper, R. "Discussion of Paul Krugman's *Growing World Trade: Causes and Consequences." Brookings Papers on Economic Activity 1.* Washington, D.C.: Brookings Institution, 1995.

_____. "Foreign Trade Wages and Unemployment." Discussion Paper 1701. Harvard Institute of Economic Research. November 1994.

Corden, William M. "Tariffs, Subsidies, and the Terms of Trade." *Economica*, n.s., 24 (Aug. 1957): 235–242.

Council of Economic Advisors. *President's Economic Report 1995.* Washington, D.C.: U.S. Government Printing Office, 1995.

_____. *President's Economic Report 1996.* Washington, D.C.: U.S. Government Printing Office, 1996.

_____. *President's Economic Report 1997.* Washington, D.C.: U.S. Government Printing Office, 1997.

_____. *President's Economic Report 1998.* Washington, D.C.: U.S. Government Printing Office, 1998.

Crosette, Barbara. "UNICEF Vows Not to Buy from Companies That Exploit Children." *The New York Times*, 25 May 1995, p. A-15.

Cushman, John H. Jr. "Nike Pledges to End Child Labor and Apply U.S. Rules Abroad." *The New York Times*, 13 May 1998, p. D-1.

_____. "Trade Group Strikes Blow at U.S. Environmental Law." *The New York Times*, 7 April 1998, p. D-1.

Das, Dilip K. "Changing Comparative Advantage and the Changing Composition of Asian Exports." *The World Economy* 21:1 (Jan. 1998): 121–140.

De Melo, Jaime, and Arvind Panagariya. "Introduction to Part One: Systemic Issues." In *New Dimensions in Regional Integration*, edited by Jaime De Medo and Arvind Panagariya, 3–21. Cambridge: Cambridge University Press, 1993.

De Melo, Jaime, and Arvind Panagariya, eds. *New Dimensions in Regional Integration*. Cambridge: Cambridge University Press, 1993.

De Melo, Jaime, Arvind Panagariya, and Dani Rodrik. "The New Regionalism: A Country Perspective." In *New Dimensions in Regional Integration*, edited by Jaime De Melo and Arvind Panagariya, 159–192. Cambridge: Cambridge University Press, 1993.

Deardorff, Alan V. "Determinants of Bilateral Trade: Does Gravity Work in a Neoclassical World?" In *The Regionalization of the World Economy*, edited by Jeffrey Frankel, 7–21. Chicago: University of Chicago Press, 1998.

———. "Market Access." In *OECD Documents: The New World Trading System*, 57–63. Paris: OECD, 1994.

Denison, Edward F. *Why Growth Rates Differ*. Washington, D.C.: Brookings Institution, 1967.

———. *The Sources of Economic Growth in the United States and the Alternatives Before Us*. New York: Committee for Economic Development, 1962.

Dixit, Avinash. "How Should the United States Respond to Other Countries' Trade Policies?" In *U.S. Trade Policies in a Changing World Economy*, edited by Robert M. Stern, 245–279. Cambridge: MIT Press, 1987.

Dollar, David, and Edward N. Wolff. *Competitiveness, Convergence, and International Specialization*. Cambridge: MIT Press, 1993.

Dutz, Mark A. "Enforcement of Canadian Trade Remedy Laws: The Case for Competition Policies as an Antidote for Protection." In *Antidumping: How It Works and Who Gets Hurt*, edited by J. Michael Finger, 203–219. Ann Arbor: University of Michigan Press, 1993.

Edwards, Sebastian. "Openness, Productivity, and Growth: What Do We Really Know?" *Economic Journal* 108 (March 1998): 383–398.

Engelberg, Stephen, with Martin Tolchin. "Foreigners Find New Ally in U.S. Industry." *The New York Times*, 2 November 1993, p. 1.

Esty, Daniel. *Greening the GATT: Trade, Environment, and the Future*. Washington, D.C.: Institute for International Economics, 1994.

Eymann, Angelika, and Ludger Schuknecht. "Antidumping Enforcement in the European Community." In *Antidumping: How It Works and Who Gets Hurt*, edited by J. Michael Finger, 221–239. Ann Arbor: University of Michigan Press, 1993.

Fahim-Nader, Mahnaz, and William J. Zeile. "Foreign Direct Investment in the United States: New Investment in 1995; Affiliate Operations in 1994." *Survey of Current Business* (July 1996): 102–130.

_____. "Foreign Direct Investment in the United States: New Investments in 1996. Affiliate Operations in 1995." *Survey of Current Business* (June 1997): 42–67.

Farber, Daniel A., and Robert E. Hudec. "GATT Legal Restraints on Domestic Environmental Regulations." In *Fair Trade and Harmonization: Prerequisites for Free Trade?* edited by Jagdish N. Bhagwati and Robert E. Hudec, vol. 2, 59–94. Cambridge: MIT Press, 1996.

Feenstra, Robert. "Voluntary Export Restraint in U.S. Autos, 1980–1981." In *The Structure and Evolution of Recent U.S. Trade Policies*, edited by Robert E. Baldwin and Anne O. Krueger. Chicago: University of Chicago Press, 1984. Reprinted in *International Trade: Selected Reading*, edited by Jagdish N. Bhagwati, 203–230. Cambridge: MIT Press, 1987.

Finger, J. Michael. "GATT's Influence on Regional Arrangements." In *New Dimensions in Regional Integration*, edited by Jaime De Melo and Arvind Panagariya, 128–147. Cambridge: Cambridge University Press, 1993.

_____. "The Origins and Evolution of Anti-Dumping Regulation." In *Antidumping: How It Works and Who Gets Hurt*, edited by J. Michael Finger, 13–34. Ann Arbor: University of Michigan Press, 1993.

_____. "Subsidies and Countervailing Measures and Anti-Dumping Agreements." In *OECD Documents: The New World Trading System: Readings*, 105–112. Paris: OECD, 1994.

Finger, J. Michael, ed. *Antidumping: How It Works and Who Gets Hurt*. Ann Arbor: University of Michigan Press, 1993.

Finger, J. Michael, and Tracy Murray. "Antidumping and Countervailing Duty Enforcement in the United States." In *Antidumping: How It Works and Who Gets Hurt*, edited by J. Michael Finger, 241–254. Michigan: University of Michigan Press, 1993.

Finger, J. Michael, H. K. Hall, and D. R. Nelson. "The Political Economy of Administrative Protection." *American Economic Review* 72 (June 1982): 452–466.

Forrester, J., and B. Meadows. *Limits to Growth*. Club of Rome, 1972.

Frankel, Jeffrey, ed. *The Regionalization of the World Economy*. Chicago: University of Chicago Press, 1998.

Freeman, Richard B. "A Hardheaded Look at Labor Standards." In U.S. Department of Labor, Bureau of International Labor Affairs. *International Labor Standards and Global Economic Integration: Proceedings of a Symposium*. Washington, D.C.: United States Department of Labor, 1994.

Freeman, Richard B., and L. F. Katz. *Difference and Changes in Wage Structures*. Chicago: University of Chicago Press, 1995.

Friedman, Thomas L. "U.S. Says Visit by Japanese Leader Could Turn into a Confrontation." *The New York Times*, 11 February 1994, p. A-8.

_____. "Roll Over Hawks and Doves." *The New York Times*, 2 February 1997, op-ed page.

Froot, K. A., ed. *Foreign Direct Investment*. Chicago: University of Chicago Press, 1993.

Gardner, Richard N. *Sterling-Dollar Diplomacy: Anglo-American Collaboration in the Reconstruction of Multilateral Trade.* Oxford: Clarendon Press, 1956.

General Agreement on Tariffs and Trade. *Basic Instruments and Selected Documents.* Geneva: GATT, 1993.

_____. *The Text of the General Agreement on Tariffs and Trade.* Geneva: GATT, 1986.

_____. *Textiles and Clothing in the World Economy.* Geneva: GATT, 1984.

_____. *Trade Policy Review: United States, 1988.* Geneva: GATT, 1989.

_____. *Trade Policy Review: United States, 1989.* Geneva: GATT, 1990.

_____. *Trade Policy Review: United States, 1992.* Geneva: GATT, 1992.

_____. *Trade Policy Review: United States, 1994.* Geneva: GATT, 1994.

Glickman, Norman, and Douglas Woodward. *The New Competitors: How Foreign Investors Are Changing the United States.* New York: Basic Books, 1989.

Golombek, K. R., and A. Rakrenud. "Do Environmental Standards Harm Manufacturing Employment?" *Scandinavian Journal of Economics* 99:1 (1997): 29–44.

Graham, Edward M., and Paul Krugman. *Foreign Direct Investment in the United States.* 3d ed. Washington, D.C.: Institute for International Economics, 1995.

Greenhouse, Steven. "Voluntary Rules on Apparel Labor Prove Hard to Set." *The New York Times*, 1 February 1997, p. 1.

_____. "Duke to Adopt a Code to Prevent Apparel from Being Made in Sweatshops." *The New York Times*, 8 March 1998, p. A-16.

Greenway, David, and Chris Milner. *The Economics of Intra-Industry Trade.* Oxford: Blackwell, 1986.

Grossman, Gene M., ed. *Imperfect Competition and International Trade.* Cambridge: MIT Press, 1992.

Grubel, Herbert. "Intra-Industry Specialization and the Pattern of Trade." *Canadian Journal of Economics and Political Science* 33 (Aug. 1967): 374–388.

Gullickson, William. "Multifactor Productivity in Manufacturing, 1984–1988." *Monthly Labor Review* (Oct. 1992): 20–32.

Harrigan, James. "Openness to Trade in Manufactures in the OECD." *Journal of International Economics* 44 (1996): 23–38.

Hart, Jeffrey A. "Maquiladorization as a Global Process." In *Foreign Direct Investment in a Changing Global Economy*, edited by Steven Chan, 25–37. New York: St. Martin's Press, 1993.

Hecksher, Eli. "The Effect of Foreign Trade on the Distribution of Income." *Ekonomick Tidscrift* 21 (1919): 497–512. Reprinted in American Economic Association, *Readings in the Theory of International Trade*, 272–300. Philadelphia: Blakiston, 1949.

Helpman, Elhanan, and Paul Krugman. *Market Structure and Foreign Trade.* Cambridge: MIT Press, 1985.

Hindley, Brian. "Competition Law and the WTO: Alternative Structures for Agreement." In *Fair Trade and Harmonization: Prerequisites for Free Trade?* edited by Jagdish N. Bhagwati and Robert E. Hudec, vol. 2, 333–348. Cambridge: MIT Press, 1996.

———. "Safeguards, Voluntary Export Restraints, and Antidumping Actions." In *OECD Documents on New World Trade System*, 91–104. Paris: OECD, 1994.

Hoekman, Bernard. "Services and Intellectual Property Rights." In *The New GATT*, edited by S. M. Collins and D. P. Bosworth, 84–120. Washington, D.C.: Brookings Institution, 1994.

Horlick, G. "The United States Antidumping System." In *Antidumping Law and Practice: A Comparative Study*, edited by John H. Jackson and Edwin A. Vermulst. Studies in International Trade Policy Series. Ann Arbor: University of Michigan Press, 1990.

Howenstine, Ned G., and William Zeile. "Differences in Foreign-Owned U.S. Manufacturing Establishments by Country of Owner." *Survey of Current Business* (March 1996): 43–56.

———. "Characteristics of Foreign-Owned U.S. Manufacturing Establishments." *Survey of Current Business* (Jan. 1994): 34–50.

Hudec, Robert E. "Discussion of J. Michael Finger's 'GATT's Influence on Regional Arrangements.'" In *New Dimensions in Regional Integration*, edited by Jaime De Melo and Arvind Panagariya, 151–155. Cambridge: Cambridge University Press, 1993.

———. "GATT Legal Restraints on the Use of Trade Measures Against Foreign Environmental Practices." In *Fair Trade and Harmonization: Prerequisites for Free Trade?* edited by Jagdish N. Bhagwati and Robert E. Hudec, vol. 2, 95–174. Cambridge: MIT Press, 1996.

———. "Thinking about the New Section 301: Beyond Good and Evil." In *Aggressive Unilateralism: America's 301 Trade Policy and the World Trading System*, edited by Jagdish N. Bhagwati and Hugh T. Patrick, 113–159. Ann Arbor: University of Michigan Press, 1990.

Hufbauer, Gary C., and Kimberly Ann Elliot. *Measuring the Costs of Protection in the United States*. Washington, D.C.: Institute for International Economics, 1994.

Hufbauer, Gary C., and Jeffrey Schott. *North American Free Trade: Issues and Recommendations*. Washington, D.C.: Institute for International Economics, 1992.

Hufbauer, Gary C., Diane T. Berliner, and Kimberly Ann Elliott. *Trade Protection in the United States: 31 Case Studies*. Washington, D.C.: Institute for International Economics, 1993.

International Labor Organization (ILO). *Guide to International Labor Standards*. Geneva: ILO.

International Monetary Fund. *International Financial Statistics* (monthly), various issues.

Irwin, Douglas A. *Against the Tide: An Intellectual History of Free Trade*. Princeton: Princeton University Press, 1996.

_____. "Multilateral and Bilateral Trade Policies in the World Trading Systems: An Historical Perspective." In *New Dimensions in Regional Integration*, edited by Jaime De Melo and Arvind Panagariya, 90–118. Cambridge: Cambridge University Press, 1993.

Ito, Takatoshi, and Anne O. Krueger, eds. *Regionalism Versus Multilateral Trade Arrangements*. Chicago: University of Chicago Press, 1997.

Jackson, John H. "The World Trade Organization: Dispute Settlement and Codes of Conduct." In *The New GATT*, edited by S. M. Collins and D. P. Bosworth, 63–83. Washington, D.C.: Brookings Institution, 1994.

_____. *The World Trading System: Law and Policy of International Economic Relations*. Cambridge: MIT Press, 1991.

Jackson, John H., and Edwin A. Vermulst, eds. *Antidumping Law and Practice: A Comparative Study*. Studies in International Trade Policy Series. Ann Arbor: University of Michigan Press, 1990.

Jaffe, A. B., S. R. Peterson, P. R. Portney, and R. N. Stavins. "Environmental Regulations and the Competitiveness of United States Manufacturing: What Does the Evidence Tell Us?" *Journal of Economic Literature* XXXIII (March 1995): 132–163.

Johnson, George E., and Frank P. Stanfford. "International Competition and Real Wages." Paper presented at American Economic Association Meetings, January 5–7, 1993.

Johnson, Harry. "Optimal Trade Intervention in the Presence of Domestic Distortions." In *Selected Readings in International Trade*, edited by Jagdish N. Bhagwati, 235–263. 2d ed. Cambridge: MIT Press, 1987.

Juhn, Chinhui, and Kevin M. Murphy. "Inequality in Labor Market Outcomes: Contrasting the 1980s and Earlier Decades." *Federal Reserve Bank of New York: Economic Policy Review* 1:1 (Jan. 1995): 26–32.

Juhn, Chinhui, Kevin M. Murphy, and Brooks Pierce. "Wage Inequality and the Rise in the Returns to Skill." *Journal of Political Economy* 101 (June): 410–422.

Kalt, J. "The Impact of Domestic Environmental Regulatory Policies on U.S. International Competitiveness." Discussion Paper Series, Energy, and Environmental Policy Center, John F. Kennedy School of Government, Harvard University. 1985.

Katz, Lawrence F., and Kevin M. Murphy. "Changes in Relative Wages, 1963–1987: Supply and Demand Factors." *Quarterly Journal of Economics* 107 (Feb. 1992): 35–78.

Kennedy, Paul. *The Rise and Fall of the Great Powers: Economic Change and Military Conflict from 1500 to 2000*. New York: Random House, 1987.

Klevorick, Alvin K. "Reflections on the Race to the Bottom." In *Fair Trade and Harmonization: Prerequisites for Free Trade?* edited by Jagdish N. Bhagwati and Robert E. Hudec, vol. 1, 459–468. Cambridge: MIT Press, 1996.

Kmitch, Janet, Pedro Labory, and Sarah Van Damme. "International Comparisons of Manufacturing Compensation." *Monthly Labor Review* (Oct. 1995): 7–10.

Kopp, R., P. Portney, and D. DeWitt. "International Comparisons of Environmental Regulation." Discussion Paper, Resources for the Future, Washington, D.C. 1990.

Kosters, Marvin H. "An Overview of Changing Wage Patterns in the Labor Market." In *Trade and Wages: Leveling Wages Down?* edited by Jagdish N. Bhagwati and M. H. Kosters, 1–32. Washington, D.C.: AEI Press, 1994.

Kristof, Nicholas D. "Experts Question Roving Flow of Global Capital," *The New York Times*, 20 September 1998, p. 18.

Krueger, Alan B. "How Computers Have Changed the Wage Structure: Evidence from Microdata, 1984–1989." Princeton University. Mimeo.

Krueger, Anne O. *American Trade Policy: A Tragedy in the Making*. Washington: AEI Press, 1995.

_____. "Overview." In *The Regionalization of the World Economy*, edited by Jeffrey Frankel, 259–274. Chicago: University of Chicago Press, 1998.

_____. "The Political Economy of U.S. Protection in Theory and in Practice." In *Trade, Welfare, and Economic Policies: Essays in Honor of Murray C. Kemp*, 215–236. Ann Arbor: University of Michigan Press, 1993.

_____. "Problems with Overlapping Trade Areas." In *Regionalism Versus Multilateral Trade Arrangements*, edited by Takatoshi Ito and Anne O. Krueger, 9–24. Chicago: University of Chicago Press, 1997.

Krugman, Paul. "Growing World Trade: Causes and Consequences." *Brookings Papers on Economic Activity 1*. Washington, D.C.: Brookings Institution, 1995.

_____. "Increasing Returns, Monopolistic Competition, and International Trade." *Journal of International Economics* 9 (Nov. 1979): 469–479.

_____. "The Move toward Free Trade Zones." In Federal Reserve Bank of Kansas City, *Policy Implications of Trade and Currency Zones*, proceedings of a symposium held in Jackson Hole, Wyoming, August 22–24, 1991.

_____. "The Myth of Asia's Miracle." *Foreign Affairs* 73:6 (Nov.-Dec. 1994): 62–78.

_____. "Regionalism Versus Multilateralism: Analytical Notes." In *New Dimensions in Regional Integration*, edited by Jaime De Melo and Arvind Panagariya, 58–78. Cambridge: Cambridge University Press, 1993.

_____. "Strategic Sectors and International Competition." In *U.S. Trade Policies in a Changing World*, edited by Robert Stern, 207–243. Cambridge: MIT Press, 1987.

Krugman, Paul., ed. *Strategic Trade Policy and the New International Economics*. Cambridge: MIT Press, 1986.

Kuttner, Robert. *The End of Laissez-Faire: National Purpose and the Global Economy After the Cold War*. New York: Alfred Knopf, 1991.

Langille, Brian A. "General Reflections on the Relationship of Trade and Labor, or Fair Trade Is Free Trade's Destiny." In *Fair Trade and Harmonization: Prerequisites for Free Trade?* edited by Jagdish N. Bhagwati and Robert E. Hudec, vol. 2, 231–266. Cambridge: MIT Press, 1996.

Lawrence, Robert Z. "Trade, Multinationals, and Labor." National Bureau of Economic Research Discussion Paper. 1994.

_____. "U.S. Wage Trends in the 1980s: The Role of International Factors." *Federal Reserve Bank of New York: Economic Policy Review* 1:1 (Jan. 1995): 18–23.

Lawrence, Robert Z., Dani Rodrik, and John Whalley, eds. *Emerging Agenda for Global Trade: High Stakes for Developing Countries*. Washington, D.C.: Overseas Development Council, 1996.

Lawrence, Robert Z., and Matthew Slaughter. "Trade and United States Wages: Great Sucking Sound or Small Hiccup?" In *Brookings Papers on Economic Activity, Microeconomics 2*. Washington, D.C.: Brookings Institution, 1993.

Leamer, Edward. "Effects of a U.S.-Mexico Free Trade Agreement." Paper presented at Brown University; also National Bureau of Economic Research Discussion Paper. 1991.

Leary, Virginia A. "Workers' Rights and International Trade: The Social Clause (GATT, ILO, NAFTA, U.S. Laws)." In *Fair Trade and Harmonization: Prerequisites for Free Trade?* edited by Jagdish N. Bhagwati and Robert E. Hudec, vol. 2, 177–230. Cambridge: MIT Press, 1996.

Leebron, David W. "Lying Down with Procrustes: An Analysis of Harmonization Claims." In *Fair Trade and Harmonization: Prerequisites for Free Trade?* edited by Jagdish N. Bhagwati and Robert E. Hudec, vol. 1, 41–118. Cambridge: MIT Press, 1996.

Leonard, H. *Pollution and the Struggle for the World Product*. Cambridge: Cambridge University Press, 1988.

Levinson, Arik. "Environmental Regulations and Industry Location: International and Domestic Evidence." In *Fair Trade and Harmonization: Prerequisites for Free Trade?* edited by Jagdish N. Bhagwati and Robert E. Hudec, vol. 1, 429–458. Cambridge: MIT Press, 1996.

Levy, Frank, and Richard Murname. "U.S. Earnings Levels and Earnings Inequality: A Review of Recent Trends and Proposed Explanations." *Journal of Economic Literature* 30 (Sept. 1992): 1333–1374.

Lewis, Paul. "Amid New Wealth of Trade, a Humanizing Movement." *The New York Times*, 25 December 1996, p. D-3.

Liemt, Gijsbert van. "Minimum Labor Standards and International Trade: Would a Social Clause Work?" *International Labor Review* 4 (1989): 128.

Lipsey, Robert E. "Foreign Direct Investment in the United States: Changes Over Three Decades." In *Foreign Direct Investment*, edited by K. A. Froot, 113–144. Chicago: University of Chicago Press, 1993.

Low, Patrick. "Market Access Through Market Presence: A Look at the Issues." In *OECD: New Dimensions of Market Access in a Globalizing World Economy*, 49–60. Paris: OECD, 1995.

_____. *Trading Free: The GATT and United States Trade Policy*. New York: Twentieth Century Fund, 1993.

Low, Patrick, ed. *International Trade and the Environment*. World Bank Discussion Paper no. 159. Washington, D.C.: World Bank, 1992.

Mabey, N., S. Hall, C. Smith, and S. Gupta. *Arguments in the Greenhouse*. London: Routledge, 1997.

Machado, Kit. "Japanese Foreign Direct Investments in East Asia." In *Foreign Direct Investments in a Changing Global Economy*, edited by Steven Chan, 39–66. New York: St. Martin's Press, 1993.

Malinowski, Bronislaw Kasper. *Argonauts of the Western Pacific: An Account of Native Enterprise and Adventure in the Archipelagoes of Melanisian New Guinea*. New York: Dutton, 1961.

Mann, M. A., D. J. Atherton, and L. L. Brokenbaugh. "United States International Sales and Purchases of Private Services." *Survey of Current Business* (Nov. 1996): 70–81.

Martins, J. O. "Market Structure, International Trade, and Relative Wages." ACCEDE Working Paper no. 134. 1993.

Mataloni, Raymond J. Jr. "A Guide to BEA Statistics on U.S. Multinational Companies." *Survey of Current Business* (March 1995): 38–53.

_____. "U.S. Multinational Companies: Operations in 1995." *Survey of Current Business* (Oct. 1997): 44–59.

Mataloni, Raymond J. Jr., and Mahnaz Fahim-Nader. "Operation of U.S. Multinational Companies: Preliminary Results from the 1994 Benchmark Survey." *Survey of Current Business* (Dec. 1996): 11–29.

McCulloch, Rachel. "New Perspectives on Foreign Direct Investment." In *Foreign Direct Investments*, edited by Kenneth A. Froot, 37–58. Chicago: University of Chicago Press, 1993.

McKinsey Global Institute. *Manufacturing Productivity*. Washington, D.C.: Oct. 1993.

Milner, Helen. *Resisting Protectionism: Global Industries and the Politics of International Trade*. Princeton: Princeton University Press, 1988.

_____. "Trading Places: Industry for Free Trade." In *International Trade Policies: Gains from Exchange Between Economics and Political Science*, edited by John S. Odell and Thomas D. Willett, 141–172. Ann Arbor: University of Michigan Press, 1990.

Mincer, Jacob. "Economic Development, Growth of Human Capital, and the Dynamics of Wage Structure." *Journal of Economic Growth* 1 (March 1995): 29–48.

_____. "Human Capital Responses to Technological Change in the Labor Market." *Research in Labor Economics* 6 (1984): 311–333.

_____. "Human Capital, Technology, and the Wage Structure." In *Studies in Human Capital: Collected Essays of Jacob Mincer*, edited by Jacob Mincer, vol. 1, 366–405. Aldershot: Edward Elgar, 1993.

Mishel, Lawrence, and Jared Bernstein. "Is the Technology Black Box Empty? An Empirical Examination of the Impact of Technology on Wage Inequality and Employment Structure." Economic Policy Institute. Mimeo.

Murphy, Kevin M., and Finis Welch. "The Structure of Wages." *Quarterly Journal of Economics* 101 (Feb. 1992): 285–326.

Murray, L. A. "Unraveling Employment Trends in Textiles and Apparel." *Monthly Labor Review* (Aug. 1995): 62–72.

Murray, Tracy. "The Administration of the Antidumping Duty Law by the Department of Commerce." In *Down in the Dumps*, edited by Richard Boltuck and Robert E. Litan, 23–63. Washington, D.C.: Brookings Institution, 1991.

Myerson, Allen R. "O Governor, Won't You Buy Me a Mercedes Plant." *The New York Times*, 1 September 1996, p. A-1.

Nelson, Richard, and Edwin Phelps. "Investments in Humans, Technological Diffusion and Economic Growth." *American Economic Review* 56 (May 1966): 69–75.

Nogués, Julio J., and Rosalinda Quintanilla. "Latin America's Integration and the Multilateral Trading System." In *New Dimensions in Regional Integration*, edited by Jaime De Medo and Arvind Panagariya, 278–312. Cambridge: Cambridge University Press, 1993.

Oates, Wallace, Paul R. Portney, and Albert M. McGartland. "The Net Benefits of Incentive-Based Regulations: A Case Study of Environmental Standard Setting." *American Economic Review* 79 (Dec. 1989): 1233–1242.

Odell, John S., and Thomas D. Willett, eds. *International Trade Policies: Gains from Exchange Between Economics and Political Science*. Ann Arbor: University of Michigan Press, 1990.

Ohlin, Bertril. *Interregional and International Trade*. Cambridge: Harvard University Press, 1933.

Olson, Mancur. *The Logic of Collective Action: Public Goods and the Theory of Groups*. Cambridge: Harvard University Press, 1988.

Organization for Economic Cooperation and Development (OECD). *OECD Documents: The New World Trading System: Readings*. Paris: OECD, 1994.

_____. *The Macro-Economic Impact of Environmental Expenditures*. Paris: OECD, 1985.

_____. *Trade, Employment, and Labor Standards: A Study of Core Workers' Rights and International Trade*. Paris: OECD, 1996.

_____. *International Capital Markets Statistics, 1950–1995*. Paris: OECD, 1997.

_____. *OECD Observer* 183 (Aug.-Sept. 1993)

Palmeter, N. David. "The Antidumping Law: A Legal and Administrative Nontariff Barrier." In *Down in the Dumps*, edited by Richard Boltuck and Robert E. Litan, 64–94. Washington, D.C.: Brookings Institution, 1991.

Pearson, C. *Down to Business: Multinational Corporations, the Environment, and Development*. Washington, D.C.: World Resources Institute, 1985.

Pearson, C., ed. *Multinational Corporations, Environment, and the Third World*. Durham, N.C.: Duke University Press and World Resources Institute, 1987.

Perot, Ross. *Save Your Jobs, Save Our Country: Why NAFTA Must Be Stopped*. New York: Hyperion Press, 1992.

Pollack, Andrew. "Japan Is Urged to Insure Foreigners' Trade Share." *The New York Times*, 14 October 1993.

_____. "Japan's New Tack on Trade: No More 1-on–1 with the U.S." *The New York Times*, 30 July 1996, p. D-1.

Porter, Michael E. *The Competitive Advantage of Nations*. New York: Free Press, 1990.

Preeg, Ernst H. *Traders in a Brave New World*. Chicago: University of Chicago Press, 1995.

Prestowitz, C. V. J. *Trading Places: How We Allowed the Japanese to Take the Lead*. New York: Basic Books, 1988.

Reich, Robert B. *The Work of Nations*. New York: Alfred A. Knopf, 1991.

Revenga, Ana L. "Exporting Jobs? The Impact of Import Competition on Employment and Wages in U.S. Manufacturing." *Quarterly Journal of Economics* 107:1 (Feb. 1992): 255–282.

Ricardo, David. *The Principles of Political Economy and Taxation* (first published in 1817). London: J. M. Dent and Sons, 1911.

Richardson, J. David. *Sizing Up U.S. Export Disincentives*. Washington: Institute for International Economics, 1993.

Rodrik, Dani. "Labor Standards in International Trade: Do They Matter and What Do We Do About Them?" In *Emerging Agenda for Global Trade: High Stakes for Developing Countries*, edited by Robert Lawrence, Dani Rodrik, and John Whalley. Washington, D.C.: Overseas Development Council, 1996.

Roessler, Frieder. "Diverging Domestic Policies and Multilateral Trade Integration." In *Fair Trade and Harmonization: Prerequisites for Free Trade?* edited by Jagdish N. Bhagwati and Robert E. Hudec, vol. 2, 21–56. Cambridge: MIT Press, 1996.

Rohter, Larry. "Hondurans in Sweatshops See Opportunity." *The New York Times*, 18 July 1996, p. 1.

Sachs, Jeffrey, and Howard Schatz. "Trade and Jobs in United States Manufacturing." *Brookings Papers on Economic Activity 1*. Washington, D.C.: Brookings Institution, 1994.

Salzman, James. *Environmental Labeling in OECD Countries*. Paris: OECD, 1991.

Samuelson, Paul. "International Factor-Price Equalization Once Again." *Economic Journal* 49 (June 1949): 181–197.

Samuelson, Paul, and Gustav Stolper. "Protection and Real Wages." *Review of Economic Studies* 9 (Nov. 1941): 58–73.

Saxonhouse, Gary R. "A Short Summary of the Long History of Unfair Trade Allegations Against Japan." In *Fair Trade and Harmonization: Prerequisites for Free Trade?* edited by Jagdish N. Bhagwati and Robert E. Hudec, vol. 1, 471–514. Cambridge: MIT Press, 1996.

_____. "Trading Blocs and East Asia." In *New Dimensions in Regional Integration*, edited by Jaime De Medo and Arvind Panagariya, 388–415. Cambridge: Cambridge University Press, 1993.

Schott, Jeffrey. *Free Trade Areas and U.S. Trade Policy*. Washington, D.C.: Institute for International Economics, 1989.

Schumpeter, Joseph. *Capitalism, Socialism, and Democracy.* 3d ed. New York: Harper and Brothers, 1950.

Servan-Schreiber, J. J. *The American Challenge.* New York: Atheneum, 1968.

Slaughter, Matthew J. "International Trade, Multinational Corporations, and American Wages." Ph.D. dissertation, Massachusetts Institute of Technology, 1994.

Solow, Robert. "Technical Progress, Capital Formation, and Economic Growth." *American Economics Review* 52 (May 1962): 76–86.

Spence, M. and Hazard, H. A. *International Competitiveness.* Cambridge: Ballinger Publishing, 1988.

Startup, J. "An Agenda for International Investment." In *OECD Documents: The New World Trading System: Readings.* Paris: OECD, 1994.

Stern, Robert M., ed. *U.S. Trade Policies in a Changing World Economy.* Cambridge: MIT Press, 1987.

Stolper, Wolfgang, and Paul A. Samuelson. "Protection and Real Wages." *Review of Economic Studies* (Nov. 1941): 58–73.

Swinnerton, Kenneth A., and Gregory K. Schoepfle. "Labor Standards in the Context of a Global Economy: A Symposium." *Monthly Labor Review* 117:9 (Sept. 1994): 52–58.

Tolchin, M., and S. Tolchin. *Buying into America: How Foreign Money Is Changing the Face of Our Nation.* New York: Times Books, 1988.

Topel, Robert. "Regional Labor Markets and the Determinants of Wage Inequality." *American Economic Review* 84 (May 1994): 17–22.

Triffin, Robert. *Gold and the Dollar Crisis.* New Haven: Yale University Press, 1960.

Tyson, Laura d'Andrea. *Who's Bashing Whom? Trade Conflict in High-Technology Industries.* Washington, D.C.: Institute for International Economics, 1992.

United Nations Conference on Trade and Development (UNCTAD). *Handbook of International Trade and Development Statistics, 1993.* New York: United Nations, 1994.

_____. *Protectionism and Structural Adjustment.* New York: United Nations, 1986.

_____. *World Investment Report 1995: Transnational Corporations and Competitivness.* New York and Geneva: United Nations, 1995.

_____. *World Investment Report 1996: Investment, Trade, and International Policy Arrangements.* New York and Geneva: United Nations, 1996.

U.S. Department of Commerce. *U.S. Direct Investments Abroad.* Washington, D.C., October 1997.

U.S. Department of Labor, Bureau of International Labor Affairs. *International Labor Standards and Global Economic Integration.* Proceedings of a Symposium. Washington, D.C., 1994.

U.S. International Trade Commission (USITC). *Operation of the Trade Agreements Program, 1988.* 40th Report. Washington, D.C.: Government Printing Office, 1988.

_____. *Operation of the Trade Agreements Program, 1989.* 41st Report. Washington, D.C.: Government Printing Office, 1990.

_____. *The Year in Trade, 1994*. Washington, D.C.: Government Printing Office, 1995.

_____. *The Year in Trade, 1995*. Washington, D.C.: Government Printing Office, 1996.

_____. *The Year in Trade, 1996*. Washington, D.C.: Government Printing Office, 1997.

_____. *The Year in Trade, 1992*. Washington, D.C.: Government Printing Office, 1993.

_____. *The Year in Trade, 1993*. Washington, D.C.: Government Printing Office, 1994.

U.S. Trade Representative. *Annual Report of the President of the United States on the Trade Agreement Proposal, 1984–1988*. Washington, D.C.: Office of United States Trade Representative, 1988.

_____. "Statement on the Protection of United States Intellectual Properties Abroad," 7 April 1986.

Viner, Jacob. *The Customs Union Issue*. New York: Carnegie Endowment for International Peace, 1950.

_____. *Dumping: A Problem in International Trade*. Chicago: University of Chicago Press, 1923.

Vimonen, Peter, and John Whalley. *Environmental Issues in the New World Trading System*. New York: St. Martin's Press, 1997.

Warnke, J. "Computer Manufacturing: Changes and Competition." *Monthly Labor Review* 119:8 (Aug. 1996): 18–29.

Wells, Louis P. Jr. "Mobile Exporters: New Foreign Investors in East Asia." In *Foreign Direct Investment*, edited by Kenneth A. Froot, 175–195. Chicago: University of Chicago Press, 1993.

Whalley, John. "Agreement on Textiles and Clothing." In *OECD Documents: The New World Trading System: Readings*, 73–81. Paris: OECD, 1994.

_____. "Regional Trade Agreements in North America: CUFTA and NAFTA." In *New Dimensions in Regional Integration*, edited by Jaime De Melo and Arvind Panagariya, 352–381. Cambridge: Cambridge University Press, 1993.

_____. "Why Do Countries Seek Trade Agreements?" In *The Regionalization of the World Economy*, edited by Jeffrey A. Frankel, 63–89. Chicago: University of Chicago, 1998.

Wilson, John Douglas. "Capital Mobility and Environmental Standards: Is There a Theoretical Basis for a Race to the Bottom?" In *Fair Trade and Harmonization: Prerequisites for Free Trade?* edited by Jagdish N. Bhagwati and Robert E. Hudec, vol. 1, 393–428. Cambridge: MIT Press, 1996.

Winters, L. Alan. "The European Community: A Case of Successful Integration?" In *New Dimensions in Regional Integration*, edited by Jaime De Medo and Arvind Panagariya, 202–227. Cambridge: Cambridge University Press, 1993.

Wood, Adrian. "How Trade Hurt Unskilled Workers." *Journal of Economic Perspectives* (Summer 1995): 57–80.

_____. *North-South Trade, Employment, and Inequality: Changing Fortunes in a Skill Driven World.* New York: Clarendon Press, 1994.

World Bank. *World Development Report 1987.* Washington, D.C.: World Bank, 1987.

_____. *World Development Report 1991.* Washington, D.C.: Oxford University Press, 1991.

_____. *World Development Report 1994.* Washington, D.C.: Oxford University Press, 1994.

Wyckoff, Andrew W. "The International Expansion of Productive Networks." *OECD Observer* 180 (Feb.–March 1993): 8–11.

Young, A. "Learning by Doing and the Dynamic Effects of International Trade." *Quarterly Journal of Economics* 106 (1991): 369–405.

Zaelke, D., P. Orbuch, and R. Houseman, eds. *Trade and the Environment: Law, Economics, and Policy.* Washington, D.C.: Island Press, 1993.

Zeile, William J. "The Domestic Orientation of Production and Sales by U.S. Manufacturing Affiliates of Foreign Companies." *Survey of Current Business* (April 1998): 29–50.

Zupnick, Elliot. *Foreign Direct Investments in the U.S.: Costs and Benefits.* New York: Foreign Policy Association, 1980.

INDEX